FAITH FOOD

Devotions

Kenneth E. Hagin

Second Printing 2000

ISBN 0-89276-045-1

In the U.S. write:
Kenneth Hagin Ministries
P.O. Box 50126
Tulsa, OK 74150-0126

In Canada write:
Kenneth Hagin Ministries
P.O. Box 335, Station D
Etobicoke (Toronto), Ontario
Canada, M9A 4X3

PREFACE

F. F. Bosworth said, "Most Christians feed their bodies three hot meals a day and their spirits one cold snack a week, and then they wonder why they are so weak in faith."

So feed your faith daily! It is of utmost importance to your walk with the Lord. I've written these bite-size pieces of "faith food" to aid you in making sure your faith is fed daily.

Study and say the confessions found on the bottom of each page aloud. Faithfully repeat them. They are based on God's Word. When you hear yourself confess God's Word, His truths will register on your spirit. And when God's Word gets down into your spirit, He will empower your life!

JANUARY 1

RESOLVED: TO GROW

Fight the good fight of faith . . . . — 1 TIMOTHY 6:12

The only fight the Christian is called upon to fight is the *fight of faith*.

If you're in any other kind of fight, you're in the wrong fight! There's no need to fight the devil — Jesus has already defeated him. There's no need fighting sin — Jesus is the cure for sin. But there is a fight (and therefore enemies, or hindrances) to faith.

The greatest enemy to faith is a lack of understanding God's Word. In fact, *all* hindrances to faith center around this lack of knowledge; because you cannot believe or have faith beyond your actual knowledge of the Word of God.

However, your *faith* will automatically grow as your *understanding* of God's Word grows (Rom. 10:17). If your faith is not growing, it's because your knowledge of God's Word is not growing. And you cannot grow or develop spiritually if you are not growing in faith.

The best resolution you can make today is that in the upcoming year, your knowledge of God's Word will grow. Then give yourself to the study of the Word! It will automatically follow that your faith will grow. Hence, you will grow and develop spiritually.

Confession: *In the upcoming year, my faith will grow. I am determined that my knowledge of God's Word will grow. My understanding of God's Word will grow. Therefore, faith will come, and my faith will grow. I will grow and develop spiritually this year!*

JANUARY 2

FAITH FOLLOWS LIGHT

The entrance of thy words giveth light . . . .   — PSALM 119:130

As a teenager, I became bedfast. Medical science said I would die. Now, I'd heard the New Birth preached all my life. I knew what God's will was concerning salvation. And when I came to the Lord while bedfast, I had no doubt that He would hear me. I had no lack of understanding along that line. Therefore, I had no doubt or unbelief concerning salvation. I received salvation, and I knew that I was saved.

But, I was still bedfast! I certainly had a lack of understanding of God's Word concerning divine healing, prayer, and faith. About all I had ever heard preachers say about healing was, "Just leave it to the Lord. He knows best." (Yes, but in His Word, God has made provision for us to *have* His best!)

In time, after much study of the Bible, I saw the exact steps I needed to take in prayer, and I saw just how to release my faith. Had I known these things earlier, I could have been off that bed months before I was. God didn't have a certain "set time" to heal me. No! He's the same every day! The trouble wasn't with God or His willingness to heal me; the trouble was on my end of the line. As soon as I found out what God's Word said about healing and acted upon it, I got results! As soon as light comes, faith is there.

Confession: *I will find out what God's Word says, and I will act on it. I will get results. I will see to it that God's Word finds entrance into my spirit. Light will come — and faith will follow.*

JANUARY 3

KNOW YOU'RE NEW

Therefore if any man be in Christ, he is a new creature: old things are passed away; behold, all things are become new.
— 2 CORINTHIANS 5:17

Today's text is one of my favorite scriptures. I got ahold of it while I was still a bedfast teenager. And when I came off that bed healed, I told everyone I met, "I am a new creature!"

Meditate on this verse today, because if you do not understand the truth of what the New Birth is, it will hinder your faith and will keep you from receiving the blessings God intends you to have.

The spiritual nature of man, you see, is a fallen nature — a satanic nature. Man received this satanic nature from Satan when Adam sinned. And no man can change his own human nature. *But God can!*

When you were born again, something went on *inside* you — instantaneously! That old, satanic nature went out of you. And the very life and nature of God came into you! God created you as a brand-new creature — a new creation. *The man on the inside — the real you, which is a spirit man — has already become a new man in Christ.*

So don't look at yourself from the physical or the natural standpoint. Look at yourself from the spiritual standpoint. See yourself as a new creature in Christ. That's how God sees you!

Confession: *I am a new creature. Old things inside me passed away. All things inside me became new. I have a new life. I have a new nature. I have the life of God!*

JANUARY 4

SAY YOU'RE NEW

I am crucified with Christ: nevertheless I live; yet not I, but Christ liveth in me: and the life which I now live in the flesh I live by the faith of the Son of God, who loved me, and gave himself for me.
— GALATIANS 2:20

I was healed on a Tuesday. That Saturday I walked to town, and I happened to run into a friend of mine. We had been bosom buddies. But during the sixteen months I had been bedfast, he had seen me only once.

He was the same old creature he had always been — but I had become a new creature. He laughed about the things we used to do. Pointing to a building down the street, he said, "Remember the night . . ." and he went on to talk about the time I had picked the lock on the door so some boys could go in and steal candy. I sat there with a mask-like look on my face, as if I didn't know what he was talking about. (I remembered it well enough, but I wanted to use this as an opportunity to witness to him.)

"What's the matter with you? You act like you don't remember — and you were the ringleader," he finally said.

"Lefty, the fellow you were with that night is dead."

"You're not dead! I know you almost died, but you're not dead! That's you sitting there!"

"Oh," I said, "you're looking at the house I live in — my body. The man on the inside who gave permission to the body to pick that lock, is gone. And this man on the inside is now a new creature in Christ Jesus."

Confession: *I am a new creature in Christ Jesus. I hold fast to the confession that I am a new creature.*

JANUARY 5

BRAND-NEW MAN

As newborn babes, desire the sincere milk of the word, that ye may grow thereby. — 1 PETER· 2:2

When the sinner comes to Jesus, his sins are remitted — blotted out. But not only are his sins blotted out — all that he was, spiritually speaking, in the sight of God — is blotted out. His sins cease to exist. He becomes a new man in Christ Jesus. *God does not see anything in that person's life before the moment he was born again!*

In today's text, Peter is writing to born-again Christians who have become new men in Christ. The Bible, you see, teaches a similarity between physical growth and spiritual growth. No one is born as a full-grown human being; we are born as babies in the natural, and then we grow up. Likewise, no one is born as a full-grown Christian. Christians are born as spiritual babies, and they grow up. Look at a newborn babe in the natural lying in its mother's arms, its outstanding characteristic is innocence. People say to the baby, "You sweet little innocent thing." No one thinks of that baby as having a past! So do you see what God is saying here through Peter? God is saying to people who have been born again and are now babes in Christ, *"As newborn babes . . . ."* In other words, God is saying, "You have become a new creature — a newborn babe! Your past is gone! I'm not remembering anything against you!"

5

Confession: *I am a brand-new creature. I'm a brand-new man [or woman]. All that I was before I was born into the family of God is blotted out. I'm God's child — His babe — His very own child.*

JANUARY 6

NO MORE

This is the covenant that I will make with them after those days, saith the Lord, I will put my laws into their hearts, and in their minds will I write them; And their sins and iniquities will I remember no more.
— HEBREWS 10:16,17

When God looks at you, He doesn't remember that you have any past — so why should you remember it? It can hinder your faith.

In talking with people, many have told me, "Brother Hagin, before I was ever saved, I lived such an awful life." Then they have told me they don't believe the Lord will do anything for them, such as heal them, or answer their prayers, because they lived such sinful lives before they were saved. They have a complete lack of understanding concerning the New Birth, and concerning the new creature they have become.

When the sinner comes to Christ, he receives *remission* — a blotting out — of sins.

And after a person is a Christian, he can receive *forgiveness* of sins that he may commit: *"If we confess our sins, he is faithful and just to forgive us our sins, and to cleanse us from all unrighteousness"* (1 John 1:9). How long do you think it takes God to forgive us? Ten minutes? Ten years? No, God instantly forgives us! And He instantly cleanses us when we come to Him according to this scripture.

Confession: *My Father God does not remember my sins and iniquities. Neither do I remember them. I stand in God's Presence as if I had never sinned.*

JANUARY 7

INSIDE-OUT

But I keep under my body, and bring it into subjection: lest that by any means, when I have preached to others, I myself should be a castaway.
— 1 CORINTHIANS 9:27

As a Christian, learn to let the new man on the inside dominate your outward man. The outward man is not a new man. The body has not been born again. The body will keep on wanting to do the things it has always done — things that are wrong. Paul's body did! This great apostle wouldn't have had to keep his body under if it were not wanting to do things that were wrong. So don't be surprised when your body wants to do wrong things.

We have the flesh to contend with in this world. The devil works through the flesh. Because we experience trials and temptations in the flesh, the devil tells Christians, "You must not even be saved! If you were saved, you wouldn't want to do that!" Satan will insinuate it's "you" who wants to do wrong, when really "you" the man on the inside — the new man — *doesn't* want to do wrong.

Do you need to break a habit? Conquer an old temptation? Walk in victory over the flesh? Do what Paul did. Say what Paul said. Paul said, "I don't let my body rule me." Who is "I"? "I" is the man on the inside. Paul called his body "it," and he called himself, the man on the inside, "I." Paul said, "I keep under my body, and bring *it* into subjection . . . ." Into subjection to what? To the inward man!

JANUARY 8

MERE MEN? NO!

And I, brethren, could not speak unto you as unto spiritual, but as unto carnal, even as unto babes in Christ. . . . For ye are yet carnal: for whereas there is among you envying, and strife, and divisions, are ye not carnal, and walk as men? — 1 CORINTHIANS 3:1,3

With most Christians, I'm sorry to say, the inward man does not rule the outward man. Instead, the body rules the inward man — and that's what makes carnal Christians. One translation of our text says "body-ruled" instead of "carnal." And that's what carnal Christians are — body-ruled.

"*. . . Ye are yet carnal . . . and walk as men,*" Paul told the Corinthians. In other words, they were living like people who had never been born again. I like the *Amplified Bible* translation of verse 3: ". . . For as long as [there are] envying and jealousy and wrangling and factions among you, are you not unspiritual and of the flesh, behaving yourselves after a human standard and like mere (unchanged) men?"

Don't do it! Refuse to live like mere men! Live like the new creature you are! Determine to let the new man in Christ dominate your being.

Confession: *I refuse to walk as a mere man. I am changed. I am a new creature in Christ. I will grow up in Christ. I will grow up spiritually. "I" — the man on the inside — will dominate my being. I will walk as a spiritual man. I will behave myself after the standard of God's Word. I will walk in love. I will walk in faith!*

JANUARY 9

SPIRITUAL SERVICE

I beseech you therefore, brethren, by the mercies of God, that ye present your bodies a living sacrifice, holy, acceptable unto God, which is your reasonable service. — **ROMANS 12:1**

"You" are to do something with your body. For if you don't, nothing will ever be done with it. "You," the inward man, have become a new man in Christ. "You" have received eternal life. When eternal life — which is the life and nature of God — is imparted to your spirit, it changes "you."

You won't have any trouble with "you," but you will have trouble with the flesh. People say, "You have to die out to the old *self.*" No, you don't. That old self is dead, and you have a new self in its place. But what you need to die out to is the *flesh.*

Isn't the flesh the old self? No, it isn't. Your flesh is the outward man, the body. And it's the same old flesh it was *before* you were saved!

Your body is the house you live in, and "you" — not God — are the caretaker of that house. "You" do something with your body. You are to present it to God as "*. . . a living sacrifice, holy, acceptable unto God . . . .*" Another translation concludes this verse with the phrase "*. . . which is your spiritual service.*"

Confession: *I am a new creature in Christ. I hold fast to this confession. And the new man on the inside of me is being manifested on the outside and through the flesh. I dominate my body. I present it to God as a living sacrifice, holy, and acceptable to Him, which is my spiritual service.*

JANUARY 10

In Him

Blessed be the God and Father of our Lord Jesus Christ, who hath blessed us with all spiritual blessings in heavenly places in Christ.
— **EPHESIANS 1:3**

From the day you were born again until the day you step off into eternity, God has already made provision for you in Christ Jesus. Everything you need, "He *hath* blessed" you with. In the mind of God, it is yours!

People often ask me how to study the Bible. Although I have many suggestions, here is the one I present everywhere I go. As a believer, a Christian, follow this method as you go through the New Testament; read or study primarily the Epistles. (I encourage you to spend most of your time in the Epistles, because they are the letters written to you, the believer. Study the Old Testament, too, but don't spend most of your time there. Spend most of your time in the New Testament. Why? Because we're not living under the Old Covenant; we're living under the New Covenant.)

In these Epistles, which are written to the Church, find and underline all expressions such as "in Christ," "by Christ," "in whom," "in Him," and so forth. Write them down. Meditate on them. Begin to confess them with your mouth. As far as God is concerned, everything you have, or are, in Christ, is already so. God has already done it all in Christ. However, it is your believing and your confessing that will make it real to you.

Confession: *I am a new creature IN CHRIST. God the Father HAS blessed me with all spiritual blessings in heavenly places IN CHRIST.*

JANUARY 11

HEART AND MOUTH

For with the heart man believeth unto righteousness; and with the mouth confession is made unto salvation. — ROMANS 10:10

It is always with the *heart* that man believes — and with the *mouth* that confession is "made unto salvation." When you *believe* something with your heart and *confess* it with your mouth, then it becomes real to you. *Faith's confessions create realities!*

For example, Hebrews 9:12 says, *"Neither by the blood of goats and calves, but by his own blood he entered in ONCE into the holy place, having obtained eternal redemption for us."* Jesus will never have to do that again; He has already done it once, and for all time. And Romans 10:10 tells us how we obtain the reality of that salvation: By *believing* with the heart — the inner man — and *confessing* with the mouth.

As you read some of the "in Christ," "in Him," and "in whom" scriptures, it may not seem like you really have what these scriptures say you have. But if you will begin to *confess* (because you do *believe* God's Word in your heart), "This is mine. This is who I am. This is what I have," then it will become real to you. It is already real in the spirit realm. But you want it to become real in this physical realm where you are living.

11

Confession: *With my heart I believe God's Word; and with my mouth I make confession of its promises and provisions. My faith confessions create the reality of those promises and provisions in my life. I am who God says I am — now! I have what God says I have — now!*

JANUARY 12

WE WERE HEALED!

Who his own self bare our sins in his own body on the tree, that we, being dead to sins, should live unto righteousness: by whose stripes ye were healed. — 1 PETER 2:24

Years ago, a woman was carried into one of my services. She had not walked in four years, and doctors said she would never walk again. I sat down beside her and placed my open Bible on her lap.

I said, "Sister, please read that verse out loud."

She read First Peter 2:24 aloud. And when she ended with ". . . *by whose stripes ye were healed,*" I asked, "Is 'were' past tense, present tense, or future tense?"

I will never forget her reaction, "*Were* is past tense," she exclaimed. "And if we *were* healed, then I *was* healed!" She accepted God's Word with the enthusiasm and simplicity of a child — the way we must.

And that's how God records it in His Word. He doesn't promise to heal us, because He's already provided healing for us almost 2,000 years ago! Healing is something we already have *in Christ.*

This woman's face lit up as she lifted her hands and said, "Praise God! Lord, I'm so glad I'm healed! Lord, I'm so glad I can walk again! [And she hadn't walked a step yet.] I'm so glad I'm not helpless anymore. I'm so glad I can wait on myself . . ."

"Rise and walk!" I said. And the woman leaped to her feet! Praise the Lord!

Confession: *By His stripes we WERE healed. If we were, then I was. I AM healed. Healing is mine. I have it now!*

JANUARY 13

REDEEMED FROM THE CURSE

... These curses shall come upon thee, and overtake thee. ... If thou wilt not observe to do all the words of this law. ... Also every sickness, and every plague, which is not written in the book of this law ....
— DEUTERONOMY 28:15,58,61

Christ hath redeemed us from the curse of the law, being made a curse for us: for it is written, Cursed is every one that hangeth on a tree.
— GALATIANS 3:13

The Bible says that all sickness and disease is a curse of the law. In Deuteronomy chapter 28, the law specifically named eleven diseases as being a curse of the law; then verse 61 encompasses all sickness and disease as a curse of the law.

But Christ has redeemed us from the curse of the law! Christ is not *going to* redeem us; He *has already* redeemed us.

Peter, looking back to the sacrifice at Calvary, said, "... *by whose stripes ye WERE healed*" (1 Peter 2:24). Not *going to be*, but *were*!

God remembers that He laid on Jesus not only the sins and iniquities of us all, but also our sicknesses and diseases (Isa. 53:4,5). Jesus remembers that He bore our sins and sicknesses for us (Matt. 8:17). Therefore, the Holy Spirit inspired Peter to write, "... *by whose stripes ye were healed.*"

Confession: *According to Deuteronomy 28, all sickness and disease is a curse of the law. But according to Galatians 3:13, Christ has redeemed me from the curse of the law. Therefore, I am redeemed from sickness!*

JANUARY 14

RECONCILED

It was God [personally present] in Christ, reconciling and restoring the world to favor with Himself, not counting up and holding against [men] their trespasses [but cancelling them], and committing to us the message of reconciliation (of the restoration to favor).
— 2 CORINTHIANS 5:19 *(Amplified)*

"Brother Hagin," a woman asked, "why don't I get healed? I know God has promised to heal me."

I understood her problem and tried to help her. "No ma'am, God hasn't promised to heal you any more than He has promised to save the lost. Nowhere in God's Word does it say, 'God has promised to save you.' No, God's Word declares that God has already done something about your salvation. God laid your sins and iniquities on Jesus."

God *has already* reconciled us to Himself by Christ. And He gave *us* the ministry of reconciliation. We are to tell people that God was personally present with Jesus Christ reconciling the world to favor with Himself. God is not imputing (counting up) or holding against men their trespasses anymore.

"Well," someone said, "we'll all be saved then, won't we?" No, people must *accept* that reconciliation God offers. We are, by nature, children of the devil, therefore, we must be born again!

Confession: *I am reconciled to God by Christ. I am restored to favor with God, and God has given me the ministry of reconciliation.*

JANUARY 15

MIGHTY WEAPON

For the weapons of our warfare are not carnal, but mighty through God to the pulling down of strong holds. — 2 CORINTHIANS 10:4

Although we have been made new creatures — created by God in Christ Jesus; and although we are transferred out from under Satan's authority, we still live in a world ruled by Satan.

The Bible calls Satan "the god of this world" (2 Cor. 4:4) and "the prince of the power of the air" (Eph. 2:2). Christ also called him "the prince of this world" (John 12:31, 14:30, 16:11).

According to the Word of God, the very air about us is filled with hostile forces attempting to destroy our fellowship with God the Father, and to deprive us of our usefulness in the Master's service.

But our Father God, in His great provision and plan of redemption, has given us a weapon to use against Satan. That weapon is given to us not only for ourselves, but also for the benefit of the Satan-ruled men and women around us. That weapon is the Name of Jesus!

Confession: *The weapons of my warfare are not carnal, but mighty through God to the pulling down of strongholds. Where Satan's forces have built strongholds, I can pull them down with the mighty Name of Jesus. Satan is no match for that Name. And that Name is a mighty weapon given to me to use against the forces of the enemy.*

JANUARY 16

BY INHERITANCE

God, who at sundry times and in divers manners spake in time past unto the fathers by the prophets, Hath in these last days spoken unto us by his Son, whom he hath appointed heir of all things, by whom also he made the worlds; Who being the brightness of his glory, and the express image of his person, and upholding all things by the word of his power, when he had by himself purged our sins, sat down on the right hand of the Majesty on high; Being made so much better than the angels, as he hath by inheritance obtained a more excellent name than they.

— HEBREWS 1:1-4

We cannot measure the vastness of the power and authority in the Name of Jesus without realizing that He *inherited* that Name from God the Creator.

Jesus is the brightness of God's glory.

Jesus is the express image of God's Person — the very outshining of God the Father.

Jesus is the heir of all things. And Jesus inherited His Name. The greatness of His Name is inherited from His Father. So the power of His Name can only be measured by the power of God.

And every believer has inherited the legal right to use the Name of Jesus!

Confession: *I know the Name of Jesus has within it the power and authority of the Creator! I know the power in the Name of Jesus can be measured only by the power of God. And I know I have a legal right to use that Name!*

JANUARY 17

BY CONQUEST

And having spoiled principalities and powers, he made a shew of them openly, triumphing over them in it. — COLOSSIANS 2:15

This is a picture of Christ in combat with the hosts of darkness!

A marginal note in my *King James Version* reads, "He put off from Himself the principalities and the powers." It is evident that when the demon hosts thought they had Jesus within their power, they intended to overwhelm Him and hold Him in bondage. But when the cry came forth from the throne of God that Jesus had met the demands of Justice — that the sin problem had been settled, and man's redemption was a fact — and Jesus overthrew the hosts of demons and Satan himself.

I think Rotherham's translation of Hebrews 2:14 makes it even clearer: ". . . in order that through death He might paralyse him that held the dominion of death, that is the Adversary." Jesus paralyzed Satan! Jesus put him to naught!

There is authority in the Name of Jesus, because Jesus achieved the authority in His Name by conquest!

Confession: *Jesus Christ spoiled principalities and powers. He made an open show of them, triumphing over them in it. Jesus paralyzed Satan and all his cohorts. Therefore, there is authority in the Name of Jesus. And I have a legal right to use that triumphant Name against the forces of the enemy!*

JANUARY 18

RESURRECTION GREATNESS

... He [Jesus] hath by inheritance obtained a more excellent name than they. For unto which of the angels said he [God] at any time, Thou art my Son, this day have I begotten thee? ... — HEBREWS 1:4,5

God hath fulfilled the same unto us their children, in that he hath raised up Jesus again; as it is also written in the second psalm, Thou art my Son, this day have I begotten thee. — ACTS 13:33

When did Jesus inherit His Name? When was it conferred upon Him?

It was conferred when Jesus was made alive out of spiritual death — when He was raised from the dead.

It was at Jesus' resurrection that God said, "*... Thou art my Son, this day have I begotten thee.*" And it was after His resurrection that Jesus revealed all authority in Heaven and in earth had been given to Him.

Every statement regarding the fact that Jesus' Name was inherited or conferred upon Him, shows that Jesus received the greatness of His Name, the fullness of it, *after* His resurrection from the dead.

Confession: *Jesus is Lord. He is risen from the dead, and He is Lord. The power and authority demonstrated in the resurrection abides in the Name and He has given that Name to me.*

JANUARY 19

God-Given

Wherefore God also hath highly exalted him, and given him a name which is above every name: That at the name of Jesus every knee should bow, of things in heaven, and things in earth, and things under the earth; And that every tongue should confess that Jesus Christ is Lord, to the glory of God the Father. — PHILIPPIANS 2:9-11

This was done when Christ ascended on High, and God seated Christ at His own right hand — far above all principality and power, and might, and dominion. Another translation of Philippians 2:10 reads, "That at the name of Jesus every knee should bow, of beings in heaven, and beings in earth, and beings under the earth." (That refers to angels, men, and demons.)

Why was this Name conferred upon Jesus? Why was this Name invested with such authority and dominion? Was it done for Jesus' benefit? No. In the 2,000 years since Jesus' resurrection, ascension, and seating at the Father's right hand, Jesus Himself has not used that Name once. In fact, the Scriptures give no inkling that Jesus has *ever* used that Name! Jesus does not need to; He rules creation by His *Word*. But the Scriptures do reveal that the Name of Jesus has been given for the benefit of the Church, the Body of Christ!

Confession: *As a member of the Body of Christ, as a believer, I have a right to use the Name of Jesus — that Name that is above every name!*

JANUARY 20

FOR HIS BODY, THE CHURCH

And what is the exceeding greatness of his power to us-ward who believe, according to the working of his mighty power, Which he wrought in Christ, when he raised him from the dead, and set him at his own right hand in the heavenly places, Far above all principality, and power, and might, and dominion, and every name that is named, not only in this world, but also in that which is to come: And hath put all things under his feet, and gave him to be the head over all things to the church, Which is his body, the fulness of him that filleth all in all.
— EPHESIANS 1:19-23

In every place where the Bible mentions the Name of Jesus, it also refers to His Body, the Church, because the Name was given to Jesus so that the Church might use it.

The ones who need to use His Name are those who have become joint-heirs with Jesus Christ; and those who are in contact with men and women in need of deliverance from Satan.

All that Jesus is by inheritance is in that Name! All Jesus has done through conquest is in that Name! And that Name belongs to the Body of Christ: It belongs to you and me! God has made this investment for the Church. The Church has a right to draw upon this deposit for her every need! That Name has within it the fulness of the Godhead.

Confession: *I have a right to use the Name of Jesus against the enemy. I have a right to use that Name in prayer. I have a right to use that Name in praise and worship.*

JANUARY 21

ALL THINGS

. . . For all things are yours. . . . And ye are Christ's; and Christ is God's.
— 1 CORINTHIANS 3:21,23

Most people wouldn't think the Corinthians could get anything from God; they were so carnal. Paul began this chapter by telling them they were carnal, yet he added, *". . . all things are yours."*

When you were born into the family of God, the right and privilege to use the Name of Jesus became yours. Everything Jesus bought and paid for automatically became yours. But it's up to you to use what belongs to you.

Consider the story of the prodigal son. If the prodigal is a type of the sinner or backslider, and the father is a type of God, then the elder brother is a type of the Christian who has not strayed. When the elder brother came in from the field, he heard music and dancing. A servant told him, "Your brother came home, and your father has killed the fatted calf." The elder brother became angry, and wouldn't go in and join the festivities. So his father went outside and entreated him. "No, I'm not coming in," the elder brother said, "I've served you faithfully all these years. I never went away. I didn't go off and spend your money — and you never made a feast for me." "Son," the father said, *". . . all that I have is thine"* (Luke 15:31).

Does God have what you need? If He does, then it is already yours. But you'll have to appropriate it.

Confession: *All things are mine. I am Christ's, and Christ is God's. The Name of Jesus belongs to me. I can use it. I will use it. All the Father has is mine!*

JANUARY 22

IN PRAYER

And in that day ye shall ask me nothing. Verily, verily, I say unto you, Whatsoever ye shall ask the Father in my name, he will give it you. Hitherto have ye asked nothing in my name: ask, and ye shall receive, that your joy may be full. — JOHN 16:23,24

This charter prayer promise is perhaps the most staggering statement that ever fell from the lips of the Man of Galilee.

What does Jesus mean "in that day"? Looking toward the future, Jesus, in effect, was saying, "I'm going away. I'm going to Calvary. I'm going to die. But I'm going to be raised from the dead. And I'm going to ascend on High. I'm going to sit down at the right hand of the Father. And a new day is coming. A New Covenant, or New Testament, is coming into being! And in that day, ye shall ask Me nothing." This day in which we live is that new day!

"Hitherto [up until now] *have ye asked nothing in my name . . . ."* The disciples did not pray in the Name of Jesus while Jesus was on the earth. It wouldn't have worked. And they didn't need to, because while Jesus was with them, He met their every need. But the time was coming when Jesus would leave them. That was when they needed His Name. *The Name of Jesus takes the place of Jesus personally in performing miracles, delivering from Satan's authority, and bringing God on the scene!*

Confession: *I am a "New Covenant" Christian. I pray to my Father in the Name of Jesus. I ask in Jesus' Name. I receive — and my joy is full!*

JANUARY 23

DEMAND

Verily, verily, I say unto you, He that believeth on me, the works that I do shall he do also; and greater works than these shall he do; because I go unto my Father. And whatsoever ye shall ask in my name, that will I do, that the Father may be glorified in the Son. If ye shall ask any thing in my name, I will do it. — JOHN 14:12-14

The verses in today's text have nothing whatsoever to do with prayer. In yesterday's devotion, we saw how Jesus said to use His Name in prayer to the Father. But here we see a different use of Jesus' Name. Here, the Greek word translated "ask" can also mean "demand."

An example of this use of the Name is seen at the gate called Beautiful. Peter said to a lame man sitting at the gate, *". . . In the name of Jesus Christ of Nazareth rise up and walk"* (Acts 3:6).

Jesus said, "Whatsoever you demand in My name, I will do it." Let that soak in a little. When we use the Name of Jesus, it is as though Jesus were here Himself. All the power and authority invested in Jesus, is in His Name!

You're not demanding anything of the Father. (After all, it wasn't God who had bound that lame man; it was the devil who had him bound.) No, you're demanding that the devil give way to the Name of Jesus!

Confession: *The Name of Jesus belongs to me. Whatever I demand in the Name of Jesus according to God's Word, He will do it!*

JANUARY 24

Delegated

And he said unto them, Go ye into all the world, and preach the gospel to every creature. . . . And these signs shall follow them that believe; In my name shall they cast out devils; they shall speak with new tongues; They shall take up serpents; and if they drink any deadly thing, it shall not hurt them; they shall lay hands on the sick, and they shall recover.
— MARK 16:15,17,18

Jesus delegated the power and authority in His Name to "them that believe." Some have relegated spiritual authority exclusively to preachers mightily used of God. But this passage of Scripture isn't just talking about evangelists, pastors, or others in the ministry; it's talking about the entire Body of Christ — the believing ones.

Authority is invested in the Name of Jesus. And authority is invested in the Church of the Lord Jesus Christ upon the earth. Some of us have touched that authority now and then, but none of us have been able to abide in it like God wants.

However, I am thoroughly convinced that in these last days, just before Jesus comes, there will arise a body of believers who will learn how to take advantage of all that belongs to them in the Name of Jesus — that Name which is above every Name!

Confession: *I am a believing one. And these signs in Mark 16:17 and 18 follow me. I will learn and know how to take advantage of the Name which belongs to me — the Name which is above every Name.*

JANUARY 25

KNOWLEDGE

My son, if thou wilt receive my words, and hide my commandments with thee; . . . Then shalt thou understand the fear of the Lord, and find the knowledge of God. For the Lord giveth wisdom: out of his mouth cometh knowledge . . . . — PROVERBS 2:1,5,6

Real faith accompanies knowledge of the Word of God. It takes no effort whatsoever on the part of the intellect or the will of man to obtain faith. *Faith accompanies knowledge.* As soon as the light of knowledge comes, faith is there. As the Psalmist of old said, *"The entrance of thy words giveth light . . ."* (Ps. 119:130).

People often pray for faith. But what they actually need is *knowledge* of God's Word! When the knowledge of God's Word comes, faith will automatically be there. You could pray forever to have faith, but if you don't get any knowledge of God's Word, you will never get faith.

Feed on God's Word. Meditate on God's Word. And remember, *". . . faith cometh by hearing, and hearing by the word of God"* (Rom. 10:17).

Confession: *I will receive God's Word. I will hide it within me. And I will find the knowledge of God, because out of the mouth of the Lord comes knowledge. I will receive knowledge of God's Word. And faith will accompany it. Faith comes by hearing, and hearing by the Word of God.*

JANUARY 26

FAITH: ACTING ON GOD'S WORD

But be ye doers of the word, and not hearers only . . . . — JAMES 1:22

Some people have such a struggle. They say they are *trying to get faith,* or else they are *trying to believe.* But all that is necessary, is just to *act on what God says.*

I use the phrase "acting on God's Word" rather than "have faith" or "believe," because that's exactly what faith is!

Someone once asked Raymond T. Richey, a man mightily used of God in the healing ministry, "What is faith?"

Richey replied, *"Faith is just acting on God's Word."*

Smith Wigglesworth would say, *"Faith is an act."*

That's what faith is — acting on God's Word.

Confession: *I am a doer of the Word. I gain knowledge of God's Word. I hear His Word. Then I act accordingly. I act on God's Word!*

JANUARY 27

REALITY

Thy word is true from the beginning . . . . — PSALM 119:160

People often make a substitution for faith — they substitute *mental assent* or *mental agreement*. They mentally agree that God's Word is true, and they call that *faith*. But mentally agreeing with the Word isn't faith. You can mentally agree that the Bible is true, but it won't become real to you until you *act* on what it says. *It's when you act on God's Word that it becomes a reality.*

For example, you can believe in the truth of the resurrection as a great doctrine (and in some circles that's all it is — a doctrine or a dogma), but it won't mean a thing in the world to you until you can say, "Jesus died *for me*! Jesus arose victorious over death, hell, and the grave — and He did that for me! Jesus arose victorious over Satan! Jesus conquered Satan for me! Therefore, Satan has no dominion over me! I'm free!"

The resurrection won't mean anything in your life until you can say these very words. Then the resurrection truth in the Word of God will become something more than just a doctrine, a dogma, a creed, or a theory — *it will become a reality*!

Confession: *I am a doer of the Word. I act on what the Word says is mine. The Word is true. I know it's true. So I act like it's true, and the Word becomes a reality in my life.*

JANUARY 28

ACT LIKE IT'S TRUE

Sanctify them through thy truth: thy word is truth. — JOHN 17:17

The crises of life come to all of us. If you do not know how to *act* on God's Word when a crisis comes, you will be at a disadvantage.

No matter what the problem is, God's Word has something to say about it. God's Word has the answer. Find out what the Word says, and act like it's true!

When someone asks the question, "What in the world are we going to do now?" Just smile and answer, "We're going to act like the Bible is true!"

Many people mentally agree that the Bible is true, but that's not enough. You must act like the Bible is true! If you know God's Word is true, and you act like it is, then it will become real in your life. *You will bring God on the scene in your life!*

Confession: *God's Word is truth. I act like God's Word is true. I act like First John 4:4 is true. I act like Matthew 6:25-34 is true. I act like Hebrews 13:5,6 is true. I act like Philippians 4:19 is true. I act like Matthew 8:17 and First Peter 2:24 are true. I act like all the "in Him" scriptures are true. I act like it, and they are a reality in my life!*

JANUARY 29

THE LORD AT WORK

. . . For the battle is the Lord's . . . . — 1 SAMUEL 17:47

"Don't get into any trouble," my mother called after me as I went to face a family crisis. "So-and-so almost whipped Dub."

"I'm not going to have any trouble," I answered. "I'll never have any trouble. I'm going to put the Lord to work."

As I approached the driveway, the wife of the man who had caused so much trouble met me. She began to rant and rave, and just plain old Texas, "cuss." I thought, *Dear Lord, here is this poor old soul, full of hate and selfishness, and she can't help being that way. She can't help having the nature of the devil in her, because she's a child of the devil.*

I didn't say a word to her, but I said to the Lord in my heart, "Thank God, the Greater One is in me" (1 John 4:4). And I *acted* like the Greater One was in me. And He *is* greater.

She must have sensed the compassion rising up in me, because she suddenly looked up at me and sputtered to a stop. Then she took hold of my hand and fell on her knees, crying, "My God, put your hands on my head and pray for me. A poor old soul like me needs something. Oh, my God, pray for me!"

I hadn't said a word to make her say that. All I had done was acted like the Bible was true.

Confession: *The Greater One is in me. And I'm going to act like it!*

JANUARY 30

HIS BATTLE

. . . Be not afraid nor dismayed . . . for the battle is not yours, but God's. — 2 CHRONICLES 20:15

I believe the Greater One lives in us if we're born again (1 John 4:4). I believe Jesus is greater than the devil. I know the Word of God says that. Therefore, I must act like it's true. That's when it becomes a reality, and that's when the Greater One goes to work for me.

If I go to pieces and act like I'm trying to fight the battle, the Greater One is not fighting it. And then I'm not taking advantage of the Greater One and what He has done for me. So I don't try to figure out the situation. I just lie down and go to sleep, no matter what's going on.

During the years I pastored, almost every church the Lord sent me to, was a church that had trouble. One church in particular no one wanted to pastor. God dealt with me before they contacted me, so I took it. But I didn't have any trouble. I rolled that church and its problems over on the Greater One. I would say to the people, "I'm not going to bother about that." I meant I wasn't going to worry, even if the deacons had a fist fight in the church yard. I would have just let them fight, and afterwards I would have gone and prayed with them, and gotten them lined up so we could go on with God.

Confession: *I refuse to battle. The battle is not mine, but God's. He is the Greater One, and I have put Him to work in my behalf by knowing His Word and by acting like it is true.*

JANUARY 31

REST

For we which have believed do enter into rest . . . . — HEBREWS 4:3

Through the years, I've had the greatest time putting the Lord to work for me — just letting Him do the work.

Since I learned about faith and that the Bible said, "*. . . we which have believed do enter into rest . . .*" I have been in a state of rest. Grasp what this scripture says! It doesn't say that we have entered into a state of fearing, fretting, griping, worrying, or fighting. No! It says we have entered into *rest*.

I haven't seen a "battle" in more than sixty-five years. When someone asks me, "How goes the battle?" I always answer, "The victory is wonderful!" There isn't any battle. I'm in the victory. *Faith always has a good report!*

31

Confession: *I have believed. I am a believing one. Therefore, I have entered into rest. I am in a state of rest. I act like I am in a state of rest. I do not fear or fret. I do not worry. I do not gripe. I do not battle. The battle is the Lord's. The victory is mine. I am in the victory.*

FEBRUARY 1

CHRIST IN YOU

. . . Christ in you, the hope of glory. — COLOSSIANS 1:27

By the power of the Holy Spirit, Christ is dwelling in you.

Is He any less Christ in you than He was when He was on the earth?

No! He's the same Christ. He has all of His power! He has all of His ability! He has all of His glory! He has all of His miracle-working power! He has all of His enablements!

And Christ is in you! You just have to know how to turn Him loose.

Someone once said to Smith Wigglesworth, "You must be someone big; someone great."

"No," Wigglesworth replied, "I just remember that the Scripture says, 'Greater is He that is in me, than he that is in the world.' I just know the Greater One is in me, and the Greater One does the work."

How do you turn Christ loose in you? How do you put the Greater One to work?

You do it by faith.

Confession: *Christ in me is the hope of glory. Christ is dwelling in me — with all His power, His ability, and His glory. Christ has already defeated all the power of the enemy, and He lives in me. I turn Him loose. I act like He's there. I allow Him to work by my faith.*

FEBRUARY 2

CASTING

Casting all your care upon him; for he careth for you. — 1 PETER 5:7

Casting the whole of your care [all your anxieties, all your worries, all your concerns, once and for all] on Him, for He cares for you affectionately and cares about you watchfully.
— 1 PETER 5:7 (*Amplified*)

Some people seem to take comfort in thinking, *God knows and He understands*, while they continue to hold on to their cares. And they never get free from them.

It's not enough to know that God understands and cares. If you want to be free from your cares, you must do what God said to do about them: You must cast all of your cares, all of your concerns, all of your anxieties, and all of your worries upon the Lord, because He cares for you.

This isn't something you do every day. It's a once-and-for-all proposition that enables you to get rid of your cares — it puts them over into God's hands.

I've done that. God has my cares. He's figured it all out, and He's working it all out. And I'm shouting while He's doing it! God is doing the work, and I'm shouting.

33

Confession: *I cast the whole of my care — all my anxieties, all my worries, all my concerns, once and for all — on God.*

FEBRUARY 3

COMMITMENT

Commit thy way unto the Lord; trust also in him; and he shall bring it to pass. — PSALM 37:5

A marginal note in the *King James Version* reads, "Roll thy way upon the Lord." Cast. Commit. Roll. Just roll your cares, your burdens, your anxieties, your worries, upon God. Isn't that what the Word tells us to do?

But God won't take your cares away from you. Some people have asked me, "Please pray that the Lord will lighten this load I'm carrying." God won't do that. God tells *you* what to do about your burdens. And if *you* don't do something about them, nothing will be done.

"You" is the understood subject of today's text: *You* commit your way unto the Lord. *You* roll your way upon the Lord. *You* cast all your care upon Him.

Some people don't get an answer to their prayers because they're not praying in line with God's Word. They're not doing what God said to do about cares, anxieties, worries, and so forth. But it won't do any good to pray about your cares unless you do what God tells you to do about them.

You can do what God says to do!

Confession: *I commit my way unto the Lord. I roll my way upon the Lord. I trust in Him. And He shall bring it to pass!*

FEBRUARY 4

WORRY

. . . Take no thought for your life . . . . — MATTHEW 6:25

Shortly after I was born again, I promised God, "I'll never doubt anything I read in Your Word. And I will put Your Word into practice."

Everything in the Word was a light and a blessing to me until I came to Matthew 6:25. I learned from a footnote that the Greek reads, "Do not be anxious about tomorrow." Cross-references pointed out that God says, "Do not worry." But I was full of worry! Not only was I nearly dead with a heart condition; I was about to worry myself the rest of the way to the grave! "Lord," I said, "if I have to live without worry, I can't be a Christian!" Suddenly everything in the Word seemed dark and fuzzy; I couldn't get any more light from the Word. My conscience smote me, because I was not practicing the Word.

Finally at 6:00 p.m. on July 4, 1933, I committed all my cares to the Lord. I said, "Lord, forgive me for worrying, for being full of anxieties, for fretting, for being discouraged, for having the blues, for feeling sorry for myself. I know You will forgive me because You said You would if I'd confess it. From this day on, because You have now forgiven me, I promise You the longest day I live, I will never worry again."

Confession: *I do not worry about tomorrow. I have no worries, no cares. I've committed them to God. I never have the blues. I am never discouraged!*

FEBRUARY 5

I CAN

I can do all things through Christ which strengtheneth me.
— **PHILIPPIANS 4:13**

Many years have come and gone since I cast my cares upon the Lord, and although I will confess that I've been sorely tempted, I have not worried. I have not fretted. I have not had the blues. I have not been discouraged, no matter what. (Some people said I didn't have enough sense to worry. But, thank God, I had too much Bible sense to worry!)

Worry was the most difficult sin for me to give up. Worry is the greatest temptation you will ever face too. But you can resist it. And you must.

Your worst enemy is the flesh. The flesh and natural human reasonings would limit you to your own ability. You look at the circumstances, influences, problems, cares, tests, storms, and winds, and you say, "I can't."

The language of doubt, the flesh, the senses, and the devil is, "I can't. I don't have the ability, the opportunity, or the strength. I'm limited."

But the language of faith says, "I can do all things through Christ who strengthens me."

Confession: *I can! I can do all things through Christ who strengthens me.*

FEBRUARY 6

STRENGTHENED

. . . The Lord is the strength of my life; of whom shall I be afraid?
— PSALM 27:1

. . . Whosoever believeth on him shall not be ashamed.
— ROMANS 9:33

The language of faith says, "I can do all things in Christ. The Lord strengthens me. I cannot be conquered. I cannot be defeated. If a natural force comes against me, it can't defeat me, because there aren't enough natural forces in all the world that could conquer the Christ who dwells within me!

"Greater is He who is in me, than he who is in the world. I am fortified from within. I've learned how to put Christ to work for me and in me. I have, dwelling in me, the Spirit of God who raised Jesus from the dead! I have God's wisdom, strength, and ability *in me*. I'm learning how to let that wisdom govern my intellect. I'm letting God speak through my lips. I'm daring to think God's thoughts after Him.

"He is the strength of my life, whom shall I fear? God has made me greater than my enemies. God has enabled me to put my heel on the neck of weakness, fear, and inability. I stand and declare that whosoever believeth in Him shall not be put to shame. Therefore, I cannot be put to shame."

Confession: *(Make up your own confession from today's scriptures and faith thoughts.)*

FEBRUARY 7

SWINGING FREE

Finally, my brethren, be strong in the Lord, and in the power of his might. — EPHESIANS 6:10

One day in 1932, two hundred sailors were holding onto ropes attached to the dirigible, the *USS Akron*, as they attempted to moor the giant airship to a steel mast in San Diego. Suddenly, however, the dirigible shot straight up into the air. Some of the men hung onto the lines and were swept up with the ship, soon falling to the ground. Several were killed. After all the rest had fallen, one man kept hanging on. He could be seen as the dirigible soared high in the sky. People were screaming and fainting. They knew this sailor couldn't hold on much longer, and any minute he might fall back to the earth and certain death.

But after an hour and forty-five minutes, when they were able to pull the dirigible back to its mooring, the sailor was still dangling from the airship. An ambulance was waiting to take him to the hospital, but he said he was all right. People asked him how he had held on for so long. He told them he had found he had about four feet of rope, so, while holding on with one hand, he tied the rope around his waist with the other, and the rope held him. He had just been swinging free the whole time!

Many Christians are also trying to hold on and hold out, but instead they give out. Some even fall. But all we really need to do is to wrap ourselves in the promises of God and *swing* free like this sailor, enjoying the scenery!

Confession: *I am strong in the Lord and in the power of His might. I am swinging free in His strength and in His power!*

FEBRUARY 8

BY FAITH

. . . The just shall live by faith. — ROMANS 1:17

The faith life is the most beautiful life in the world! It is the life God wants us to live, and the walk God wants us to walk (2 Cor. 5:7).

Let both your words and your actions agree. If you *talk* faith, you must *walk* faith — you must *act* faith. Your actions and your words must agree that you are a believer. It won't do any good to talk faith if you're not going to act faith. And if it were somehow possible to act faith without talking faith, that wouldn't do any good, either, because your words and your actions must agree.

Some people declare one minute, "I'm trusting God to meet my needs." Then, with the next breath, they say, "Well, it looks like I'm going to lose my car. I can't make the payments." One minute it sounds like they're talking faith, but in a few moments their actions prove otherwise.

Some even quote God's Word, saying, "I know the Lord said in Philippians 4:19, *'But my God shall supply all your need according to his riches in glory by Christ Jesus.'* And I'm trusting Him to meet our needs — but it looks like we'll have to have the phone taken out. We can't pay the bill." They mentally agreed to the truth of this scripture, but they didn't *act* as if it were so.

Start acting like God's Word is true.

Confession: *I live by faith — faith in the Word of the Living God. I act like His Word is true.*

FEBRUARY 9

KEEPING HIS WORD

. . . I am watching over my word to perform it.
— **JEREMIAH 1:12** (*NASV*)

You may be certain that if you accept God's Word and act on it, He is watching over that Word to make it good in your life. All you need to do is to *act on the Word*. It is very important that you learn this simple little lesson. Acting on the Word is not struggling. It is not crying. It is not praying. It is simply acting on what God has spoken, and that brings results.

Several years ago, after I had spent hours struggling and praying about finances and healing for my family, I lay exhausted on the altar of a church. Once I was finally quiet, the Lord could speak to me.

"What are you doing?" He asked.

"I came out here to pray through," I said.

"What do you mean by 'pray through'?"

"I guess I was going to pray until I had some kind of feeling or a witness that these needs are met. I'm 365 miles from home. I thought I would know somehow when my children were healed and our financial needs were met."

"Isn't My Word sufficient for you? You are not acting like My Word is so," the Lord said. "In fact, you're acting as if it were not so. You're acting as though you think if you pray long enough and loud enough, you might eventually talk Me into the notion of not being a liar and of keeping My word."

Confession: *I believe God. And I act like I believe Him!*

FEBRUARY 10

LOVE BORN

. . . God is love. — 1 JOHN 4:8

. . . The love of God is shed abroad in our hearts by the Holy Ghost . . . .
— ROMANS 5:5

When you were born again, God became your Father. God is a love God. You are a love child of a love God. You are born of God, and God is love; therefore, you are born of love. The nature of God is in you — and the nature of God is love.

In fact, you can't say you don't have this divine love, because *everyone* in the family of God has it — or else they're not in the family! They may not be exercising it. They may be like the man who wrapped his one talent in a napkin and buried it (Matt. 25:25), but the Bible says that the love of God has been shed abroad in our hearts by the Holy Spirit. That means the God-kind of love has been shed abroad in our heart, our spirit, our inner man.

Romans 5:5 is not talking about the baptism in the Holy Spirit. It's talking about the New Birth — when you are born of the Spirit of God — that's when the love of God came in. When you were born spiritually, you partook of God's life and nature.

Confession: *God is love. I am born of God; therefore, I am born of love. I am a love child of a love God. The love of God is shed abroad in my heart by the Holy Spirit. My nature is love. It is natural for me to walk in love.*

FEBRUARY 11

MATURING FRUIT

But the fruit of the Spirit is love . . . . — GALATIANS 5:22

I am the vine, ye are the branches: He that abideth in me, and I in him, the same bringeth forth much fruit . . . . — JOHN 15:5

Love is the fruit of the recreated human spirit, produced because of the life of Christ within.

Picture a fruit tree. Where does the fruit grow? Fruit grows on the branches. Jesus used the illustration of the tree. Who are the branches? We are.

How does natural fruit grow on the branch? It receives nourishment from the trunk — the vine — of the tree. Life from the trunk flows out into the branches. It's the same in the spiritual realm. God is life. God is love. His life and love flow out to the believers — the branches.

Fruit grows. It doesn't come fully mature. The Bible says, *"But whoso keepeth his word, in him verily is the love of God perfected . . ."* (1 John 2:5). The word "perfected" means matured. John was talking about maturing in the fruit of love. (I don't think any of us have completely matured in it yet, but some of us are making progress.)

Confession: *The fruit of the spirit is love. Christ is the vine. I am the branch. I abide in Christ, and Christ abides in me. Therefore, I bring forth fruit. As I keep God's Word, I mature in the fruit of love. I am making progress.*

FEBRUARY 12

THE LOVE LAW

A new commandment I give unto you, That ye love one another; as I have loved you, that ye also love one another. — JOHN 13:34

God's family is a love family.

And the love law of the family of God is, "... *That ye love one another; as I have loved you* . . . ."

How did God love us? Did He love us because we deserved it? No. God loved us while we were yet unlovely. God loved us while we were yet sinners! (And think about this: If God loved us with so great a love while we were yet sinners and unlovely — when we were His *enemies* — do you think He loves us any less now that we are His *children*? No, a thousand times no!)

Love is the only commandment of the love family. If you love another person, you won't steal from him. If you love someone, you won't kill him. You won't covet his house. You won't tell a lie about him. Therefore, divine love is the fulfilling of the law.

Since love is the law of the family of God, one step out of love is a step into sin. If you've made such a step, repent and get back into walking in love. To fellowship with your Father, to walk with God, to walk in God's realm, you must walk in love — for God is love.

Confession: *I love others as Christ loved me. Love is the law I am under. I walk in love. Therefore, I have fellowship with my Father Who is love.*

FEBRUARY 13

KNOWN BY OUR LOVE

By this shall all men know that ye are my disciples, if ye have love one to another.
— JOHN 13:35

How is the world going to know us?

By our love. By this divine love. By this God-kind of love. By this unselfish love. *"God so loved — He gave."*

Now, His love isn't natural human love. Natural human love is selfish. As a usual thing, even a mother's love is a natural human love. It's selfish: "That's *my* baby!"

But if we would learn to let the divine love of God which is shed abroad in our hearts dominate us, it would make a real difference in our lives. It would cure the ills in our homes. Natural human love can turn to hatred when it doesn't get its way. It will fight and fuss, claw and knock, "cuss" and be mean. Divine love, when it is reviled, reviles not again. The God-kind of love is not interested in *what I can get*, but in *what I can give*. Do you see how that can solve all the problems in your home?

As children of God, the nature of God is in us — and God's nature is love. So it is *natural* for love to be in our spirit, our heart. However, if we allow our outward man and our mind to dominate us, that love nature in our heart is kept prisoner. Let's release the love of God that is within us!

Confession: *The world will know me by my love. I will release the love nature within me!*

FEBRUARY 14

LOVE ATMOSPHERE

Beloved, let us love one another: for love is of God; and every one that loveth is born of God, and knoweth God. He that loveth not knoweth not God; for God is love. . . . If we love one another, God dwelleth in us, and his love is perfected in us. — 1 JOHN 4:7,8,12

Husbands and wives need to let the love of God dominate them — and not just natural human love — because natural love is so shallow.

Christians have an advantage over other people. Not only can they love their spouse with natural affection, but they can add to it divine love which never seeks its own, but always seeks the other's welfare.

In all the years of our marriage, my wife and I have walked in love. I never consider myself or what I want; I consider what Oretha wants. I never want to be self-seeking; I always want to put her first. And Oretha reciprocates. We always try to outdo one another in love. And how blessed it is! Praise God! Our home is like Heaven on earth.

A troubled person who had visited us once said, "When I visit in your home, it's like heaven. You can feel a *presence* there the minute you go into the house."

We create atmospheres in our homes.

Confession: *I will walk in divine love toward those I love. I will let the unselfish love of God pour through me to them, creating an atmosphere of love!*

FEBRUARY 15

THE BRETHREN

We know that we have passed from death unto life, because we love the brethren. He that loveth not his brother abideth in death. Whosoever hateth his brother is a murderer: and ye know that no murderer hath eternal life abiding in him. — 1 JOHN 3:14,15

A minister's wife came to me greatly disturbed. "Brother Hagin," she said, "I can't go to Heaven. I hate my mother-in-law!"

After letting her stew a little, I was able to help her. I asked her to look me straight in the eye and say, "I hate my mother-in-law." And I asked her to check on the inside of her — in her spirit — as she was saying that.

She said, "I hate my mother-in-law." Then she exclaimed, "Why, something seems to be 'scratching' me on the inside!"

"Yes," I said, "that's the love of God in your born-again human spirit that loves everyone. The real you doesn't hate your mother-in-law. But you're letting the outward man dominate the situation."

"You're right," she said, "I don't really hate my mother-in-law." And she made the spiritual adjustment of allowing the man on the inside, where love lives, to dominate the outward man.

Confession: *I know that I have passed from death unto life because I love the brethren. And I allow that love to dominate my being. I walk in love toward everyone!*

FEBRUARY 16

AN EXPOSÉ ON LOVE

Love endures long and is patient and kind; love never is envious nor boils over with jealousy . . . . — 1 CORINTHIANS 13:4 (*Amplified*)

What about this God-kind of love?

What are its characteristics?

They are given to us in First Corinthians 13. It is to be regretted that the translators of the *King James Version* translated the Greek word for divine love, *agape*, as "charity." My favorite translation on this "exposé on love" is found in *The Amplified Bible*. I think every Christian should read the *Amplified* translation of First Corinthians 13 every few days, if not every day — and practice it!

Let's look at it, beginning with verse four:

"Love endures long and is patient and kind . . . ." Many people endure long — but they aren't very kind while they're doing it! They just suffer along with people and things because they have to. A wife will put up with a husband, but she's not too kind while she does it (and vice versa).

". . . Love never is envious nor boils over with jealousy . . . ." Natural human love is the kind of love that boils over with jealousy. The God-kind of love doesn't boil over with jealously.

Confession: *I am a love person. Therefore, I endure long and I am patient and kind. I am never envious, nor do I boil over with jealousy.*

FEBRUARY 17

LOVE ARISES

Love . . . is not boastful or vainglorious, does not display itself haughtily. It is not conceited (arrogant and inflated with pride); it is not rude (unmannerly) and does not act unbecomingly . . . .
— 1 CORINTHIANS 13:4,5 *(Amplified)*

It's always flesh that is boastful, haughty, conceited, arrogant, inflated with pride, rude, and unmannerly.

And by an act of your own will, you can decide not to give in to these fleshly temptations. You can decide rather to walk in love — to walk in the Spirit.

The battle is there between your human spirit and your flesh. But the Bible says, ". . . *Walk in the Spirit, and ye shall not fulfil the lust of the flesh*" (Gal. 5:16).

Decide to allow your spirit to dominate. When the temptation comes, stand still a moment and begin to speak the Word of God. Begin to say, "I am born of love. I will allow the love of God within me to dominate." When the temptation comes, begin to speak the Word of God. Begin to say, "I am born of love. I will allow the love of God within me to dominate this situation."

And the love of God will rise up big within you!

Confession: *I am a love person. Therefore, I am not boastful or vainglorious. I do not display myself haughtily. I am not conceited — arrogant and inflated with pride. I am not rude. I am not unmannerly. I do not act unbecomingly. I act in love.*

FEBRUARY 18

THE BEST WAY

. . . Love (God's love in us) does not insist on its own rights or its own way, for it is not self-seeking . . . .
— 1 CORINTHIANS 13:5 (*Amplified*)

Take time to let today's text sink into your heart.

Too many people would rather declare, "Well, I know what's mine, though. I've got *my* say-so, and I'm going to have it. I've got *my* rights, and I'm going to have them." And they insist on having their own way, no matter how much their actions may hurt someone else.

I was only twenty years old and unmarried when I pastored my second church, and I rented a room from a couple in the church. The man of the house knew the Bible, and he had a marvelous experience with God. But he was the type of person who said, "I've got my say-so, and I'm going to have it. I'm a member of that church just as much as anyone else, and I've got my say-so." He had his say-so all right, and so did some of the others, until they wrecked the church.

This text says that love does not insist on having its own rights. Start believing in God and believing in love. It's the best way — and it's your way!

Confession: *I believe in God. And I believe in love. I am a love person. I do not insist on my own rights. I do not insist on my own way. I am not self-seeking. I am a love person.*

FEBRUARY 19

LOVE GAUGE

... Love ... is not touchy or fretful or resentful; it takes no account of the evil done to it [it pays no attention to a suffered wrong].
— 1 CORINTHIANS 13:5 *(Amplified)*

Here is the love thermometer — the love gauge! It's very easy to find out whether or not you're walking in love. When you begin to take account of the evil done to you, you're not walking in love. As long as you walk in God and stay full of the Holy Spirit, you won't take account of the evil done to you.

Through the years when unjust things have happened to me, people have told me, "I wouldn't take that. I wouldn't put up with that — not me!" But I just kept my mouth shut and never said a word, smiled, and stayed happy. Why, I wouldn't take time to deny it if they claimed I'd killed my grandma! I'd just keep shouting, "Hallelujah! Praise God! Glory to God!"

I suggest you walk in love, too, toward those who treat you in an evil manner. If you walk in love regardless of suffered wrongs, you'll come out on top in the long run!

However, some people will regard your attitude as a weakness. Even ministers have told me, "There must be a weakness in your character; you never take up for yourself." No, it's a strength! *Love never fails.*

I simply refuse to hold any resentment in my heart against anyone.

Confession: *I am a love person. Therefore, I am not touchy, fretful, or resentful. I have no resentment in my heart toward anyone.*

FEBRUARY 20

A SECOND LOOK

... Love ... is not touchy or fretful or resentful; it takes no account of the evil done to it [it pays no attention to a suffered wrong].
— 1 CORINTHIANS 13:5 (*Amplified*)

The subject of walking in the God-kind of love is so important — and so overlooked by Christians — that we're going to take some extra time examining it.

"... Love ... takes no account of the evil done to it ...." This has to be the God-kind of love, because we were enemies of God, and God didn't take account of the evil we had done to Him. He sent Jesus to redeem us. He loved us while we were yet sinners.

"... Love ... pays no attention to a suffered wrong ...." We might just as well admit it — there aren't too many people walking in God's love, even though they have it! No, they're walking in natural human love, and they surely pay attention to a suffered wrong! They get huffy about it. A husband and wife, both Christians, will become angry and won't speak to each other for a week because of some wrong that one of them suffered.

Can't you see how it would straighten things out in the home, the church, and the nation for people to become children of God, get the love of God in them, and then live in the family of God as children of God?

Confession: *I am a love person. I am not touchy. I am not fretful. I am not resentful. I take no account of the evil done to me. I pay no attention to a suffered wrong.*

FEBRUARY 21

LOVE CHARACTERISTICS

. . . [Love] does not rejoice at injustice and unrighteousness, but rejoices when right and truth prevail. Love bears up under anything and everything that comes, is ever ready to believe the best of every person . . . .
— 1 CORINTHIANS 13:6,7 *(Amplified)*

"Love bears up under anything and everything that comes . . . ." If you have the God-kind of love within — and if you walk in the God-kind of love — you will make it every time!

". . . Love . . . is ever ready to believe the best of every person . . . ." Natural human love is ever ready to believe the *worst* about every person! I've traveled across this country for many years in the ministry, and it's amazing what you hear about this preacher and that preacher, this person and that person, this singer and that singer. I don't pay the least bit of attention to any of those stories. I don't believe a word of them. I believe the *best* of everyone.

Children ought to have the right to be brought up in this love atmosphere in the home. Then they'll go out in life's fight and win. But when you always see the worst in the children and always tell them, "You'll never amount to anything," they'll live up to what you say. But when you see the best in them and love them, it will bring out the best in them. They will grow up to amount to something.

Confession: *I am a love person. I do not rejoice at injustice and unrighteousness. I rejoice when right and truth prevail. I bear up under anything and everything that comes. I am ever ready to believe the best of every person.*

FEBRUARY 22

UNFAILING LOVE

. . . [Love's] hopes are fadeless under all circumstances, and it endures everything [without weakening]. Love never fails [never fades out or becomes obsolete or comes to an end] . . . .
— 1 CORINTHIANS 13:7,8 (*Amplified*)

If you walk in love, you will not fail — because love never fails!

We are interested in spiritual gifts (1 Cor. 12 and 14), and we ought to be. The Bible tells us that prophecies will fail, tongues will cease, and knowledge will vanish away. But thank God, love never fails.

Yes, I believe in prophecy and prophesying. I believe in speaking in tongues. Thank God for these gifts! But if you exercise these gifts outside of love, they become as sounding brass and tinkling cymbals.

Let's have prophecy. Let's have tongues. Let's have faith. Let's have knowledge. But let's have love with it. Let's put love first, because we are in the family of love, and we have become acquainted with our Heavenly Father, who is love.

We ought to want to learn and grow in love until we are made perfect in love. I haven't been made perfect in love yet, have you? But I'm going to keep working toward that goal!

Confession: *I am a love person. My hopes are fadeless under all circumstances. I endure everything without weakening. I never fail!*

FEBRUARY 23

Fear Not

But straightway Jesus spake unto them, saying, Be of good cheer; it is
I; be not afraid.   — MATTHEW 14:27

God never comes with a message of fear. You can start in the Old Testament and trace all the way down through the New, and you will see that every time God manifested Himself to people, or sent angels or Jesus Himself, they always came with the message, "Be not afraid! Fear not!"

Fear doesn't come from God. It comes from the devil. And Christians, including preachers and teachers, have no business going around putting fear into people.

We hear so much fear preached: Fear of sickness and disease; fear of what's going to happen in the world; and fear of the devil. The way some people preach about demons causes people to be afraid. I preach about the devil and demons, too, but I preach that we've got authority over them. I preach that we should always remember, in all our encounters with the devil, that He's a defeated foe.

Fear is not the message of the Church. Faith is the message of the Church. Good cheer is the message of the Church. "Be not afraid" is the message of the Church.

Confession: *I am of good cheer. I am not afraid. I fear not. That is the*
message of God my Father to my heart. It is also His message to oth-
ers. Therefore, my message to others is: Faith and good cheer. Be not
afraid. Fear not!

FEBRUARY 24

RESISTING FEAR

For God hath not given us the spirit of fear; but of power, and of love, and of a sound mind. — 2 TIMOTHY 1:7

Today's text calls fear a spirit, and it states definitely that the spirit of fear does not come from God. Today's faith thought is a confession you can use to successfully resist fear when it attempts to come upon you.

Fear,
I resist you,
in the Name of the Lord Jesus Christ.

In His mighty Name,
I resist you.
I refuse to fear;
I refuse to be afraid.

It is written in His Holy Word
that He hath not given me
the spirit of fear;
But of power,
and of love,
and of a sound mind.

I no longer have the spirit of fear.
I have the spirit of love.
I have the spirit of power.
I have the spirit of a sound mind.

55

FEBRUARY 25

DON'T TALK FEAR

Thou art snared with the words of thy mouth, thou art taken with the words of thy mouth.
— **PROVERBS 6:2**

With your mouth, you are either going to give God or Satan dominion over you.

When you were born again, you confessed the lordship of Jesus Christ (Rom. 10:9,10). You confessed Jesus as your Lord. Jesus began to have dominion over you and to rule in your life. But, when you confess Satan's ability to hinder you, to keep you from success, to cause you to fear — even though you are a Christian — you are giving Satan dominion over you. And, naturally, when Satan has dominion over you, you are filled with weakness and fear.

Don't ever confess your fears.

"But what if I'm afraid?" you might ask.

"You" are not really afraid. The Bible says that God has not given you — the real "you" — the spirit of fear, but He's given you the spirit of power, of love, and of a sound mind. Fear isn't something that is coming from the inside of you, trying to get hold of you. Fear is from the enemy. *You* have a spirit of power — so say you have! *You* have a spirit of love — so say you have. *You* have a spirit of a sound mind — so say you have. When you confess it, then it will begin to dominate you.

Confession: *I am never afraid. I do not know fear. I have a spirit of power. I have a spirit of love. I have a sound mind.*

FEBRUARY 26

GODLINESS IS PROFITABLE

For bodily exercise profiteth little: but godliness is profitable unto all things, having promise of the life that now is, and of that which is to come. — 1 TIMOTHY 4:8

Some people would have you believe that godliness — living for God, being born again, walking in fellowship with the Lord — has no profit in this life. They think we must simply endure life with all its ups and downs, struggles and trials, always bearing in mind that "this life will soon be o'er."

I'm glad Paul gave us a balanced viewpoint by saying that godliness is not only profitable "over yonder" in the next life, but it has promise of *". . . the life that now is . . . ."*

As sinners, we were bankrupt, but God had mercy on us, and He sent Jesus to redeem us. Jesus came not only to save us from our sins — but to live within us (Col. 1:27). And Jesus wants us to bring as much glory to His Name, and to pay as rich dividends to Him as possible in this life. Instead of saying that godliness is a hindrance to success, the Apostle Paul says the exact opposite in our text scripture.

It doesn't *cost* to serve God — it *pays!*

Confession: *I live a godly life. I am born again. I live for God. I walk in fellowship with the Lord. This is profitable for me — here on earth in the life that now is, and also in the life which is to come!*

FEBRUARY 27

Is Your Profit Showing?

Meditate upon these things; give thyself wholly to them; that thy profiting may appear to all. — 1 TIMOTHY 4:15

If your profiting is to appear to all, then it is to show! Why is godliness profitable? Why is living for God, being God's child, walking in fellowship with God, keeping God's commandments, profitable?

It is because God has made some promises to His faithful children. Notice the word "promise" in yesterday's text: ". . . *having PROMISE of the life that now is* . . ." (1 Tim. 4:8). God has made us promises in this life. Our profiting is because of these promises.

And when our profiting (which is due to God's promises) appears to all, we are able to show the world there is a God in the Church — just as when Israel was walking with God, she could show the earth "there is a God in Israel" (1 Sam. 17:46).

Confession: *I will meditate upon God's promises and give myself wholly to them, that my profiting may appear to all.*

FEBRUARY 28

PROMISE OF PROTECTION

Read Psalm 91.

Paul said, in writing to the Church *". . . ye are God's husbandry* [garden, farm], *ye are God's building"* (1 Cor. 3:9). That means we belong to God. Now, if you have a building worth anything, even your own home, you are going to protect it every way you possibly can. And God, in His Holy Word, has promised us protection. I think the greatest such promise is Psalm 91.

Many years ago, I read this Psalm from a Swedish translation. I found that verse 10 translated in the *King James Version* as *"There shall no evil befall thee . . . ,"* was translated in the Swedish version as, "There shall no accident overtake thee . . . ." I researched it and found that this meaning is, indeed, included in the original text. I then claimed this protection.

Some years later, I did some checking and found that I had driven nearly two million miles preaching the Gospel without having a single accident! Understand, I'm not bragging on my driving; I'm bragging on the Word — Psalm 91.

Verse 10 continues, *". . . neither shall any plague come nigh thy dwelling."* I claimed that part of the verse, as well as verse 11: *"For he shall give his angels charge over thee, to keep thee in all thy ways."*

God has made promises and provisions for us. If our faith is not in God's promises, we live way beneath our privileges.

Confession: *(Make your personal confession of Psalm 91.)*

FEBRUARY 29

PROMISE OF PROSPERITY

Blessed is the man that walketh not in the counsel of the ungodly, nor standeth in the way of sinners, nor sitteth in the seat of the scornful. But his delight is in the law of the Lord; and in his law doth he meditate day and night. And he shall be like a tree planted by the rivers of water, that bringeth forth his fruit in his season; his leaf also shall not wither; and whatsoever he doeth shall prosper. — PSALM 1:1-3

60

When God's Word has a part in your life, and when you live by those principles of the Word, then what the Bible promises will come to pass in your life. Whatever you do shall prosper!

One translation of the last portion of Joshua 1:8 reads, ". . . Thou shalt be able to deal wisely in the affairs of life."

The Bible says concerning King Uzziah, ". . . *as long as he sought the Lord, God made him to prosper*" (2 Chron. 26:5). The Bible says of Joseph, ". . . *that which he did, the Lord made it to prosper*" (Gen. 39:23).

Confession: *I walk in godliness. I do not walk in the counsel of the ungodly, nor stand in the way of sinners, nor sit in the seat of the scornful. But my delight is in the law of the Lord. In God's Word I meditate day and night. Therefore, I am like a tree planted by the rivers of water. I bring forth fruit. My leaf does not wither. Whatsoever I do shall prosper.*

MARCH 1

By Thy Words

For by thy words thou shalt be justified, and by thy words thou shalt be condemned. — MATTHEW 12:37

Jesus Himself made the above statement.

Words are much more important than many people realize.

Do you remember Job — and his three so-called "friends" who came to comfort him? Job's cry to those who came as comforters and stayed as tormentors was, *"How long will ye vex my soul, AND BREAK ME IN PIECES WITH WORDS?"* (Job 19:2).

Words make us or break us.

Words heal us or make us sick.

According to the teaching of the Bible, words destroy us, or words make us full of life, happiness, and health.

Words that we spoke yesterday make life what it is today.

That agrees with what Jesus said in Mark 11:23, *". . . he shall have whatsoever he SAITH."*

Those things which you say are words. In fact, you could read that last phrase like this: "He shall have the WORDS that he speaks."

Confession: *By my words I shall be justified. I know that I shall have whatsoever I say. I shall have the words that I speak. Therefore, I speak words full of life, happiness, and health. I speak words that make, rather than break!*

61

MARCH 2

POWER OF LIFE

Death and life are in the power of the tongue: and they that love it shall eat the fruit thereof. — **PROVERBS 18:21**

"No, I won't pray for your son," I told the startled widowed mother of a fifteen-year-old boy. "It won't do any good. As long as you keep telling your son he'll never amount to anything, you'll undo the praying."

"Did the Lord reveal that to you?" she asked.

"No," I said, "I just know that the condition in life that we or our children are in was created by *words.*"

"What shall I do?" she said.

"There are some things you should have done when your son was younger, but he's fifteen now. So first, quit nagging him about being saved. Second, instead of lying in bed at night worrying about him, say, 'Lord, I don't know where he is, but wherever he is, I surround him with faith and love.' You've been surrounding him with doubt, fear, and condemnation. Say, 'Lord, I'm going to tell You what I believe. I don't believe he'll end up in the penitentiary. I'll never tell him again he won't amount to anything. I believe he will amount to something.'"

I was back in this woman's city fifteen months later. To make a long story short, she came to me and shared, "It was hard, but I did just what you told me. Before, my son was all out for the devil — but now he's all out for God!"

Confession: *Life is in the power of my tongue, and I will minister life with it. I speak words of life!*

MARCH 3

WELL OF LIFE

The mouth of a righteous man is a well of life . . . .
— **PROVERBS 10:11**

Immediately after the birth of our son and daughter, I took those little ones into my hands and said, "Lord, I thank You for this child. Because I know the Bible, I realize it is my responsibility to train up this child in the way it should go, and when it is old, it will not depart from it.

"I realize Your Word says to bring our children up in the nurture and admonition of the Lord, and I'm going to do that. I know that children are taught in two ways: By precept and by example. So I'm going to live right in front of this child. I will set the right example. Then, too, I know that you can have what you say, so I say over this child that it will grow up strong physically, without sickness and without disease; it will be alert mentally; and stalwart spiritually."

Our children grew up without sickness and disease. I never prayed a prayer that they would be saved. I never prayed a prayer that they would be filled with the Holy Spirit. But both were saved and filled with the Holy Spirit at an early age.

Children are a product of words!

Confession: *According to the New Testament, in Christ I am righteous. Therefore, my mouth is a well of life. I speak words of life concerning others as well as myself!*

MARCH 4

PLEASANT WORDS

Pleasant words are as an honeycomb, sweet to the soul, and health to the bones.
— **PROVERBS 16:24**

Words bless or words curse.

Words heal or words make us sick.

Words that we hear in the morning will linger with us throughout the day. Wives and husbands need to realize that a biting, stinging word in the morning will rob their companion of efficiency the whole day long. But a loving, tender, beautiful word, a little prayer word, will fill that loved one with music, and lead them into victory.

Parents and children need to realize that the home atmosphere is a product of words.

Learn to make words work *for* you. Learn to fill words with power that cannot be resisted. How do you do that? By filling your words with faith and love.

Confession: *My words work for me. I fill them with a power that cannot be resisted. I fill my words with faith and love. My words bless. My words heal. My words lead my loved ones into victory. My words charge the atmosphere of my home with faith and love!*

MARCH 5

ATMOSPHERE

*In the lips of him that hath understanding wisdom is found. . . .
Through wisdom is an house builded; and by understanding it is
established: And by knowledge shall the chambers be filled with all
precious and pleasant riches.* — PROVERBS 10:13, 24:3,4

Spiritual things are created by words. Even natural, physical things are
created by words! God, who is a Spirit, said, "Let there be an earth,"
and there was an earth. Jesus said, ". . . *whosoever shall SAY . . . shall
have whatsoever he SAITH*" (Mark 11:23,24). Atmospheres are created with words.

For example, if you go into a room where fish has been fried, the fish
smell is still in the atmosphere. And if you go into a room where harsh
words have been spoken, they also linger in the atmosphere. The air is
heavy with them.

Children brought up in an atmosphere of wrong words become warped.
They fail in life, because right words were not spoken to them.

Why is it that some children grow up strong and go out in life's fight and
win? It's because the right kind of words were spoken in their home!
Words make children love an education. Words bring children to church.

Confession: *I create the very atmosphere around me with my words. I
speak words of wisdom — God's words. I speak words of faith —
God's words. I speak words of love — God's words. And the chambers
round about me are filled with precious and pleasant riches!*

MARCH 6

WRONG WORDS

Whoso keepeth his mouth and his tongue keepeth his soul from troubles.
— **PROVERBS 21:23**

When trouble comes, most people want to blame God. "Why did God let this happen?" they ask.

After Job's troubles came, he said, *"For the thing which I greatly feared is come upon me, and that which I was afraid of is come unto me"* (Job 3:25). Job opened the door and let the devil in!

66

We cause our troubles ourselves much of the time. Many dear Christian people don't keep their mouths and tongues under control. They're always saying wrong words. Just about all they ever talk about is what a battle they've had with the devil. Words of defeat are wrong. Words of failure are wrong. Words about how the devil is hindering you, how he's keeping you from success, how he's making you sick and keeping you sick, are wrong. Such words give Satan dominion over you and create troubles.

But when you have God's Word in your heart, and speak it out of your mouth — right in the face of apparent contradictions, right in the face of pain, right in the face of alarming symptoms, right in the face of excruciating circumstances — such adverse conditions will disappear.

Confession: *I keep my mouth, and I keep my tongue. Therefore, I keep my soul from troubles. I believe God's Word in my heart. I purpose that the Word shall be in my mouth and on my tongue, and I shall only speak according to God's Word!*

MARCH 7

HEALTH WORDS

There is that speaketh like the piercings of a sword: but the tongue of the wise is health. **— PROVERBS 12:18**

I first learned the secret of words — faith words — when I spent sixteen months on the bed of sickness, given up to die by five doctors.

But one August day in 1934, as I lay in that bed, I acted on Mark 11:23 and 24, and I *said* . . . ! *Words* were spoken!

I *said*, "I believe that I receive healing for the deformed heart. I believe I receive healing for the incurable blood disease. I believe I receive healing for the paralysis. I believe I receive healing from the top of my head to the soles of my feet." Within the hour, I was standing on my feet beside the bed — healed!

Now more than sixty-five years have come and gone, and I haven't even had a headache. And I won't have one. But if I did have one — which I haven't — I wouldn't say my head hurt. Why? Because Jesus said, "*. . . he shall have whatsoever he saith*" (Mark 11:23). If someone were to ask me in such a case, "How are you feeling?" I'd reply, "I'm fine, thank you. You see, the Word of God says that by His stripes I am healed. So I believe that I am healed. And the Word of God says . . ." And I would speak the right words — for the tongue of the wise is health!

Confession: ***My tongue is health. It speaks words of life and health. I talk health. Therefore, I walk in health.***

MARCH 8

TRANSFORMED TALK

Blessed is the man that walketh not in the counsel of the ungodly . . . .
— PSALM 1:1

. . . Be not conformed to this world: but be ye transformed by the renewing of your mind . . . .
— ROMANS 12:2

When God's Word tells us not to be conformed to this world, notice that it relates conformity to the area of the mind. In other words, we are told not to think like the world thinks; we are to get our mind renewed with the Word of God and *think* in line with the Word of God. Then we will *talk* and *believe* in line with the Word of God.

The world is programmed negatively. The world thinks sickness, fear, doubt, defeat, and failure. That's because the world without God is in spiritual death. Therefore, it is programmed to death instead of life. Listen to what people say: "That scares me to death."

If Christians do not renew their minds with the Word of God, they will make the same mistake the world makes. They'll talk themselves into sickness. But if we'll renew our mind with the Word of God, we'll know that God says, ". . . *the tongue of the wise is health*" (Prov. 12:18).

Confession: *I never talk sickness; I don't believe in sickness. I talk health. The tongue of the wise is health. I believe in healing and health. I never talk failure; I don't believe in failure. I believe in success. I never talk doubt; I refuse to doubt. I never talk defeat; I don't believe in defeat. I never talk about what the devil is doing; I talk about the works of God.*

MARCH 9

OVERCOMING FAITH

For whatsoever is born of God overcometh the world: and this is the victory that overcometh the world, even our faith. — 1 JOHN 5:4

I may be in the world, but I am not of the world. I am of God. My citizenship is in Heaven. And while I am in this world, I have the Greater One living in me. Greater is He that is in me, than he that is in the world (1 John 4:4).

Who is in the world? The devil. He's called the god of this world in Second Corinthians 4:4.

What is in the world? Sin. But the Greater One in me is greater than sin. The Greater One conquered sin.

What else is in the world? Sickness. It's not of God. It doesn't come from Heaven. There's no sickness up there. Sickness is of this world. But the Greater One in me is the Healer.

What else is in the world? Trouble. Adverse circumstances. Seeming impossibilities. But when I've faced such things, I've just remembered who is on the inside of me and what the Bible says. I didn't even have to pray about it. I just looked that circumstance right in the face and laughed as I said, "If I don't make it *over* you, I'll make it *around* you. If I don't make it *around* you, I'll make it *under* you. If I don't make it *under* you, I'll make it *through* you, because the Greater One is in me!" Even while I laughed, that circumstance ran off and hid!

69

Confession: *I am born of God. And by releasing my faith in words through my mouth, I overcome the world!*

MARCH 10

FRUIT OF THE MOUTH

*A man's belly shall be satisfied with the fruit of his mouth; and with
the increase of his lips shall he be filled.* — **PROVERBS 18:20**

You won't get the blessings of God just because you believe.

You don't get saved, healed, or get answers to prayer just because you
believe.

Most Christians think that is the case, but it isn't what the Bible teaches.
The Bible teaches that you must believe and you must say something.

For example, in order to be saved, Romans 10:9 and 10 says, *"That if
thou shalt CONFESS WITH THY MOUTH the Lord Jesus, and shalt
believe in thine heart that God hath raised him from the dead, thou shalt
be saved."* Notice it doesn't say you'll be saved just because you believe.
The very next verse says, *"For with the heart man believeth unto righteousness; AND WITH THE MOUTH CONFESSION IS MADE
UNTO SALVATION."*

Jesus didn't conclude Mark 11:23 by saying you'd have whatsoever you
believed. He concluded it by saying, *". . . he shall have whatsoever he
SAITH."*

Faith is always expressed in WORDS! The words that you speak — not
just on Sunday, in church, or when you pray, but the words you speak
in your everyday life, at home, with your friends, and on your job —
determine what you have in life.

Confession: *I purpose that I shall speak only according to God's Word!*

MARCH 11

SAYING THE SAME THING

Seeing then that we have a great high priest, that is passed into the heavens, Jesus the Son of God, let us hold fast our profession [confession]. — **HEBREWS 4:14**

The Greek word translated "profession" here is translated *confession* elsewhere in the *King James Version*. The literal Greek meaning of this word is *to speak the same thing*. So instead of saying, "Let us hold fast our confession" we could say, "Let us hold fast to speaking the same thing." Notice that *words* are involved here.

The thing that defeats many people is that they have a double confession. One time they confess one thing, and the next time they confess something else.

For example, they may say to you, "Yes, the Lord is my Shepherd, and I shall not want. According to Philippians 4:19, my God shall supply all of my need according to His riches in glory by Christ Jesus — and I'm believing God to supply my needs."

But when they leave you and meet someone else, their mind may revert back to their problems, so they'll say, "We're not doing so good. We can't pay our phone bill. We're going to have to take the phone out. And it even looks like we're going to lose our car . . ."

What about that first confession they made? It was nullified by the second.

Confession: *I make my mouth do its duty. I see to it that I speak in line with God's Word. Then I hold fast to my confession.*

MARCH 12

A PSALM

Let the word of Christ dwell in you richly in all wisdom; teaching and admonishing one another in psalms and hymns and spiritual songs . . . .
— COLOSSIANS 3:16

Here is the psalm the Holy Spirit gave me on the subject of words.

> Words seem so insignificant and small
>   that men oft times take no note of them at all.
>
> But words spoken in faith, create realities . . .
> So rise up and speak, like the Creator of the universe,
> Who, in faith, said, LET THERE BE — and THERE WAS.
>
> Words — you speak them all the time,
>   filled with negativism and defeat,
> Those words create defeat, and make you
>   unsuccessful, unhealthy, and unwise.
>
> But Words given by God, inspired by His Spirit,
>   called by men, the Holy Writ,
> These words heard with the ear of faith,
> And spoken out of a heart filled with faith,
> Will create in your life, and your family's too,
> Success and victory; health and healing;
> Circumstances and darkness and troubles too,
>   will run away from you.
>
> Filled with His Word, inspired by His Spirit,
> Make your tongue do its duty.
> See to it that you speak only truth . . .
> His Word is truth.
> Speak words of faith and love; words that are true,
> And no longer will spiritual realities unto you,
>   seem unreal and far away.
>
> But all of the blessings of life;
>   spiritual, material, physical, and financial too,
> Will come to make their abode with you.

MARCH 13

GOD'S MEDICINE

My son, attend to my words; incline thine ear unto my sayings. Let them not depart from thine eyes; keep them in the midst of thine heart. For they are life unto those that find them, and health [medicine] to all their flesh. — PROVERBS 4:20-22

A marginal note in a good reference Bible will show that the last phrase of the above text can read *"and medicine to all their flesh." This means that God has "prescribed" His words for our healing and for our health!*

But medicine, even in the natural, won't do any good unless you take it according to directions. You could go to a doctor, get a prescription, have it filled, take it home, set it on your bedside table — and still grow steadily worse! You could call the doctor and complain, "I don't understand it. I paid good money for this prescription, but I'm getting worse." The doctor might ask, "Are you taking your medicine according to the directions?" "Well, no, but I've got it right here in the bottle at my bedside." The medicine won't work just because it's in the bottle. You've got to get it *in you*!

And God's medicine (your Bible) won't work just because you have it on your bedside table. But it will work if you'll get it down on the inside of you — into your heart, or spirit. And not just by reading it and forgetting it; but by meditating upon it until it becomes a part of your inward man.

Confession: *I hide God's words in the midst of my heart. They are life to me. They are medicine to my flesh!*

MARCH 14

OBSTACLES

. . . And much people followed him [Jesus], *and thronged him. And a certain woman, which had an issue of blood twelve years. . . . When she had heard of Jesus, came in the press behind, and touched his garment.*
— MARK 5:24,25,27

To receive her healing, this woman had a number of obstacles to overcome. In her religious tradition, a woman with an issue of blood was considered in the same category as a leper. She was not supposed to mingle in public. If anyone came close to her, she was to cry, "Unclean! Unclean!" In fact, the women in ancient Israel didn't have the same rights and privileges to mix freely in public that most women in the modern world have.

You could say that a multitude of people stood between this woman and her healing. Public sentiment and her own religious teachings stood between her and getting to Jesus. But she overcame all obstacles. She got into the very midst of the crowd, and she reached through to touch Jesus' clothes.

This woman didn't pray that God would overcome the obstacles; she did something about them herself! You, too, will have to do something about the obstacles that confront you. Too many people expect God to do everything, leaving no part for them to play in receiving His blessings. But we do have a part to play. Receiving from God is a faith proposition.

Confession: *I am a believer. I am not a doubter. I have faith. I am an overcomer. No obstacle to the blessings of God can stand in my way. I overcome all obstacles by faith in God's Word!*

MARCH 15

STEP 1: SAY IT

For she said, If I may touch but his clothes, I shall be whole. And straightway the fountain of her blood was dried up; and she felt in her body that she was healed of that plague. . . . And he [Jesus] said unto her, Daughter, thy faith hath made thee whole; go in peace, and be whole of thy plague.   — MARK 5:28,29,34

The Lord Jesus Christ gave me a sermon during a vision in 1953. He told me to get pencil and paper and to write down 1, 2, 3, 4. Then He said, "If anyone, everywhere, will take these four steps, or put these four principles into operation, they will always receive whatever they want from Me, or from God the Father."

The steps Jesus gave me are simple. They are (1) *Say it*; (2) *Do it*; (3) *Receive it*; and (4) *Tell it*. Jesus used the healing of the woman with the issue of blood to illustrate these four steps.

Step 1: Say it. What was the woman's first step toward being healed? *"For she SAID . . . ."* Jesus told me, "Positive or negative, according to what the individual says, that shall he receive. This woman could have made a negative statement instead of a positive one. She could have said, 'There's no use. I've suffered so long. All the best doctors have given up on my case. I might as well go ahead and die.' And that would have been what she received. But she made a positive statement — and it came to pass."

What this woman said was her faith speaking.

Confession: *I have what I say. I speak positively — and I receive accordingly. What I say is my faith speaking. And what I say makes me whole.*

MARCH 16

STEP 2: DO IT

What good is it, my brethren, if a man professes to have faith, and yet his actions do not correspond. . . . some one will say, "You have faith, I have actions: prove to me your faith apart from corresponding actions and I will prove mine to you by my actions. . . ." You notice that his [Abraham's] faith was co-operating with his actions, and that by his actions his faith was perfected.
— JAMES 2:14,18,22 *(Weymouth)*

Step 2: Do it. It wouldn't have done that woman with the issue of blood any good to have said, "If I may but touch His clothes I shall be whole," if she hadn't *acted* on what she said.

Jesus said to me in that vision, "Your actions defeat you, or they put you over. According to your actions, you receive, or you are kept from receiving."

That's important. Read it again.

The Book of James is written to *believers.* James said, "What doth it profit, *my brethren.*" Most people think James was writing about salvation, but he was writing to people who were already saved, pointing out that faith without corresponding actions won't work. It is a great mistake to confess faith in the Word of God and, at the same time, contradict your confession by wrong actions. Actions must correspond with your saying and believing in order to receive from God.

This woman said, "If I may touch but His clothes, I shall be whole," and then she acted on that — and she received!

Confession: *My actions line up with God's Word. My actions put me over. By my actions I receive from God!*

MARCH 17

STEP 3: RECEIVE IT

And straightway the fountain of her blood was dried up; and she felt in her body that she was healed of that plague. And Jesus, immediately knowing in himself that virtue had gone out of him, turned him about in the press, and said, Who touched my clothes? — MARK 5:29,30

Jesus knew that *power* had gone out of Him. At that time, Jesus was the only representative of the Godhead at work upon the earth. He was anointed with the Holy Spirit (Acts 10:38). In that day, to get to where the power was, you had to go where Jesus was. Today, the Holy Spirit in the Person of the Godhead is at work upon the earth. He is everywhere present — and wherever the Holy Spirit is, there is *power.*

Nuclear bombs release radioactivity into the atmosphere — a power that can neither be seen nor felt, but a power that is both dangerous and deadly. However, there is a power working upon the earth this moment that is neither dangerous nor deadly; a power that is good, that heals, and that sets men free — the power of the Holy Spirit!

Jesus said to me when He gave me these four steps, "Power is always present everywhere. Faith gives it action, or puts it to work, or uses it."

This woman's faith caused the power to flow from Jesus into her. With our faith, we can plug into the power of God that is everywhere present, and we can put that power to work for us!

Confession: *I recognize that God's power is everywhere present. And I know how to plug into that power and put it to work for me. Faith is the plug.*

MARCH 18

STEP 4: TELL IT

O give thanks unto the Lord; call upon his name: make known his deeds among the people. Sing unto him, sing psalms unto him: talk ye of all his wondrous works. — PSALM 105:1,2

Step 4: Tell it. This woman, *". . . knowing what was done in her, came and fell down before him, and told him all the truth"* (Mark 5:33). Not only did Jesus hear her, but the whole crowd heard her. Jesus said to me concerning this step, "Tell it so that others may believe it and receive it."

There is a difference between this step and the first step. The first is, *Say it.* This fourth step is *Tell it.*

The woman *said* what she believed. Then, after she received, she *told* what had happened to her.

1. Say it.
2. Do it.
3. Receive it.
4. Tell it.

I asked Jesus, when He gave me these steps, "Are You telling me that any believer, anywhere, can write a ticket of victory over the world, the flesh, and the devil?"

"Emphatically, yes," Jesus answered. "And if they don't do it, it won't be done. They'll be wasting their time to pray that I will give them the victory. They'll have to write their own ticket."

Confession: *I give thanks unto the Lord. I make known His deeds among the people. I sing unto Him. I sing psalms unto Him. I talk of all His wondrous works!*

MARCH 19

DAVID AND GOLIATH

Then said David to the Philistine, Thou comest to me with a sword, and with a spear, and with a shield: but I come to thee in the name of the Lord of hosts, the God of the armies of Israel, whom thou hast defied. This day will the Lord deliver thee into mine hand; and I will smite thee, and take thine head from thee; and I will give the carcases of the host of the Philistines this day unto the fowls of the air, and to the wild beasts of the earth; that all the earth may know that there is a God in Israel. And all this assembly shall know that the Lord saveth not with sword and spear: for the battle is the Lord's, and he will give you into our hands. — 1 SAMUEL 17:45-47

79

I asked the Lord to give me more scriptures which use these same principles.

Jesus smiled and said, "All right. They're in an Old Testament story you've known from your youth — the story of David and Goliath."

"Is that what David did?" I asked.

"Exactly," Jesus said. "Those are the four steps David took."

After the vision was over, I reread the story of David and Goliath. I discovered that five times David *said it* before he acted on it! Read it yourself. David knew you could have what you say. He knew you could write your own ticket with God. How did David know God would do it? David knew God would do anything he would believe Him for — and God will do it for you too!

Confession: *I am a believer. I am not a doubter. I believe God for total victory. Then the world will see that God is for me!*

MARCH 20

THE PRODIGAL

And when he came to himself, he said, How many hired servants of my father's have bread enough and to spare, and I perish with hunger! I will arise and go to my father, and will say unto him, Father, I have sinned against heaven, and before thee, And am no more worthy to be called thy son: make me as one of thy hired servants. And he arose, and came to his father . . . . — LUKE 15:17-20

Jesus gave me this example from the New Testament of these four principles being followed.

Notice that the first thing the prodigal son did was, *he said it*!

Then, *he did it*. He climbed out of that hog pasture, and he started down the road toward home.

Next, *he received it*. His father saw him coming afar off, and had compassion, and ran, and fell on his neck, and kissed him. His father said, "Bring the robe and put it on him. Bring the ring and put it on his finger. Bring shoes and put them on his feet. Kill the fatted calf."

Then they had a celebration and *told it*.

Confession: *I know that God will do anything I believe Him to do which is in line with His Word. And I know how to write my own ticket with God. First, I say it. Next, I do it. Then, I receive it. Finally, I tell it!*

MARCH 21

WISDOM AND REVELATION

[I] *Cease not to give thanks for you, making mention of you in my prayers.* — EPHESIANS 1:16

Ephesians 1:17-23 and 3:14-21 are Spirit-given prayers which apply to the Church everywhere. The turning point in my life came when I prayed them a thousand times or more for myself. I would kneel, open my Bible, and say, "Father, I'm praying these prayers for myself. Because they are Spirit-given prayers, this has to be Your will for me, just as it was Your will for the Church at Ephesus." Then I would continue to pray by reading from these passages, except wherever Paul said, "you," I would substitute "me," as follows:

> *That the God of our Lord Jesus Christ, the Father of glory, may give unto "me" the spirit of wisdom and revelation in the knowledge of him:*
> *The eyes of "my" understanding being enlightened; that "I" may know what is the hope of his calling, and what the riches of the glory of his inheritance in the saints,*
> *And what is the exceeding greatness of his power to usward who believe, according to the working of his mighty power,*
> *Which he wrought in Christ, when he raised him from the dead, and set him at his own right hand in the heavenly places . . . .*

After about six months, the first thing I was praying about started to happen: The revelation of God's Word began to come to me!

Confession: (*Pray the prayer in Ephesians chapter one for yourself.*)

MARCH 22

FOR THIS CAUSE

For this cause I bow my knees unto the Father of our Lord Jesus Christ.
— EPHESIANS 3:14

The second prayer I would pray was this one from Ephesians chapter 3.
And I'd pray it for myself like this:

> *For this cause I bow my knees unto the Father of our Lord*
> *Jesus Christ,*
> *Of whom the whole family in heaven and earth is named,*
> *That he would grant "me," according to the riches of his*
> *glory, to be strengthened with might by his Spirit in "my"*
> *inner man;*
> *That Christ may dwell in "my" heart by faith; that "I," being*
> *rooted and grounded in love,*
> *May be able to comprehend with all saints what is the breadth,*
> *and length, and depth, and height;*
> *And to know the love of Christ, which passeth knowledge, that*
> *"I" might be filled with all the fulness of God.*
> *Now unto him that is able to do exceeding abundantly above*
> *all that we ask or think, according to the power that worketh*
> *in us,*
> *Unto him be glory in the church by Christ Jesus throughout*
> *all ages, world without end. Amen.*

I suggest that you pray these Ephesian prayers for yourself. Stay at it. It
won't work if you pray them just on a hit-and-miss basis. But if you'll
stay with it, praise God, they will work for you!

Confession: (*Pray yesterday's and today's prayers for yourself.*)

MARCH 23

FOR ANOTHER

I have no greater joy than to hear that my children walk in truth.
— 3 JOHN 1:4

When a Spirit-filled relative of mine couldn't seem to grasp certain important Bible truths, I prayed the Ephesian prayers for him every morning and night, inserting his name in the appropriate places.

> Lord, I'm praying this prayer for "Joe." God of our Lord Jesus Christ, the Father of glory, give unto "Joe" the spirit of wisdom and revelation in the knowledge of Him. I pray that the eyes of "Joe's" understanding be enlightened; that "Joe" may know what is the hope of His calling, and what is the riches of the glory of His inheritance in the saints . . . .

And I continued on through both prayers. I prayed these prayers for him morning and night for ten days. Finally he wrote me, saying, "It's amazing how things have opened up to me. I'm beginning to see what you've been talking about." No human teacher had talked to him about spiritual matters.

People frequently want to know how to pray for friends and loved ones. Some people just pray, "God, bless them." But God has already blessed them with all spiritual blessings in heavenly places in Christ Jesus (Eph. 1:3). They just don't know it, so they can't take advantage of it. Pray these Ephesian prayers for your friends and loved ones. Stay with it morning and night, and more frequently if you can.

Confession: (*Pray the Ephesian prayers for someone you desire to walk in the truth.*)

MARCH 24

Authority

Behold, I give unto you power [authority] *to tread on serpents and scorpions, and over all the power of the enemy: and nothing shall by any means hurt you.* — LUKE 10:19

The Greek word "exousia" means *authority*. However, it is often translated as "power" in the *King James Version* of the New Testament. In our text, for example, two different Greek words are translated as "power," yet the correct translation of the first word is "authority." Our verse should read, "I give you *authority* to tread on serpents and scorpions, and over all the *power* of the enemy . . . ."

What is the difference between power and authority?

Well, what can one uniformed police officer do to direct the flow of rush hour traffic? He can do a great deal. Is it because the policeman has the *power* to hold back these mighty machines? No! His most strenuous efforts couldn't stop the swiftly passing cars. He doesn't have the power to do it, but he has something far better. He is invested with the *authority* of the government he serves. Even a stranger in the city recognizes this authority and obeys it.

Authority is delegated power.

Confession: *I have been given authority to tread on serpents and scorpions, and over all the power of the enemy. Nothing shall by any means hurt me.*

MARCH 25

DELEGATED POWER

And Jesus came and spake unto them, saying, All power [authority] *is given unto me in heaven and in earth. Go ye therefore . . . .*
— MATTHEW 28:18,19

The authority on earth that is invested in the Name of Jesus Christ and was obtained by Him through His overcoming Satan was then delegated by Jesus Christ to the Church.

Jesus spoke these words in Matthew 28 after His death on the cross, after His burial, after His defeat of Satan in hell, after His resurrection, after His ascension with His own blood to the heavenly Holy of Holies — but just *before* His ascension to be seated at the right hand of the Father. Jesus said that all authority in Heaven and on earth is given to Him. Then He immediately transferred this authority on earth to His Church, saying, *"Go ye therefore . . . ."*

Mark records that Jesus said at this same time, *"And these signs shall follow them that believe; In my name shall they cast out devils; they shall speak with new tongues; They shall take up serpents; and if they drink any deadly thing, it shall not hurt them; they shall lay hands on the sick, and they shall recover"* (Mark 16:17,18).

Confession: *The authority in the Name of Jesus that is above every name has been given to the Church. It has been given to me. I have authority over all the power of the enemy.*

MARCH 26

BE STRONG

Finally, my brethren, be strong in the Lord, and in the power of his might. Put on the whole armour of God, that ye may be able to stand against the wiles of the devil. — EPHESIANS 6:10,11

What would you think if you saw a traffic policeman in front of a car, trying to hold it back? You'd think, *He can't do that. He's no match for that car!*

Some people read Ephesians 6:10 and think that the Lord is telling them to be strong in themselves. And they're trying to be strong. They'll say, "Oh, pray for me that I'll hold out faithful to the end!" But God didn't say a word about our being strong in ourselves or in the power of our might.

That traffic policeman steps right out in front of those cars and holds up his hand, because he knows they're going to stop for him. He doesn't have to exert any strength himself; he's strong in the authority that's been given to him.

That is what the Lord is telling us. He's saying, "Be strong in the Lord. Be strong in the authority of His might. Just step out there in front of that oncoming devil. Hold up your hand in the Name of Jesus, and say, 'Thus far, and no further! Stop right now!'"

Confession: *I am strong in the Lord and in the power of His might. I am invested with authority from the Lord Jesus Christ. When I hold up my hand in the Name of Jesus and say, "Thus far, and no further," the devil stops in his tracks!*

MARCH 27

WHOM RESIST

Be sober, be vigilant; because your adversary the devil, as a roaring lion, walketh about, seeking whom he may devour: Whom resist stedfast in the faith . . . . — 1 PETER 5:8,9

In 1942, I had a battle with symptoms in my body. I prayed, appropriated the promises of God, and stood my ground. But at times it looked like I wasn't going to make it.

One such night I had a dream. I dreamed another man and I were on some kind of a parade ground. It was like a football field. There were stands on either side. As we walked along talking, suddenly the man looked back and yelled, "Look!" and he started running. I turned and saw that two ferocious lions were almost upon me. I ran about two steps. Then I hollered to the other man, "You'll never make it! You can't outrun them!" I stopped still, turned around, and faced them. I was trembling. My flesh was covered with goose pimples. But I said, "I stand against you. I refuse to budge in the Name of Jesus Christ." The lions stopped, came right up to me, sniffed around my feet, and just trotted off. I awoke, and First Peter 5:8 came to my mind. I knew my physical battle was won. I received healing immediately. I had almost run, but I stood my ground. I had used my authority.

Confession: *I resist the devil steadfast in the faith. I stand my ground. I use my authority. And the devil runs from me as if in terror.*

MARCH 28

SOURCE

Behold, I have given you authority to tread upon serpents and scorpions, and over all the power of the enemy; and nothing shall in any wise hurt you. — LUKE 10:19 *(ASV)*

Authority is delegated power.

Its value depends on the force behind the user.

Jesus said, "I have given you authority." Who gave it? Jesus did. Who is Jesus? *Jesus is God manifested in the flesh!* That means that God said it. Therefore, God said "I have given you authority to tread upon serpents and scorpions, and over all the power of the enemy."

(Serpents and scorpions represent demons and evil spirits and the power of the enemy.)

God Himself is the Power, the Force, behind this authority. The believer who is fully conscious of divine authority can therefore face the enemy without fear or hesitation.

Behind the authority possessed by the believer is a Power far greater than the power that backs our enemies. And those enemies are compelled to recognize that authority!

No wonder John says, ". . . *greater is he that is in you, than he that is in the world*" (1 John 4:4).

Confession: *I am a believer. Jesus has given me authority. God has given me authority. God Himself is the Power behind this authority. And this authority God has given me is over all the power of the enemy.*

MARCH 29

RESURRECTION POWER

That I may know him, and the power of his resurrection . . . .
— **PHILIPPIANS 3:10**

Paul was actually praying in Ephesians that the Church would receive revelation knowledge of spiritual things. If you've been praying the Ephesian prayers for yourself, as I've suggested, you know that Paul wanted the believers at Ephesus to know:

> ". . . the exceeding greatness of his power to us-ward who believe, according to the working of his mighty power, Which he wrought in Christ, when he raised him from the dead, and set him at his own right hand in the heavenly places, Far above all principality, and power, and might, and dominion, and every name that is named, not only in this world, but also in that which is *to come*" (Eph. 1:19-21).

There was such a manifestation of the divine omnipotence of God's power in raising Jesus from the dead that it is actually the mightiest working of God! And God wants us to know what happened when this occurred.

The resurrection was opposed by all the tremendous powers of the air. These evil forces endeavored to defeat the plan of God. But these powers were overthrown by our Lord Jesus Christ, and He has been enthroned far above them, ruling with the authority of the Most High. Thus, the source of our authority is found in this resurrection and seating of Christ by God.

Confession: *The Power that raised Jesus from the dead is the Corporation behind the authority!*

MARCH 30

To Usward

Many, O Lord my God, are thy wonderful works which thou hast done, and thy thoughts which are to us-ward . . . . — PSALM 40:5

Did you notice this phrase in Ephesians 1:19, ". . . *the exceeding greatness of his power to usward who believe* . . ."?

All the demonstration of the glory of God shown in the manifestation of His omnipotence pointed to man — "to usward."

The Cross of Christ — with what is revealed of obedience to God, atonement for sin, and crushing defeat for the enemies of divine authority — shows us a representative Man.

Christ was our Representative, our Substitute — overcoming for mankind and preparing a throne and a heavenly ministry for those who should overcome through Him.

Therefore, the source of our authority is found in the resurrection and seating of Christ by God. In the Book of Ephesians, we learn that God wants the Church to gain revelation knowledge of all that this means to us.

Confession: *I am a believer. I am receiving the spirit of wisdom and revelation in the knowledge of God. The eyes of my understanding are being enlightened that I may know what is the exceeding greatness of God's power to usward who believe!*

MARCH 31

RAISED TOGETHER

And what is the exceeding greatness of his power. . . . Which he wrought in Christ, WHEN HE RAISED HIM from the dead, and set him at his own right hand in the heavenly places. . . . AND YOU hath he quickened, who were dead in trespasses and sins.

— EPHESIANS 1:19,20, 2:1

If you were to open your Bibles to Ephesians 2:1. A *King James Version* would look something like this:

CHAPTER 2

AND you *hath he quickened*, who were dead in trespasses and sins.

When a word is italicized in the *King James Version*, that means the word is not in the original manuscripts; the translators have added it. So the original reads, "And you who were dead in trespasses and sins."

I wanted you to see that the verb which controls Ephesians 2:1 is back in Ephesians 1:20! (Paul didn't write in chapter and verse; men divided Paul's writings later for easy reference.) Our text today makes it clearer for you. Notice the capitalized words: ". . . *WHEN HE* [GOD] *RAISED HIM* [Christ] *from the dead. . . . AND* [raised] *YOU . . . who were dead in trespasses and sins.*" The same verb that expresses the reviving of Christ also expresses the reviving of Christ's people! So the mighty act of God which raised Christ from the dead also raised His Body!

Confession: *The same mighty Power that raised Jesus from the dead also raised me!*

APRIL 1

Seated Together

Even when we were dead in sins, [God] hath quickened us together with Christ, (by grace ye are saved;) And hath raised us up together, and made us sit together in heavenly places in Christ Jesus.
— EPHESIANS 2:5,6

The very act that raised the Lord from the dead also raised His Body. (The head and the body are naturally raised together.)

Furthermore, the very act that seated Christ also seated His Body. Where are we sitting? In heavenly places! Right now! We're not going to sit there *sometime*; God has made us sit together *now* in heavenly places in Christ Jesus.

Christ is seated at the Father's own right hand. Therefore, we are seated at the Father's own right hand! (The right hand is the place of authority. God carries out all of His plan and program through His right hand — through Christ, through His spiritual Body, which is the Church.)

The right hand of the throne of Majesty in the heavens is the center of power of the whole universe (Heb. 8:1)! The exercising of the power of that throne was committed to the ascended Christ — and that authority belongs to us.

Confession: *God has quickened me with Christ. God has raised me up together with Him. God has made me sit together with Christ in heavenly places. As I go about in the earth, working with God in carrying out His plan, I am seated, as far as authority goes, at the Father's right hand.*

APRIL 2

UNDER OUR FEET

. . . And set him at his own right hand in the heavenly places, Far above all principality, and power, and might, and dominion, and every name that is named, not only in this world, but also in that which is to come: And hath put all things under his feet, and gave him to be the head over all things to the church, Which is his body, the fulness of him that filleth all in all. — EPHESIANS 1:20-23

The Church is the Body of the Lord Jesus Christ. We are the Body of Christ.

Now for a question: Where are the feet? Are they in the head, or are they in the body? They're in the body, of course.

Look again at today's text. It describes positionally where we are seated.

God has put all things under Christ's feet. Christ's feet are in His Body. Therefore, all things have been put under *our* feet!

What are the "all things" Paul is talking about? Principalities, powers, might, and dominion. In other words, all the power of the enemy is under our feet!

Someone has said that if we have anything to say to Satan, we should write it on the bottoms of our shoes!

Confession: *I am seated with Christ in heavenly places. I am a member in particular of the Body of Christ. All the power of the enemy is under my feet!*

APRIL 3

BECAUSE I GO

Verily, verily, I say unto you, He that believeth on me, the works that I do shall he do also; and greater works than these shall he do; because I go unto my Father. — JOHN 14:12

Dr. John Alexander Dowie (1847-1907) was used by God to reintroduce divine healing to the modern Church.

Dr. P. C. Nelson, founder of Southwestern Assemblies of God College, said, "You can't follow Dowie's doctrine, but you can follow his faith."

I heard Dr. Nelson tell about how when he himself was a young Baptist minister, he saw Dowie minister to a woman with a purplish-blue cancerous growth that covered most of her face.

Nelson said, "I saw Dowie, in the presence of us six denominational ministers and three medical doctors, just reach out and take hold of that cancer, saying, 'In the Name of the Lord Jesus Christ!' — and then strip it off that woman's face. The doctors present examined her immediately, and said the skin on her face was like the skin of a newborn baby."

The reason Jesus gave, was so those who believe on Him would be able to do the works He did, "because He did go unto His Father." It's because of Jesus' seating at the right hand of the Father on High in the place of authority that believers can do these same works.

Confession: *I believe on Jesus. Because Jesus went to His Father and mine, and is seated at the right hand of Majesty on High — and I am seated with Him — I can do the works of my Father, in Jesus' Name.*

APRIL 4

THE WORKS THAT I DO

Now it came to pass on a certain day, that he [Jesus] went into a ship with his disciples: and he said unto them, Let us go over unto the other side of the lake. And they launched forth. But as they sailed he fell asleep: and there came down a storm of wind on the lake; and they were filled with water, and were in jeopardy. And they came to him, and awoke him, saying, Master, master, we perish. Then he arose, and rebuked the wind and the raging of the water: and they ceased, and there was a calm. And he said unto them, Where is your faith? . . .
— LUKE 8:22-25

95

John Alexander Dowie was born in Edinburgh, Scotland, and moved to Australia as a young man. In 1875, while Dowie was pastoring a Congregational church in Newton, Australia, a terrible plague swept through that part of the country. It was during this plague that Dowie first received light on divine healing and the authority that believers possess.

I read that Dowie once said, "I have crossed the ocean fourteen times by ship. During those fourteen crossings, many storms arose. But every time a storm came up, I always did like Jesus did: I rebuked that storm. And every single one ceased."

Dowie knew that Jesus had said, *"He that believeth on me, the works that I do shall he do also . . . ."* Dowie knew that he was linked up with God. You and I are linked up with God just as much as Dowie or anyone else ever was.

Confession: *I believe on Jesus. The works that Jesus did on the earth, I can do. Jesus said I could, so I can.*

APRIL 5

EDGE OF AUTHORITY

. . . And they awake him, and say unto him, Master, carest thou not that we perish? And he arose, and rebuked the wind, and said unto the sea, Peace, be still. And the wind ceased, and there was a great calm.
— MARK 4:38,39

A tornado arose one spring day in Texas. Most people had gone into their storm cellars. We didn't have one. I was bedfast and almost totally paralyzed anyway. I became fearful. If the tornado were to strike, it would strike my corner room first, because the wind was coming from that direction. The house would cave in right where I was!

In desperation, and without thinking whether or not I could do it, I said, "Dear Lord, I'm Your child. When those disciples were about to sink, they awakened You and said, 'Carest thou not that we perish?' And You did care. You awoke and rebuked the wind. I know You don't want me to perish, but I can't get out of here. I'm here on this bed, and this wall is about to blow in on top of me. So I now rebuke this storm in Jesus' Name!"

As fast as you'd snap your fingers, the storm stopped. It grew calm. I rejoiced. I didn't know then the great truths about the believer's authority. I had gotten to the edge of it and had exercised it without really knowing what I had done. But God wants us to get the revelation of the truth of His Word so we can understand what belongs to us and use it in our lives.

Confession: *I will get the revelation of the truth of God's Word and understand and use what belongs to me.*

APRIL 6

DETHRONED POWERS

We do discuss 'wisdom' with those who are mature; only it is not the wisdom of this world or of the dethroned Powers who rule this world, it is the mysterious Wisdom of God . . . .
— 1 CORINTHIANS 2:6,7 *(Moffatt)*

God's Word teaches that Satan and evil spirits are rebel holders of authority, and that they have been dethroned by the Lord Jesus Christ. Notice how Moffatt's translation calls them "dethroned Powers who rule this world."

God made the earth and the fullness thereof. Then He gave Adam dominion, or authority, over all the works of His hands (Gen. 1:27,28; Ps. 8:3-6). Adam had dominion on the earth. In fact, Adam was made the god of this world. When he committed high treason and sold out to Satan, then Satan became the god of this world through Adam (2 Cor. 4:4), and a rebel holder of Adam's authority.

But the Bible calls Jesus Christ the last Adam (1 Cor. 15:45). Jesus came as our Representative — our Substitute — and defeated Satan! Jesus didn't do it for Himself; He did it for us! All that Jesus did belongs to us.

We believers are to remember that we are in the world, but we're not of the world. Satan is not to dominate us; we are to dominate him. We can dominate Satan. We have authority over him. Jesus defeated him for us.

Confession: *Jesus dethroned Satan and all his cohorts for me. Satan cannot dominate me. I dominate him. Jesus gave me authority over Satan, and I will use it.*

APRIL 7

HIS BODY

Now ye are the body of Christ, and members in particular.
— 1 CORINTHIANS 12:27

We've sometimes prayed about the Lord's work upon the earth like this: "Lord, *You* do this. Lord, *You* do that."

But think about what Jesus said in Matthew 28:18 and 19, " . . . *All power* [authority] *is given unto me in heaven and in earth. Go ye therefore* . . . ." The Lord Jesus Christ conferred the authority on the earth upon us. He commissioned us to go.

Actually, the authority that Christ can exercise on the earth has to be exercised through the Church. The Church is His Body. And the Church is here. Christ is not here. He's at the right hand of the Father. Christ is the Head of the Church, but all of His orders have to be carried out through His Body. Everything Christ does on the earth has to be done through His Body.

You're a member in particular of Christ's Body. He has conferred upon you authority over all the power of the enemy!

Confession: *I am a member in particular of the Body of Christ. I am a worker together with God in the completing of His work upon the earth. I am well-equipped. I am endued with power and authority in Jesus' Name. And I will faithfully fulfill my part in God's plan.*

APRIL 8

Permitted

Verily I say unto you, Whatsoever ye shall bind on earth shall be bound in heaven: and whatsoever ye shall loose on earth shall be loosed in heaven. — MATTHEW 18:18

Many things exist because believers *permit* them to — they just don't do anything about them. Sometimes believers don't know they can do anything to change these situations.

Years ago, when I was meditating and studying about the authority believers have, I sensed the Lord challenging me. At that time, I had been praying for about fifteen years for my older brother to be saved. I had often prayed and fasted three days at a time for his salvation — but he would get worse instead of better. I'd pray, "God, save him. God, save him." But nothing ever happened. As I lay across the bed studying on this particular day, I heard the Lord in my spirit. He challenged me: "*You* do something about that situation. You've got the authority. You've got my Name!"

I rose up off that bed and said, "In the Name of Jesus Christ, I break the power of the devil over Dub's life. And I claim his salvation and deliverance!"

In less than two weeks, I got word that Dub had been born again.

Confession: *Jesus said that Heaven backs us up in whatever we believers prohibit or permit. In Jesus' Name, I prohibit, or bind, the work of the enemy. And in Jesus' Name I loose, or permit, the power of God to flow in my realm of operation.*

APRIL 9

FLEE FROM YOU

. . . Resist the devil, and he will flee from you. — JAMES 4:7

Every passage in the New Testament that deals with the devil always instructs you and me to do something about the devil. New Testament believers are never told to pray that God would do something about the devil!

In James 4:7 "you" is the understood subject of the sentence. "*You* resist the devil and he will flee from *you*." Notice it's not, "Pray to God for Him to do something about the devil." Nor is it, "Pray that Jesus won't let the devil get you."

Also notice that the Bible doesn't say, "When you feel like it, you can resist the devil, and it will work for you." No. Whether you feel like it or not, the authority still belongs to you. *You can't feel authority; you just exercise it!*

I once sensed in my spirit that there was special significance about the word "flee" in James 4:7. In a huge dictionary I found the definition that seemed to fit what my spirit called for: "To flee: to run from as in terror."

Act on James 4:7. Don't just consider it as a fairy tale, but as the Word of God, which is to be acted upon. If you'll act on it, the devil and all his cohorts will run from you as in terror!

Confession: *I resist the devil according to God's Word. The devil runs from me as in terror. He's scared to death of Jesus Christ — so he's scared to death of me!*

APRIL 10

CAST OUT DEVILS

And these signs shall follow them that believe; In my name shall they cast out devils . . . . — MARK 16:17

The very first sign Jesus said would follow any and every believer was: *". . . In my name shall they cast out devils . . . ."*

Jesus wasn't talking necessarily about casting the devil out of people who are demon-possessed. Jesus was simply saying that in His Name believers would have authority over the devil. They would break the power of the devil over their own lives and the lives of their loved ones. They would be free from the enemy, because they would exercise authority over him.

Notice again that Jesus didn't say a word about praying to God or Jesus to do something about devils. Jesus said that believers would do it. Believers will cast out devils. Believers would speak with new tongues. Believers would lay their hands on the sick and they would recover.

Don't pray that God would lay hands on the sick — you do it! And don't pray that God would cast out the devil — you do it!

Confession: *I am a believer, and this sign follows me. In Jesus' Name, I cast out devils. I keep them out of my path. I break the power of the devil over my life. I break the power of the devil over the lives of my loved ones. I walk free of the enemy, because I exercise authority over him.*

APRIL 11

YOUR DOMAIN

For if because of one man's trespass (lapse, offense) death reigned through that one, much more surely will those who receive [God's] overflowing grace (unmerited favor) and the free gift of righteousness [putting them into right standing with Himself] reign as kings in life through the one Man Jesus Christ (the Messiah, the Anointed One).
— ROMANS 5:17 (*Amplified*)

In the time when Paul wrote this, kings reigned over certain countries or domains.

You are to reign in your domain too. This doesn't mean you're to reign and rule over other people, but you're to rule and reign in your life, your dominion. You're to rule and reign over circumstances, poverty, sickness, disease — everything that would hinder. You're to reign because you have authority!

How do you have it? Through the One, Jesus Christ.

Don't let the devil cheat you out of the blessings God intended you should have. God never intended that you should be poverty stricken and destitute. He didn't intend that the devil should rule and reign over your family and dominate them. Just get angry at the devil. Tell him, "Take your hands off of my children! You've got no right here. I'm ruling over this domain!" If he says anything about it, quote him Romans 5:17.

Confession: *I reign in my domain. I have the authority to do so. I reign by the One, Jesus Christ. The enemy cannot rule over my family. He cannot rule over me!*

APRIL 12

To the Church

*And hath put all things under his feet, and gave him to be the head
over all things to the church, Which is his body . . . .*
— EPHESIANS 1:22,23

What a need there is for the Church to awaken to the appreciation of
her mighty place and privilege — to be exalted to the place God wants
her, and to realize she is to rule over the powers of the air!

How often the Church has failed in her ministry of authority, actually
bowing down in defeat and being overcome with fear.

*". . . And gave him to be the head over all things TO THE
CHURCH . . . ."* To the Church! The reason Jesus is Head over all
things — the devil, demons, sickness, poverty, and everything else that's
evil — is for the benefit of the Church! We need to sit reverently and
meditate before these mighty truths so their tremendous meaning can
grasp our hearts. In this attitude, the Spirit of Truth can lift us into the
place where we can see the full meaning of what God's Word is saying:
That God made Christ to be the head over all things for the sake of the
Church, so that the Church, through the Head of the Church, might
exercise authority over all things.

Confession: *Jesus is my Head. Jesus is Lord over all. Jesus has given me
authority over all the hosts of the enemy. Greater is Jesus that is in me
than he that is in the world. I am more than a conqueror through Him
that loved me and gave Himself for me.*

APRIL 13

FIRSTBORN FROM THE DEAD

Who [his dear Son] is the image of the invisible God, the firstborn of every creature: For by him were all things created, that are in heaven, and that are in earth, visible and invisible, whether they be thrones, or dominions, or principalities, or powers: all things were created by him, and for him: And he is before all things, and by him all things consist. And he is the head of the body, the church: who is the beginning, the firstborn from the dead; that in all things he might have the preeminence. For it pleased the Father that in him should all fulness dwell; And, having made peace through the blood of his cross, by him to reconcile all things unto himself; by him, I say, whether they be things in earth, or things in heaven. — COLOSSIANS 1:15-20

Although He is coequal with the Father, the eternal Son of God accepted a subordinate place and undertook the task of reconciling the world to God through the blood of His Cross.

For this purpose, Jesus yielded Himself to death (Matt. 27:50). When Jesus was made to be sin (2 Cor. 5:21), He was turned over by God to spiritual death, which is separation from God. This occurred when that heartbreaking cry fell from Jesus' lips, "My God, My God, why hast thou forsaken Me?" Jesus' spirit was delivered up for our offenses, that He might be raised for our justification (Rom. 4:25). It was the wisdom of the Father that yielded Jesus, the Righteous One, to death, that our debt might be paid, and Jesus might become THE FIRSTBORN FROM THE DEAD!

Confession: *Thank You, Jesus, for dying for my sins. Thank You, Jesus, that You paid my debt so that I might be free!*

APRIL 14

STRIPPED

And having spoiled principalities and powers, he made a shew of them openly, triumphing over them in it. — COLOSSIANS 2:15

And the hostile princes and rulers He shook off from Himself, and boldly displayed them as His conquests . . . .
— COLOSSIANS 2:15 (*Weymouth*)

The Bible teaches us here that Jesus put Satan to naught and He triumphed over him. Another translation reads, "He stripped him." What did He strip Satan of? His authority over man.

When Jesus put Satan to naught and stripped him of his authority, it was you in Christ who did the work. Christ acted in your stead — in your place. He did it for you.

What Christ did was marked to your credit. He did it as your substitute. (He did it in your place, and God marked it to your credit as though you were the one who did it!)

No, we're not bragging about what you are in the flesh. (You don't amount to much in the flesh.) We're talking about who you are *in Christ*.

You can say, "*In Christ*, I conquered Satan. I stripped him of his authority. And *when Jesus arose from the dead, I arose with Him*!"

Confession: *Christ Jesus satisfied the claims of Justice against me. He paid the penalty of sin for me. He stripped the hosts of darkness of their authority over me. Satan, therefore, has no dominion over me!*

APRIL 15

Paralyzed

Forasmuch then as the children are partakers of flesh and blood, he also himself likewise took part of the same; that through death he might destroy him that had the power of death, that is, the devil.
— HEBREWS 2:14

. . . That He might paralyse him that held the dominion of death, That is the Adversary. — HEBREWS 2:14 (*Rotherham*)

106

Jesus put to naught the hosts of darkness! He paralyzed their death-dealing power! And when Jesus met John the Revelator on the Isle of Patmos, Jesus said, *"I am he that liveth, and was dead; and, behold, I am alive for evermore, Amen; and have the keys of hell and of death"* (Rev. 1:18).

Keys represent authority. Jesus conquered Satan and stripped him of his authority. Jesus was the Master of all hell!

But Jesus did not conquer Satan for Himself. He conquered him for us. It was as though you and I personally had met Satan and had conquered him, stripped him of his authority, and stood as master over him.

Confession: *Jesus is my Head. Jesus is Lord over all. Jesus conquered Satan for me. Jesus stripped Satan of his authority over me. In the eyes of Heaven, hell, and this universe, it was as though I personally had met Satan and had conquered him, stripped him of his authority, and stood there as master over him. Therefore, in Christ Jesus, I am more than a conqueror. I am a holder of authority. I stand as master over Satan and all his cohorts!*

APRIL 16

THE AGENT: GOD

And ye are complete in him, which is the head of all principality and power. . . . Buried with him in baptism, wherein also ye are risen with him through the faith of the operation of God, who hath raised him from the dead. And you, being dead in your sins and the uncircumcision of your flesh, hath he quickened together with him . . . .
— COLOSSIANS 2:10,12,13

Notice the expression "through the faith of the operation of God." Jesus was quickened (made alive) by the faith of the operation of God — and we were made alive at the same time. It was God who raised Jesus from the dead. It was God who gave Jesus a Name above every name. It was God who blotted out "the handwriting of ordinances" against us, took it out of the way, and nailed it to His Cross (Col. 2:14). It was God who stripped the powers of darkness of their authority and handed it to the Son (Col. 2:15). And it was God who quickened us "together with Him."

In the mind of God, legally speaking, it was when Jesus was quickened and made alive, that we were recreated. *"For we are his workmanship, created in Christ Jesus . . ."* (Eph. 2:10). This fact of our re-creation becomes a vital reality in our lives when we were individually born again (made new creatures).

Raised with Christ! Quickened with Him! Seated with Him (Eph. 2:4-6)!

Confession: *Through the faith of the operation of God, I was quickened together with Christ and was seated with Him in heavenly places.*

APRIL 17

ANALOGY

And he is the head of the body, the church: who is the beginning, the firstborn from the dead; that in all things he might have the preeminence.
— COLOSSIANS 1:18

Here's where we believers have missed it! We've recognized that Jesus is the Head of the Church, and we've exalted Him to His position of Power, all right. But we've failed to see that the Head is wholly dependent upon its body for carrying out its plans. We've failed to see that we are seated with Christ in heavenly places. We've failed to see that Jesus has authority over Satan's power. If this authority is ever exercised, it will have to be exercised through the Body. We've been so sure that *we* couldn't do anything, that we've left everything up to Christ the Head of the Church — and the Head is powerless without the Body.

Take your own physical head as an example. It is powerless to carry out any of its plans without the cooperation of the body. Your head might see a songbook on a rack in front of you, but unless your body cooperates, your head will never be able to sing from that book.

The ministry God wants to accomplish through His Son in this world will be carried out through the Body of Christ. And we — the Body of Christ — have the same authority the Head has!

Confession: *The ministry God wants to accomplish through His Son in this world will be carried out through the Body of Christ. I am a member of the Body, and I will exercise my authority!*

APRIL 18

WHAT YE WILL

If ye abide in me, and my words abide in you, ye shall ask what ye will, and it shall be done unto you. — JOHN 15:7

The Lord has said to me as I prayed about the impending death of loved ones, "Whatever you say about it, that's what I'll do."

In one particular case, as I pled my rights in prayer concerning a situation, the Lord came to me in a vision and said, "All right, I'm going to give them _____ more years. And I'm going to do it just because you asked Me to. No earthly father ever desired to do more for his children than I do for Mine, if they would only let Me."

Why doesn't God just do it?

Because we must cooperate with God in faith!

The idea that God is a tyrant who rules over people, knocks heads together, and does what He wants to, whether man cooperates or not, is pure ignorance.

We have a part to play! And, thank God, we can take our rightful place. The Lord Jesus Christ — Head over all things to His Body — is hindered in His mighty plans and workings because His Body fails to appreciate the deep meaning of His exaltation, and the fact that we are seated with Him at the right hand of the Father!

Confession: *I abide in Christ, and His Word abides in me. Therefore, I ask what I will, and it shall be done unto me!*

APRIL 19

TAKING YOUR PLACE

If ye then be risen with Christ, seek those things which are above, where Christ sitteth on the right hand of God. Set your affection on things above, not on things on the earth. — COLOSSIANS 3:1,2

The elevation of the believer to be seated with Christ at the right hand of the Father took place potentially at the resurrection (Eph. 2:5,6). Meditate on this passage until it becomes real to you. Remember, every heavenly blessing is yours (Eph. 1:3). But you have to take your place there to enjoy them. The believer whose eyes have been opened to his throne rights in Christ may: (1) Accept his seat, and (2) Begin to exercise the spiritual authority that seating confers on him.

The devil bitterly resents our entrance into his domain. He has been used to exercising authority and ruling over someone's life, so he will concentrate his forces against us when we come into these mighty truths. And no truth encounters such opposition as the truth of the authority of the believer!

The only place of safety is to be seated with Christ in heavenly places, far above all principality, power, might, and dominion. If the believer abides steadfastly, by faith, in this place, he cannot be touched by the enemy. So take your seat in heavenly places and keep it!

Confession: *I set my affection on heavenly facts. I keep myself mindful that I am seated with Christ in heavenly places far above the enemy!*

APRIL 20

THE ARMOR

Wherefore take unto you the whole armour of God, that ye may be able to withstand in the evil day, and having done all, to stand.
— **EPHESIANS 6:13**

The message of the armor tells us how to take our place and maintain it against the devil (Eph. 6:10-18).

"Stand therefore, having your loins girt about with truth . . . ." The girdle of truth is a clear understanding of God's Word. It holds the rest of the armor in place like a soldier's belt.

". . . And having on the breastplate of righteousness." The breastplate has two meanings: (1) Jesus is our righteousness, so we put Him on; (2) The breastplate represents our active obedience to the Word of God.

"And your feet shod with the preparation of the gospel of peace." This is faithful ministry in proclaiming the Word of God.

"Above all, taking the shield of faith, wherewith ye shall be able to quench all the fiery darts of the wicked." This is complete safety by faith in the blood. No power of the enemy can penetrate the blood!

"And take the helmet of salvation . . . ." This is the covering of our Lord Jesus Christ.

". . . The sword of the Spirit, which is the word of God." All other parts of the armor are for protection (defense); this one is to be used offensively against the enemy.

"Praying always with all prayer and supplication in the Spirit . . . ." You've got on the armor. Now you're ready for the prayer fight.

Confession: *(Confess yourself in the armor. Say, "I stand therefore, having my loins girt about with truth . . . ," and so forth.)*

APRIL 21

UNSEEN FORCES

For we wrestle not against flesh and blood, but against principalities, against powers, against the rulers of the darkness of this world, against spiritual wickedness in high places. — EPHESIANS 6:12

We are called upon to bind unseen forces. We have authority over the devil and evil spirits. But we do not have authority over men or their wills.

Years ago, a pastor friend of mine accompanied me from Fort Worth to a campmeeting in California. This man had diabetes, and he had to check his urine every morning for sugar content to see how much insulin he would need for his daily injection.

As we were leaving for California, I said, "You won't register any sugar as long as you're with me." He looked at me as if he didn't believe me, but in the almost two weeks he was with me, he never registered any sugar, even though he ate pies and cakes. He later told me he was home for three days before he registered sugar again.

Why? I took authority over his sickness. I had control over unseen forces, but I didn't have control over his will. As long as he was with me, and this unseen force was in my presence, I could control it. I tried to convince him he could do the same thing, but he expected it to come back, and it did.

Confession: *I have authority over all unseen forces in my realm of domain. And I bind them and stop their activity in Jesus' Name!*

APRIL 22

BLINDED

But if our gospel be hid, it is hid to them that are lost: In whom the god of this world hath blinded the minds of them which believe not, lest the light of the glorious gospel of Christ, who is the image of God, should shine unto them. — 2 CORINTHIANS 4:3,4

No man in his right mind would speed down the highway at one hundred miles an hour past flashing red lights and signs that said, "Danger! Danger! Bridge Out!" But a man who was drunk or on drugs would.

Likewise, no man in his right mind would go through life and plunge off into eternity and hell, lost. But people do it. Why? Because the devil has them doped and blinded.

In the case of my Brother Dub's salvation, I realized it was the devil who had bound Dub and was keeping him from being saved. So I said, "Satan, in the Name of Jesus Christ, I break your power over my brother Dub's life, and I claim his deliverance and salvation."

We do not have control over human wills, but we do have control over evil spirits that bind and blind men. I'm convinced this is an area we're going to know more about and take advantage of in the future.

Confession: *The god of this world will not blind the eyes of my loved ones, because I will take the Name of Jesus and break his power over them!*

APRIL 23

FOUNDATION

Study to shew thyself approved unto God, a workman that needeth not to be ashamed, rightly dividing the word of truth.
— 2 TIMOTHY 2:15

Someone who reads about how I took my authority over the spirits binding my brother might say, "I believe I'll *try* that." It won't work if you *try* it. I didn't just *try* it — I *did* it!

Just because someone sees a traffic policeman exercising his authority doesn't mean they can run out in front of the cars and say, "I believe I'll try that." No one would obey them. Now, if they would put on a policeman's uniform and put a whistle in their mouth, people would stop. They would recognize the authority behind the policeman.

Believers sometimes hear how someone else used their authority, and they think, *I'll try that because I heard him say it. It worked for him, so it will work for me.* Satan knows they are not convinced of their authority, and when they try to act on God's Word without really having the Word built into their spirits, and without having the solid foundation of it built into their lives, the devil will defeat them — and defeat them soundly.

But when you've built a foundation of the Word of God in you, and you act on God's Word, you'll defeat the devil in every combat!

Confession: *I study to shew myself approved unto God. I build the truths of God's Word into my life and spirit. I am convinced by God's Word of my authority. I cannot be defeated. And the devil knows it!*

APRIL 24

LORD, TEACH US TO PRAY

And it came to pass, that, as he was praying in a certain place, when he ceased, one of his disciples said unto him, Lord, teach us to pray . . . .
— LUKE 11:1

Someone said, "It is more important that men learn to pray than that they gain a college education." Notice he did not say that having an education is not important; he said, that learning to pray is more important.

I feel sorry for people who don't know how to pray. When the crises of life come, they know how to say words — but just spouting off words into the atmosphere isn't praying! Simply talking into the air is not praying. Taking up twenty minutes on a Sunday morning giving God a homily on what His duties are toward the church is not praying. And giving the congregation a lecture pretending to be praying to God is not praying.

Christianity, from a practical side, is a living religion whose believers are in touch with the living God who hears and answers prayer. And prayer may be defined as joining forces with God the Father — fellowshipping with Him — carrying out His will upon the earth.

It is of utmost importance that all Christians — *including you* — learn how to pray!

Confession: *I am in touch with the living God who hears and answers prayer. I fellowship with Him. I join forces with Him in carrying out His will upon the earth.*

APRIL 25

LIMITING GOD

Yea, they turned back and tempted God, and limited the Holy One of Israel. — PSALM 78:41

Can you limit God? The Bible says Israel did. And we have limited Him. We have limited God with our prayer life.

John Wesley, founder of Methodism, said, "It seems God is limited by our prayer life. He can do nothing for humanity unless someone asks Him to do it."

Why is that?

God made the world and the fullness thereof. Then God made man and gave him dominion over all the works of His hands. Adam was made the god of this world. However, Adam committed high treason and sold out to Satan. Then Satan became the god of this world (2 Cor. 4:4).

God didn't just move in and destroy Satan. If He had, Satan could have accused God of doing the same thing he had done. But God devised a plan of salvation. And He sent His Son, whom Satan could not and did not touch, to consummate that plan. Through Jesus, God redeemed mankind!

Now authority has been restored to us through Jesus Christ — and when we ask God, then He can and will move. That is why it seems He can do nothing unless someone asks Him to do it.

Confession: *I take my place in prayer. I join forces with my Father in carrying out His will upon the earth!*

APRIL 26

COVENANT FRIEND

And Abraham drew near, and said, Wilt thou also destroy the righteous with the wicked? Peradventure there be fifty righteous within the city: wilt thou also destroy and not spare the place for the fifty righteous that are therein? That be far from thee to do after this manner, to slay the righteous with the wicked: and that the righteous should be as the wicked, that be far from thee: Shall not the Judge of all the earth do right?
— GENESIS 18:23-25

God refused to destroy Sodom and Gomorrah until He had talked it over with Abraham, His blood covenant friend!

Abraham's prayer in Genesis chapter 18 is one of the most suggestive and illuminating prayers in the Old Testament. Abraham was taking his place in the covenant that God had made with him — the Old Covenant, the Old Testament.

Through the covenant, Abraham had received rights and privileges we understand little about. The covenant Abraham had just solemnized with the Lord Jehovah gave Abraham a legal standing with God. Therefore, we hear Abraham speak plainly as he intercedes for Sodom and Gomorrah, "Shall not the Judge of all the earth do right?"

Confession: *I have a covenant with God, the New Covenant. I have covenant rights and privileges. I have a standing with God. I commune with God. I use my covenant rights and privileges in prayer. I join forces with my Father in carrying out His will and plan upon the earth.*

APRIL 27

A BETTER COVENANT

But now hath he obtained a more excellent ministry, by how much also he is the mediator of a better covenant, which was established upon better promises. — HEBREWS 8:6

All through the Old Testament, we find men who understood and took their place in the covenant. Joshua could open the River Jordan. He could command time to stand still. Elijah could bring fire out of Heaven to consume not only the sacrifice, but the altar as well. David's mighty men were utterly shielded from death in time of war as long as they remembered the covenant. When you read about them, you think you're reading about "supermen."

Nearly all the prayers in the Old Testament were prayed by covenant men. Those prayers *had* to be answered.

The believer today has the same covenant rights as believers who lived under the Old Covenant. In fact, we have a *better* covenant established upon better promises. Therefore, we ought to be able to do all that they did and more, because we have a New Covenant, a better covenant — established on greater promises.

Confession: *Through Jesus, I have a covenant with God. It is a better covenant, based on better promises. I have better covenant rights than Abraham, Joshua, Elijah, and David had. I take my place as a New Testament believer in prayer. My prayers have to be answered.*

APRIL 28

PLEAD YOUR CASE

Put me in remembrance: let us plead together: declare thou, that thou mayest be justified. — ISAIAH 43:26

"Put me in remembrance . . . ." What does God mean by that? It means that we are to remind God of His promises about prayer.

When you pray, stand before the throne of God and remind Him of His promises. Lay your case legally before Him, and plead it as a lawyer. A lawyer is continually bringing up law and precedent. You bring up God's Word. Bring up His covenant promises.

The margin of my *King James* reference Bible says "set forth thy cause" as another meaning of "declare thou" in this verse. God is asking you to bring His Word; to put Him in remembrance, and to plead your covenant rights. This is a challenge from God to lay your case before Him!

If your children are unsaved — find scriptures which cover your case. Then lay the matter before God. Be definite in your requests. Find scriptures that definitely promise you those things you need. When you come to God according to His Word, His Word does not fail.

Confession: *I accept the challenge of the covenant-keeping God! I put God in remembrance of His promises. I plead my case. I set forth my cause legally. I find scriptures that cover my case, and I lay the matter before God. I come according to God's Word, and God's Word does not fail!*

APRIL 29

HE KEEPS HIS WORD

For as the rain cometh down, and the snow from heaven, and returneth not thither, but watereth the earth, and maketh it bring forth and bud, that it may give seed to the sower, and bread to the eater: So shall my word be that goeth forth out of my mouth: it shall not return unto me void, but it shall accomplish that which I please, and it shall prosper in the thing whereto I sent it. — **ISAIAH 55:10,11**

Isaiah 55:11 is a verse you should continually use in prayer. It is the very backbone of the prayer life. No word that has gone forth from God can return to Him void.

God said, "*. . . I will hasten my word to perform it*" (Jer. 1:12). A marginal note in the *King James* version reads, "I will watch over my word to perform it."

God will make His Word good if you dare to stand by it!

The greatest answers to prayer I have received came when I brought God's Word to Him and reminded Him of what He had to say.

Praise God, He keeps His Word!

Confession: *God's Word shall not return to Him void, but it shall accomplish that which God pleases, and it shall prosper in the thing whereto God sent it. I bring God's Word to Him in prayer. And God makes it good. He keeps His Word. And I receive the benefits.*

APRIL 30

PRAYER FRUIT

If ye abide in me, and my words abide in you, ye shall ask what ye will, and it shall be done unto you. Herein is my Father glorified, that ye bear much fruit; so shall ye be my disciples. — JOHN 15:7,8

"If ye abide in me . . . ." If we are born again, we do abide in Christ. If Jesus had said that and that alone, we would have had it made, but He continued, *". . . AND my words abide in you . . . ."*

Jesus' words abide in us in the measure that they govern our lives — in the measure that we act upon them.

If Jesus' words abide in us, we are bound to have faith, because the Bible says, *"So then faith cometh by hearing, and hearing by the word of God"* (Rom. 10:17). It would be impossible for Jesus' words to abide in someone and that person not have faith!

Unbelief and doubt are a result of ignorance of the Word of God. If we live the Word, then when we come to pray, that Word dwells in us so richly that it becomes Jesus' Word on our lips. It will be as the Father's words were on the lips of Jesus.

Confession: *I abide in Christ. And His words abide in me. I hide His words in my heart. I believe them. I pray them. When I come to prayer, the Word that dwells in my heart becomes God's Word on my lips, and it cannot return to God void. It will accomplish what it promises!*

MAY 1

ACCORDING TO HIS WILL

And this is the confidence that we have in him, that, if we ask any thing according to his will, he heareth us: And if we know that he hear us, whatsoever we ask, we know that we have the petitions that we desired of him. — 1 JOHN 5:14,15

People have remembered John's phrase "according to his will," and thought they had to pray, "Lord, do this or that, *if it be thy will.*" But inserting this expression into a prayer when God's Word already states that what we're praying for is His will — is confessing that we don't believe God's Word. And that kind of praying will not work.

How can we find out what God's will is?

God's Word is His will! We can find out God's will for us in the Bible — because the Bible is God's will, His covenant, and His testament. And it is God's will for us to have whatever God has provided for us!

First we must find the scriptures that reveal God's will for us. Then we can go before God with great boldness: "*. . . this is the CONFIDENCE that we have in him . . . .*" When we pray for things that God's Word tells us *are* His will, we *know* that He hears us! And when we *know* God hears us, we *know* we have the petitions we ask of Him. We *know* we have them, praise God!

Confession: *I have this boldness toward God: When I ask anything according to God's Word, I know He hears me! And I know that when God hears me, I have the petitions I desired of Him!*

MAY 2

SAVING THE LOST

The Lord is not slack concerning his promise, as some men count slackness; but is longsuffering to us-ward, not willing that any should perish, but that all should come to repentance. — 2 PETER 3:9

We know that saving the lost is God's will — because it was to save the lost that Jesus laid down His life.

Therefore, knowing this, we would not pray, "God, save my mother, *if it is Your will.* Don't let her go to hell, *if it is Your will. If it's not Your will,* let her go to hell."

No! Why? *Because we know God's will in the matter.* God's will — His Word — makes it clear in such scriptures as John 3:16 an Second Peter 3:9. It is God's will for men and women to be saved. Therefore, we can pray for the lost with great boldness.

Believers especially can exercise great authority in praying for the salvation of their families. I used some of the scriptures we have been studying as I prayed for my relatives. I said something like this: "This is the confidence that we have in God, that, if we ask anything according to His will, He hears us. What I am asking for is according to God's will; therefore, He hears me. That is what the Word says. *'And if we know that He hears us, whatsoever we ask, we know that we have the petitions that we desire of him.'* Then according to the Word, I have that petition."

Then I stopped asking and started thanking God. It's amazing how it works. I don't mean that your entire family will necessarily come to the Lord overnight, but as you stand in faith, thanking God, they will come.

Confession: *I can pray in faith for the lost, because I know God's will in the matter!*

MAY 3

SUPPLYING OUR NEEDS

But my God shall supply all your need according to his riches in glory by Christ Jesus. — PHILIPPIANS 4:19

It is God's will that our needs be met. All of them!

Philippians 4:19 includes *all* of your needs (*all* means *all!*), whether spiritual, physical, material, or financial.

Believe that!

Lest someone think that God is not concerned about our financial needs, this verse is set in a context which discusses material and financial affairs. Read it and you will see that the Philippians had taken up an offering of money and goods to send to other Christians. Paul was telling them, "Because you have given to others and have helped them, my God shall supply all your need." So Paul was talking about material and financial matters.

With what boldness, then, we can pray for finances to meet our obligations! Having all of our needs met is according to God's will!

Confession: *When I pray concerning finances, I pray according to God's Word — His will. Therefore, I am confident that God hears me. That's what His Word says. And if I know that God hears whatever I ask of Him, I know that I have the petition I desired of Him. According to the Word of God, I have my petition. And I thank God for it!*

MAY 4

THE GOOD

If ye be willing and obedient, ye shall eat the good of the land.
— ISAIAH 1:19

If you are willing and obedient, it is God's will that you have the best. (Of course, you can't walk in disobedience and enjoy the good things of God.)

God is not a miser or a tightwad. And He didn't put everything here in this world for the devil and his crowd to enjoy.

Some people have the idea that if you're a Christian, you should never have anything, financially or materially. They believe that you should go through life poor and beaten down.

But Jesus said, *"If ye then, being evil* [natural], *know how to give good gifts unto your children, HOW MUCH MORE shall your Father which is in heaven give good things to them that ask him?"* (Matt. 7:11).

Oh, God wants to give us good gifts! He wants us to have the best! He wants us to prosper and have the good things of this life! But we must cooperate with Him.

Confession: *I am willing to love and serve God my Father. I am obedient to walk in the light of His Word, His will. Therefore, I shall eat the good of the land. And with confidence I can pray for the good things in life, because it is my Father's will that I have them.*

MAY 5

HIS RICHES

A good man leaveth an inheritance to his children's children: and the wealth of the sinner is laid up for the just. — PROVERBS 13:22

The Lord Jesus said to me once as He came and sat by my bedside and talked to me for an hour and a half about being led of the Spirit, "My Spirit will lead all of My children. The Bible says, *'For as many as are led by the Spirit of God, they are the sons of God'* (Rom. 8:14). I will lead you, and not only you, but any child of God. I will show you what to do with your money. I will show you how to invest it. In fact, if you'll listen to Me, I will make you rich. I am not opposed to My children being rich. I am opposed to their being covetous."

(Someone could be covetous and not have a dime.)

People misquote the Bible when they claim that it says, "Money is the root of all evil." But the Bible doesn't say that at all. It says, *"For the love of money is the root of all evil . . ."* (1 Tim. 6:10).

It is all right for you to have money. It is wrong for money to have you!

Confession: *I am a child of God. I am led by the Spirit of God. My trust is in God, not in riches. But I trust God to lead me concerning my finances. I honor God with tithes and offerings of all that I have. And all of my needs are supplied according to God's riches in glory by Christ Jesus.*

MAY 6

HEALING: GOD'S WILL

For I came down from heaven, not to do mine own will, but the will of him that sent me. — JOHN 6:38

Healing the sick is God's will.

Yet Christians who need healing have said to me, "Maybe God put this sickness on me for some purpose."

Did Jesus ever put sickness on anyone? When people came to Jesus for healing, did He ever turn even one away, saying, "No, it's not My will. Just suffer a little longer. Wait until your piety gets deepened enough"?

No! Not once!

Do you want to know what God is like? Look at Jesus. Do you want to see God at work? Look at Jesus! Did Jesus go about making people sick? No! He went about doing good and healing (Acts 10:38). Do you want to know the will of God? Look at Jesus. Jesus is the will of God in action.

We can pray for healing with great confidence — knowing it is the will of God!

Confession: *When I pray concerning healing, I know that I pray according to God's will. It is God's will that we have what Jesus bought for us. Therefore, I am confident that God hears me. And since I know that God hears me, I know that I have the petition I desire of Him. And I thank Him for it!*

MAY 7

DON'T BLAME GOD

. . . He that hath seen me hath seen the Father. . . . Believest thou not that I am in the Father, and the Father in me? the words that I speak unto you I speak not of myself: but the Father that dwelleth in me, he doeth the works. — JOHN 14:9,10

Many of the laws that govern this earth today came into being when Adam sinned and the curse came upon the earth.

Because people don't understand this, they accuse God of causing accidents, sicknesses, the death of loved ones, storms, catastrophes, earthquakes, floods, etc. Even insurance policies call such things "acts of God." They are not acts of God! They are acts of the devil!

Jesus set aside these natural laws to bless humanity. We don't see Jesus bringing any storms on people. In fact, we see Jesus stilling the storms. Therefore, God didn't send the storm. Jesus wouldn't rebuke something God did! But Jesus did rebuke what the devil stirred up.

When you see Jesus at work, you see God at work. Jesus' description of the Father, and His statement that ". . . *he that hath seen me hath seen the Father* . . ." (John 14:9), make it impossible to accept the teaching that sickness and disease are from God. The very nature of God refutes such an idea!

Confession: *God is love. And I don't blame love for what the devil does. I look at Jesus, and I see love at work.*

MAY 8

PURPOSE

. . . For this purpose the Son of God was manifested, that he might destroy the works of the devil. — 1 JOHN 3:8

During the Korean Conflict, I read an article by a well-known newspaper columnist. He said, "I don't claim to be a Christian, but I'm not an atheist or an agnostic either. The atheist says there is no God. The agnostic says there may be a God; he doesn't know. I believe there is a God. I don't believe everything just happened into being. What hinders me from being a Christian is what I hear preachers say. They say that God is running everything. Well, if He is, He's sure got things in a mess."

Then the columnist alluded to the wars, children being killed, poverty, disease, and so forth, that plague the world. He said, "I believe there is a Supreme Being somewhere, and that everything He made was beautiful and good. I can't believe these other things are the works of God."

No, these things came with the fall, when Satan became the god of this world (2 Cor. 4:4). And the Bible teaches that when Satan is finally eliminated from the earth, there will be nothing here that will hurt or destroy. It ought to be obvious where all the hurts and destruction come from. If evil came from God, we would still have it after Satan is destroyed from the scene, because God will still be here. But we know that evil does not come from God.

Confession: *The Son of God was manifested so that He might destroy the works of the devil. As part of Christ's Body, I take authority over the works of the devil!*

MAY 9

SOURCE OF SICKNESS

And ought not this woman, being a daughter of Abraham, whom Satan hath bound, lo, these eighteen years, be loosed from this bond on the sabbath day? — LUKE 13:16

The Bible is progressive revelation. It is in the New Testament that we get full light, full truth, and full revelation. There Jesus plainly taught that sickness is of the devil, not God.

In Luke 13, we see Jesus going into the synagogue on the Sabbath. A woman was there whose body was bowed together in a fixed position. She couldn't straighten up. She may have had arthritis. Jesus called her to Him, and said, "Woman, thou art loosed from thine infirmity!" Then Jesus laid hands on her, and immediately she stood straight. The ruler of the synagogue, like the leaders of some churches today, got angry about it!

Then, as recorded in our text, Jesus elaborated on the fact that Satan is the author of sickness. Jesus made three enlightening statements: (1) The woman ought to be loosed; she ought not to be bound; she ought to be free from this physical infirmity; (2) It was Satan who had bound her, not God; and (3) The reason this woman ought to be loosed was because she was a daughter of Abraham.

Confession: *Since Satan is the author of sickness, I ought to walk free from sickness. And Jesus has made the provision for me to do so. Divine health is my covenant right!*

MAY 10

Healing Is Good

How God anointed Jesus of Nazareth with the Holy Ghost and with power: who went about doing good, and healing all that were oppressed of the devil; for God was with him. — ACTS 10:38

Who anointed Jesus of Nazareth? God did! And Jesus said, ". . . *the Father that dwelleth in me, he doeth the works*" (John 14:10). How did God do these works of healings through Jesus? By anointing Jesus with the Holy Spirit and with healing power.

What did Jesus do with the anointing that God anointed Him with? *He went about doing good!* And what was the good Jesus did? *Healing!*

Therefore, it was actually God healing the people when Jesus healed them, because it was God who had anointed Jesus. God is in the healing business! He's not in the sickness business!

Who was it Jesus healed? All that were oppressed of the devil. All! *ALL!* Everyone healed under the ministry of Jesus were oppressed of the devil. (This doesn't mean that everyone had an evil spirit, but it does mean that the devil is behind all sickness.)

Yet to hear some people talk — even ministers — they would lead you to believe that God and the devil had swapped jobs in the last 2,000 years, and God is putting sickness on people, and the devil is healing them. But no! The devil is the same devil he has always been. And God is the same God!

Confession: *Satan is the oppressor, not God. Jesus is the Deliverer!*

MAY 11

SET AGAINST SICKNESS

And he said unto them, Go ye into all the world, and preach the gospel to every creature. . . . And these signs shall follow them that believe; In my name . . . they shall lay hands on the sick, and they shall recover.
— MARK 16:15,17,18

Let's stop and analyze something here: Which of the sick did Jesus say we were to lay hands on?

Jesus just said "the sick" — period.

Then, if God were the author of sickness — if God did put sickness and disease on people — if it were the will of God for some to be sick — this statement would be confusing. Because in it, Jesus authorized us to lay hands on ALL sick.

If God weren't in the healing business, Jesus would have had to say something like, "Lay your hands on those that it is the will of God to heal, and they shall recover. And those that it isn't — they won't recover."

But, no! God set the Church against sickness — period!

Confession: *God is in the healing business. God is not in the sickness business. God is in the delivering business. God is not in the bondage business. I refuse to allow the enemy to try to get me to accept sickness or bondage as being from God. Satan is the author of sickness. God has set me against sickness!*

MAY 12

ANY

Is any sick among you? let him call for the elders of the church; and let them pray over him, anointing him with oil in the name of the Lord: And the prayer of faith shall save the sick, and the Lord shall raise him up; and if he have committed sins, they shall be forgiven him.

— JAMES 5:14,15

"*Is any sick among you?*"

Among whom?

The Church!

Then it *must* be God's will to heal "any" of the sick in the Church!

And it *can't* be God's will for "any" in the Church to be sick!

"But, Brother Hagin, you've forgotten," one person said.

"Forgotten what?"

"The Bible says that if we *suffer* with Him, we'll reign with Him."

"No, I haven't forgotten," I explained. "Let's read it again: '. . . *if . . . we suffer WITH HIM . . .*' (Rom. 8:17). Suffer what: Pneumonia? Cancer? Tuberculosis? No! Jesus didn't suffer from any of these things.

What did Jesus suffer? *Persecution.* And you will, too, if you live right. Especially if you preach divine healing, the gifts of the Spirit, and faith. I've suffered persecution for more than sixty-five years, but I haven't suffered sickness and disease.

Confession: *It is God's will for the Church, His Body, to walk in divine health. It is God's will for me to be well!*

133

MAY 13

CHASTENING

That he might sanctify and cleanse it [the Church] *with the washing of water by the word.*
— EPHESIANS 5:26

"You've forgotten," someone said to me.

"What did I forget?"

"In the Book of Hebrews it says, '. . .*whom the Lord loveth he chasteneth . . .*'" (Heb. 12:6).

"No, I didn't forget. That verse is still in there. But it doesn't say, 'whom the Lord loveth He makes sick.'"

People put their own interpretation on verses. "Chasten" in the Greek means *to child train, to educate.* You train your children. You send them to school. But did you ever tell the teacher, "If Johnny doesn't do right, knock his eye out," or "If Johnny is disobedient, break his leg," or "Give him cancer." No! That isn't the way you discipline or train a child! And that's not the way God does it either!

Confession: *I am trained by the Word and the Spirit of God. I am educated by the Word and the Spirit of God. I am disciplined by the Word and the Spirit of God. With the washing of water by the Word, I am cleansed!*

MAY 14

EVERY GOOD GIFT

Every good gift and every perfect gift is from above, and cometh down from the Father of lights, with whom is no variableness, neither shadow of turning. — JAMES 1:17

What is good?

Acts 10:38 says that Jesus went about doing good *and healing.* Healing is good! Sickness is not good. Every healing comes down from the Father. Every sickness does not come down from the Father.

In the first place, where in the world would God get sickness to put on you? He doesn't have any in Heaven. He would have to borrow some from the devil! (You can't give someone something you don't have.) The Bible says there is no sickness in Heaven. Therefore, sickness can't come from Heaven.

What does come down from Heaven?

Every good gift and every perfect gift!

Confession: *Every good gift and every perfect gift is from above, and comes down from my Father, the Father of lights. Only good gifts can come down from God, for God is good, and Heaven holds only good. There is no sickness in Heaven. Therefore, sickness cannot come from God. Healing comes from God. So I purpose to receive only what my Father gives — healing!*

MAY 15

HOW ABOUT JOB?

And the Lord turned the captivity of Job, when he prayed for his friends: also the Lord gave Job twice as much as he had before.
— JOB 42:10

"But you've forgotten, Brother Hagin, that God made Job sick," someone said.

"No, He didn't — the devil did."

"Yeah, but God gave him permission!"

But God didn't commission Job's problem. God will *permit* you to rob a gas station (you have a free will), but He won't *commission* you to do it.

Actually, God has only given the devil "permission" in a sense. If you allow Satan to attack you, God will permit it, because Satan is the god of this world (2 Cor. 4:4), and you are living on his territory. Job himself opened the door to the devil by being afraid. Job said, *"For the thing which I greatly feared is come upon me, and that which I was afraid of is come unto me"* (Job 3:25).

Many Bible scholars agree that the entire Book of Job took place over a nine- to eighteen-month period. Afterwards, we see that God turned Job's *captivity*. Therefore, when Job was sick, he was in captivity to the devil. When Job was in poverty, he was in captivity to the devil. But God turned Job's captivity! God gave Job twice as much as he had to begin with. That's God at work!

Confession: *God turns our captivity! He doesn't put us in bondage. God sets us free! Through Jesus, I am free! I will never accept sickness and disease as being from God! I know where it comes from — and I stand against it!*

MAY 16

WHAT ABOUT PAUL'S THORN?

But if ye will not drive out the inhabitants of the land from before you; then it shall come to pass, that those which ye let remain of them shall be pricks in your eyes, and thorns in your sides, and shall vex you in the land wherein ye dwell. — NUMBERS 33:55

"Don't you remember, though, Brother Hagin — Paul was sick all his life."

"No, I don't remember that."

"But he had a *thorn in the flesh.*"

"Where did you ever read in the Bible that a thorn in the flesh is sickness? Nowhere!"

Study the Scriptures. See how the Bible uses that term. In the Old Testament, God said to Israel, "If you don't kill those Canaanites when you possess the land, they will be thorns in your side. They will torment you" (Num. 33:55; Joshua 23:13; Judges 2:3).

Paul tells exactly what the thorn was: ". . . *the messenger of Satan to buffet me . . .*" (2 Cor. 12:7). Everywhere Paul went to preach, this evil spirit went before and behind him, and stirred up everything it could. (And Paul couldn't command the evil spirit to leave the earth, because the devil has the right to be here until Adam's lease runs out.)

So there is no separating sickness and disease from Satan — he causes them. Jesus' attitude toward sickness was uncompromising warfare against Satan.

Confession: *Since sickness and disease are of the devil, I follow in the footsteps and attitude of Jesus, and deal with them as Jesus did!*

MAY 17

THE LORD THAT HEALETH

. . . If thou wilt diligently hearken to the voice of the Lord thy God, and wilt do that which is right in his sight, and wilt give ear to his commandments, and keep all his statutes, I will put [literal Hebrew: I will permit] *none of these diseases upon thee, which I have brought* [permitted] *upon the Egyptians: for I am the Lord that healeth thee.*
— EXODUS 15:26

When Israel crossed the Red Sea and started toward their homeland, the Lord spoke these words to them and revealed Himself as Jehovah-Rapha. Jehovah-Rapha translated is, "I am the Lord thy Physician," or *"I am the Lord that healeth thee."* God didn't put diseases upon Israel or upon the Egyptians. It is Satan, the god of this world, who makes man sick. Jehovah declares that He is the Healer.

In his book *Christ the Healer*, F. F. Bosworth said, "This name [Jehovah-Rapha] is given to reveal to us our *redemptive* privilege of being healed. . . . The fact is, that the very first covenant God gave after the passage of the Red Sea, which was so distinctively typical of our redemption, was the covenant of healing, and it was at this time that God revealed Himself as our Physician, by the first *redemptive* and covenant name, Jehovah-Rapha, 'I am the Lord that healeth thee.' This is not only a promise, it is 'a statute and an ordinance.'"

Confession: *Jehovah-Rapha* — *"I am the Lord that healeth thee"* — *is the name of my Lord.*

MAY 18

COVENANT BLESSING

And ye shall serve the Lord your God, and he shall bless thy bread, and thy water; and I will take sickness away from the midst of thee. There shall nothing cast their young, nor be barren, in thy land: the number of thy days I will fulfil. — EXODUS 23:25,26

As long as Israel walked in the covenant, there was no sickness among them. There is no record of a premature death as long as they kept the covenant. No babies, no young people, no middle-aged people died. With sickness taken away from the midst of them, they lived their whole lives out without disease, and then they just fell asleep in death. When it was time for them to go, they would lay hands on their children, pronounce blessings upon them, gather their feet up into bed, give up the ghost, and go home.

What does that have to do with us? God is the same God now that He was then! The Bible says that He does not change. God was against sin in the Old Testament (Old Covenant), and God is against sin in the New Testament (New Covenant). God was against sickness in the Old Testament — and God is against sickness in the New Testament. God made provision for healing in the Old Testament — and God has made provision for healing in the New Testament!

Confession: I love and serve the Lord my God as a New Covenant believer. Jesus has taken sickness away from the midst of me. If He tarries His coming, the number of my days I will fulfill!

MAY 19

WITH LONG LIFE

The days of our years are threescore years and ten; and if by reason of strength they be fourscore years . . . . — PSALM 90:10

With long life will I satisfy him, and shew him my salvation.
— PSALM 91:16

If Jesus tarries His coming, I don't mind telling you at all, I'll live to a great age. And I'll know before I go. I will tell everyone good-bye and before I leave here, I'll look over there and say, "There it is, folks — and I'm going. I want to leave you all shouting and happy, because that's the way I'm going."

"But, Brother Hagin, you can't ever tell."

Oh yes, you can! You can have what God said you can have. We've got a better covenant than Israel had. If it was God's plan for Israel — who were servants, not sons, and who lived under a covenant not as good as ours — to live out their full length of time with no sickness, then what a plan God must have for us, the sons of God! If God didn't want His *servants* sick, I don't believe He wants His *sons* sick!

I believe it is the plan of God our Father that no believer should ever be sick, and that every believer should live his full length of time if Jesus tarries, to fall asleep in Jesus.

Confession: *I can believe God for anything His Word promises. I can believe God for a long, productive life. If Jesus tarries, I will live out my days in His service without sickness and disease!*

MAY 20

FOR MY BENEFIT

And he will love thee, and bless thee, and multiply thee: he will also bless the fruit of thy womb, and the fruit of thy land, thy corn, and thy wine, and thine oil, the increase of thy kine, and the flocks of thy sheep, in the land which he sware unto thy fathers to give thee. Thou shalt be blessed above all people: there shall not be male or female barren among you, or among your cattle. And the Lord will take away from thee all sickness, and will put [permit] none of the evil diseases of Egypt, which thou knowest, upon thee . . . .
— DEUTERONOMY 7:13-15

"And he will love thee . . . ." Love thee! Love thee!

And put sickness upon you? And cause you to die when you're a baby? And cause some of you to be stillborn, and some of you to be sick and crippled?

No! No! No! That's not the Holy Scriptures!

"But that's not for us today, Brother Hagin."

Are you sure? First Corinthians is in the New Testament, isn't it? Let's look at First Corinthians 10:11 to see if divine health is for us: *"Now all these things happened unto them [Israel] for ensamples [examples, types]: and they are written [Who are they written for — the Jews? No!] for OUR admonition, upon whom the ends of the world are come."*

Glory! Deuteronomy 7:13-15 was written for my benefit. It was written for my admonition!

Confession: (*Make your own confession of Deuteronomy 7:13-15. The Lord loves me . . . He blesses me . . . He blesses my children . . . and so on*).

MAY 21

JOINT-HEIRS

The Spirit itself [Himself] *beareth witness with our spirit, that we are the children of God: And if children, then heirs; heirs of God, and joint-heirs with Christ . . . .* — ROMANS 8:16,17

Do you think the people who lived under the Old Covenant could be more blessed than those in the Church of the Lord Jesus Christ?

Do you think the people who lived under the Old Covenant could be blessed financially, and be well and healed, but those in the Church couldn't?

Do you think that the Church, the Body of Christ, the Body of the Son of God, the Body of the Beloved, would have to struggle through life poverty-stricken, emaciated, wasted away with starvation, sick and afflicted, singing, "Here I wander, like a beggar, through the heat and cold"?

Away with such ideas!

The Bible declares that we are joint-heirs with Christ! Sons of God! Children of God! In the Kingdom of God!

We're not beggars! We're new creatures.

We're blessed above all people.

Confession: *The Holy Spirit Himself bears witness with my spirit that I am a child of God. God is my very own Father. I am His very own child. And since I am His child, then I am His heir. I am an heir of God — the Creator of the universe — and I am a joint-heir with Jesus Christ!*

MAY 22

GOD'S STAMP

He [God] brought them forth also with silver and gold: and there was not one feeble person among their tribes. — PSALM 105:37

You can see from the Scriptures that it was God's plan for everything connected with Israel to bear the stamp of prosperity and success. Furthermore, disease and sickness were not to be tolerated among them.

And so it should be with the Church. Everything connected with the Body of Christ, the New Testament Church, should bear the stamp of prosperity, success, healing, surplus, and health.

143

What God said concerning Israel, He said in so many words concerning the Church. Romans 1:16 says, *"For I am not ashamed of the gospel of Christ: for it is the power of God unto salvation . . . ."* Scofield's footnote on the word "salvation" states that the Greek and Hebrew words translated "salvation" imply the ideas of deliverance, safety, preservation, healing, and health (soundness). The Gospel of Jesus Christ, then, is the power of God unto deliverance. It is the power of God unto safety and preservation. It is the power of God unto healing and health.

Confession: *I am a child of God. I am a member of the Body of Christ. I bear the stamp of prosperity, success, healing, surplus, and health. The Gospel of Jesus Christ is the power of God unto deliverance, safety, preservation, healing, and health for me.*

MAY 23

FORGIVENESS AND HEALING

Who forgiveth all thine iniquities; who healeth all thy diseases.
— **PSALM 103:3**

Disease came upon the children of Israel when they disobeyed the law. Forgiveness for their disobedience meant the healing of their diseases.

It was when the children of Israel took themselves out from under the protection of their covenant by wrongdoing that their distresses came (Ps. 107:11,17,18). But when they cried unto the Lord, *". . . he saveth them out of their distresses. He sent his word, and healed them, and delivered them from their destructions"* (Ps. 107:19,20).

We have protection under our better covenant — but it is possible to take ourselves out from under the protection of our covenant.

Since I have known the truth of God's Word concerning divine health and healing, the only time some physical disorder touched me was when I got out from under God's protection. Now, I don't mean I stole something or told a lie; I just wasn't obeying God like I should have been. (Usually, I wasn't ministering the way God said to minister.) Therefore, I got out from under the protection of the covenant and opened myself up to the enemy's attacks. So I had to repent and get back in line. The moment I did, I was healed physically.

Confession: *God forgives iniquities. God heals diseases. He sent His Word and healed me. He delivered me from destruction.*

MAY 24

ONLY OUR DISEASES

He was despised and shunned by men; a man of pains, and acquainted with disease; and as one who hid his face from us was he despised, and we esteemed him not. But only our diseases did he bear himself, and our pains he carried: while we indeed esteemed him stricken, smitten of God, and afflicted. Yet he was wounded for our transgressions, he was bruised for our iniquities: the chastisement for our peace was upon him; and through his bruises was healing granted to us.

— ISAIAH 53:3-5 (*Leeser*)

I want to boldly state that it is not the will of God my Father that we should suffer from cancer and other dread diseases that bring pain and anguish. It is God's will that we be healed!

How do I know? Because healing is provided for us under the New Covenant.

Isaiah chapter 53 gives us a graphic picture of the coming Messiah. This chapter deals with the disease and sin problems that confront the Church today.

God dealt with man's body, as well as with his spirit and soul. God laid our iniquities and our sins upon Jesus — and Jesus bore them. God laid our diseases and our sicknesses upon Jesus — and Jesus bore them. Why? So that we might be free!

Confession: *Jesus Christ, the Lamb of God, bore my sins and iniquities. So I don't have to bear them. He also bore my diseases and pains. So I don't have to bear them. Because of Jesus, I am free. By His stripes, I was healed!*

MAY 25

HIMSELF TOOK ... AND BARE

That it might be fulfilled which was spoken by Esaias the prophet, saying, Himself took our infirmities, and bare our sicknesses.
— MATTHEW 8:17

In our text today, Matthew is quoting Isaiah 53.

When I first understood what this verse really meant, I rejoiced in it. Because when I read it, I was able to emphasize the word "our." Jesus took *our* infirmities and bore *our* sicknesses. I am included in that "our"! He took *my* infirmities, and bore *my* sicknesses!

At this realization, I felt as the elderly woman did who suddenly turned up missing in London during World War II. Her neighbors didn't see her in the bomb shelters during enemy air raids, so they assumed she had either been killed or had left town. When some of them saw her on the street several days later, they asked her where she had been. She answered that she hadn't been anywhere.

"But what did you do during the bombing?" they asked.

She said, "I just stayed in bed and slept."

"Weren't you afraid?"

"No, after I read in the Bible that God neither slumbers nor sleeps, I decided there wasn't any need for both of us to stay awake!"

Since Christ Himself took our infirmities and bore our sicknesses, there isn't any need for us to bear them. Jesus bore them so that we might be free!

Confession: *Because Christ took my infirmities and bore my sicknesses, there is no need for me to bear them. I accept what Jesus has provided!*

MAY 26

BY HIS STRIPES

Who his own self bare our sins in his own body on the tree, that we, being dead to sins, should live unto righteousness: by whose stripes ye were healed. — 1 PETER 2:24

Some years ago, I was awakened at 1:30 a.m. with severe symptoms in my heart and chest. I knew something about such symptoms because I had been bedfast and given up to die with a heart condition as a teenager.

The devil said to my mind, "You're going to die. This is one time you're *not* going to get your healing."

I pulled the covers over my head and began to laugh. I didn't feel like laughing, but I just laughed anyway for about ten minutes. Finally, the devil asked me what I was laughing about.

"I'm laughing at you!" I said. "You said I wasn't going to get my healing. Ha, ha, Mr. Devil. I don't *expect* to get my healing! Jesus already *got* it for me! Now, in case you can't read, I'll quote First Peter 2:24 for you." And I did.

After quoting the last phrase, ". . . *by whose stripes ye were healed,*" I said, "Now if we *were* — I *was!* So I don't have to get it — Jesus already got it! And because Jesus got it for me, I accept it, and claim it, and I have it. Now you just gather up your little symptoms and get out of here, Mr. Devil!"

And he did!

Confession: *Jesus has already obtained healing for me. I accept it. I claim it. I have it. By Jesus' stripes, I was healed!*

MAY 27

TRAVEL SAFETY

And the same day, when the even was come, he saith unto them, Let us pass over unto the other side. — MARK 4:35

Jesus got into a ship with His disciples and said, "Let us pass over unto the other side." And that settled it! Jesus did not say, "Let us go halfway and sink." Therefore, when a storm arose and Jesus' disciples were frightened, He rebuked them, saying, "How is it that you have no faith?"

At a Full Gospel Business Men's convention, a woman asked me to pray for her. She said, "I'm a nervous wreck. It just scares me to death to travel by plane. I actually become sick with fright. I'm not going to attend any more conventions, even though I love to, because I'm so afraid to fly."

"You don't have to be afraid," I replied. "And really, you don't even have to pray about it. All you have to do is get on the plane and say, 'Let us pass over to Los Angeles or Chicago or wherever.' And the plane can't go down. Then you can do just what Jesus did: You can go to sleep, knowing the plane is going to get there, because you have spoken in faith."

I saw this woman at several conventions afterwards. She told me, "It works just like you said. I get on board the plane and say, 'Let's go over to the other side.' Then I lie back, relax, and praise the Lord. I'm really enjoying flying now."

Confession: *Wherever I travel, I can say, "Let us pass over to the other side" — and I will have what I say!*

MAY 28

No Accident

The angel of the Lord encampeth round about them that fear him, and delivereth them. — PSALM 34:7

In May 1952, my wife and children were traveling with me to a tent meeting in New Mexico. When my mother learned of our travel plans, she said, "Be careful on the road! There are so many wrecks. When you're traveling, I stay awake all night praying for your safety and just waiting for the phone to ring with the news that you've been in a wreck. But I know that you're praying every minute you're on the road."

"No, I never do," I replied.

"Oh, Son, what's gotten into you?" she said.

"Nothing but the Word," I said, "Jesus has already said, ' . . . *I will never leave thee, nor forsake thee'* (Heb. 13:5). So I don't have to go down the road begging Jesus to be with me. I always start out by saying, 'Heavenly Father, I'm so thankful for Your Word. I'm so glad Jesus is with me. I'm so glad the Father, Son, and Holy Spirit are inside me.' Then I go singing and rejoicing. God has already told me in Psalm 91 that no evil will overtake me. And the Swedish translation of that passage reads, 'No *accident* shall overtake thee.'"

Confession: *Jesus never leaves me. Angels are encamped around me. The Father, the Son, and the Holy Spirit live inside of me. No accident can overtake me!*

MAY 29

THE LAW OF LIFE

For the law of the Spirit of life in Christ Jesus hath made me free from the law of sin and death. — ROMANS 8:2

Dr. John G. Lake went as a missionary to Africa in 1908. The deadly bubonic plague broke out in his area. Hundreds died. He cared for the sick and buried the dead. Finally the British sent a relief ship with medical supplies and a corps of doctors. The doctors sent for Lake to come aboard. They asked him, "What have you been using to protect yourself?"

"Sirs," Lake replied, "I believe the law of the Spirit of life in Christ Jesus has set me free from the law of sin and death. And as long as I walk in the light of that law of life, no germ will attach itself to me."

"You had better use our preventatives," the doctors urged.

"No," Lake said, "but I think you would like to experiment with me. Take some of the foam that comes from the victims' lungs after death, and examine it under the microscope. You will find the masses of living germs remain alive for a while after the man is dead. Fill my hand with the foam and examine it under the microscope. Instead of remaining alive, the germs will die instantly."

The doctors made the experiment and what Lake said proved true. When the doctors expressed wonder at what caused it, Lake told them, "That is the law of the Spirit of life in Christ Jesus."

Confession: *The law of the Spirit of life in Christ Jesus has made me free from the law of sin and death.*

MAY 30

MORE THAN CONQUERORS

Nay, in all these things we are more than conquerors through him that loved us. — ROMANS 8:37

If God's Word had just told us we were conquerors, it would have been enough — but it tells us that we are *more than conquerors* through Jesus Christ.

Rather than saying, "I'm defeated," rise up and say what the Bible says about you. Say, "I am a conqueror!"

It may not seem to you that you are a conqueror, but your confession of it because of what you see in God's Word will create the reality of it in your life.

Sooner or later you will become what you confess!

You will not be afraid of any circumstances, if you make the right confession.

You will not be afraid of any disease, if you make the right confession.

You will not be afraid of any conditions, if you make the right confession.

You will face life fearlessly, as a conqueror!

Confession: *In all things I am more than a conqueror through Him that loves me. I am not afraid of any circumstances. I am not afraid of any disease. I am not afraid of any condition. I face life fearlessly, a conqueror! I am a conqueror! In fact, I am more than a conqueror!*

MAY 31

WORKING IN ME

For it is God which worketh in you both to will and to do of his good pleasure. — **PHILIPPIANS 2:13**

Another translation of this verse reads, "For it is God who is at work within you . . . ."

I like to put Philippians 2:13 together with First John 4:4: ". . . *greater is he that is in you* [and that means me] . . . ." God is in me!

What is God doing in me?

He is at work in me.

What is God working at?

Both to will and to do of His own good pleasure.

What is His own good pleasure?

His pleasure is that I have everything the Word of God says I can have — that I do everything the Word of God says I can do. God is enabling me!

God is in me, and my spirit rejoices. My heart is glad that I can turn God loose in me. I can let God have right-of-way in me. I can put God to work even to a greater degree in my life.

How can I do this?

First, I can do it by believing in my heart that God is in there, and that the Word of God is true. Then, I can boldly confess with my mouth, for I will not enjoy the reality of what the Word states is mine or what I believe until I confess it with my mouth. The Bible teaches that ". . . *with the heart man believeth . . . and with the mouth confession is made unto . . .*" (Rom. 10:10).

Confession: *God is in me. God is at work within me. God works through me!*

JUNE 1

GOD IS A SPIRIT

But the hour cometh, and now is, when the true worshippers shall worship the Father in spirit and in truth: for the Father seeketh such to worship him. God is a Spirit: and they that worship him must worship him in spirit and in truth. — JOHN 4:23,24

God is a Spirit.

Spiritual things are more real than *material* things. They have to be, because God, who is a Spirit, created all material things.

God's unseen ability brought into being everything we know upon the earth in the natural realm by simply saying, "Let there be . . . ."

You cannot know God, or touch God, or become acquainted with God *physically*.

You cannot know God, or touch God, or communicate with God *mentally*.

God is a Spirit. And, thank God, you can reach Him with *your* spirit. Your human spirit can come to know God. Your spirit can become acquainted with God. Your spirit can communicate with God. Your spirit can worship God!

Confession: *The hour now is when the true worshippers worship the Father in spirit and in truth. I am a true worshipper. God is a Spirit. I worship God in spirit and in truth. My spirit knows God. My spirit becomes better and better acquainted with God every day. My spirit communicates with God. My spirit worships God.*

JUNE 2

IN HIS IMAGE

And God said, Let us make man in our image, after our likeness . . . .
So God created man in his own image, in the image of God created he
him . . . .   — GENESIS 1:26,27

For the Lord taketh pleasure in his people . . . .   — PSALM 149:4

If man is made in the likeness of God, and God is a Spirit, then man, of necessity, must be a spirit.

God made man for His own pleasure. He made man to fellowship with Him. Man is not an animal. Man is in the same class with God; otherwise, he couldn't fellowship with God.

Did you ever try to fellowship with a cow? Cows are in a different kingdom than you are in. They are in a different class. You can't fellowship with them.

But we can fellowship with one another. And we can fellowship with God, because we are in the same class of being as God.

God is a Spirit. And man, created in the image and likeness of God, is also a spirit being.

Confession: *God is a Spirit, and I am a spirit. I am created in God's image and in His likeness. I am in the same class of being as God. I can give God pleasure. I can fellowship with Him.*

JUNE 3

MAN OF THE HEART

Whose adorning let it not be that outward adorning of plaiting the hair, and of wearing of gold, or of putting on of apparel; But let it be the HIDDEN MAN OF THE HEART, in that which is not corruptible, even the ornament of a meek and quiet SPIRIT, which is in the sight of God of great price. — 1 PETER 3:3,4

No one knows what you look like! They may think they do, but they don't. You — the real you — are a hidden man. You are a spirit; you have a soul; and you live in a body (1 Thess. 5:23). What people see is only the "house" you live in.

I've heard ministers quote two-thirds of First Peter 3:3 and say that women shouldn't fix their hair and shouldn't wear gold. But if that's what Peter meant, then women shouldn't wear clothes, either! Because if Peter told women not to plait their hair and not to wear gold, then he also told them not to put on apparel. (Apparel is clothing.)

No, Peter is really saying — probably because women are more prone to do this — "Don't spend all of your time on your hair, on your clothes, and on the *outward* man. See to it, first of all, that *the hidden man of the heart* — that's the spiritual man, the real man, the inward man — is adorned with a meek and a quiet *spirit*."

Confession: *I am a spirit. I am a child of the Father of spirits. I have a soul. And I live in a body. I see to the adorning of the real me — the hidden man of the heart.*

JUNE 4

THE INWARD MAN

For which cause we faint not; but though our outward man perish, yet the inward man is renewed day by day. — 2 CORINTHIANS 4:16

The outward man, or the body, is decaying. It's growing older, just as the house you may live in at 504 Chestnut Street is growing older.

But do you know what? *You* are not getting any older!

What does the scripture text say about the real you? Does it say, "Yet the inward man is perishing"? No. "Is decaying"? No. "Is growing older"? No! It says, ". . . *the inward man is RENEWED DAY BY DAY*"!

You will never be any older than you are right now!

You're no older now than you were a few years ago. You may know more, but you're not any older.

The inward man — the real you — is renewed day by day!

Confession: *I am a spirit being. I am the child of the Father of spirits. The real me is a "hidden man," an inward man. I am not getting any older. I am an eternal spirit being. I am being renewed day by day.*

JUNE 5

ETERNAL UNSEEN THINGS

While we look not at the things which are seen, but at the things which are not seen: for the things which are seen are temporal; but the things which are not seen are eternal. . . . For we know that if our earthly house of this tabernacle were dissolved, we have a building of God, an house not made with hands, eternal in the heavens.
— 2 CORINTHIANS 4:18, 5:1

The outward man is seen.

The inward man is that "hidden man." He is unseen. Paul is still talking about this inward man we read about in yesterday's scripture text, Second Corinthians 4:16. Paul is saying that this inward man is unseen — and that he is eternal.

Our "earthly house of this tabernacle" is the outward man Paul was talking about in verse 16. Our earthly house (body) is decaying. When it dies, is put into the grave, is dissolved, and goes back to dust — *that is not the end*!

The inward man is eternal!

The hidden man of the heart is eternal!

The hidden man is a spirit man — and he is eternal!

You are a spirit — and you are eternal!

Confession: *I am an eternal spirit being. I look not to the things which are seen. I look at the things which are not seen. For the things which are seen are temporal, but the things which are not seen are eternal!*

JUNE 6

CONFIDENT, KNOWING

Therefore we are always confident, knowing that, whilst we are at home in the body, we are absent from the Lord: (For we walk by faith, not by sight:) We are confident, I say, and willing rather to be absent from the body, and to be present with the Lord.

— 2 CORINTHIANS 5:6-8

". . . We are always confident, knowing . . . ." I like that! Not *hoping.* Not *guessing.* Not *maybe so.* But *knowing!* Knowing that while "we" are at home in the body, "we" are absent from the Lord. Yes, God's Spirit is in our hearts, crying, "Abba, Father," but Jesus Christ, with a physical, flesh-and-bone resurrected body is at the right hand of the Father in Heaven. And when "we" are absent from the body, "we" will be present with Him there.

Who is "we"?

At the time of his physical death, man leaves his body. When he does, he is no less man than when he had his body. I don't have space here to recount my entire testimony concerning my experience of dying (for the complete account, please see my minibook entitled, *I Went to Hell*). But I do want to say this: When I was *outside* my body, I was no less man than I was when I was *inside* my body. To me, I was just as real as I am now. I had the same shape. I had the same form. I had the same size. And I knew everything I knew before I left my body.

Confession: *The real me lives inside my body. The real me is an eternal spirit being that will never die!*

JUNE 7

GAIN!

For to me to live is Christ, and to die is gain. — PHILIPPIANS 1:21

When the body dies, the inward man still lives. In today's text, Paul was talking about physical death — and he said it is *gain*.

That does away with the theory that when a man is dead, he's dead like a dog, and that's the end of it. There certainly wouldn't be any gain to that.

It also does away with the theory that when you die, you just float around like a cloud in the sky. There wouldn't be any gain to that, either.

And it also does away with the theory of reincarnation. (That's all it is — a theory! It's certainly not scriptural.) Some people think they will be born again into this life — that the next time they might be a cow, or a horse, or even a fly. There wouldn't be any *gain* to coming back as a cow — you might get eaten. If you were a mosquito, you might get squashed. How foolish people can become when they leave the Bible and get off into false teachings!

The truth is just as the Bible presents it: At physical death, the born-again believer — an eternal spirit being — departs to be with Christ, and that is gain!

Confession: *For "me" to live in this physical body is Christ. The life of Christ dwells within the real me — the man on the inside, the eternal spirit being.*

JUNE 8

OUR CHOICE

For to me to live is Christ, and to die is gain. But if I live in the flesh, this is the fruit of my labour: yet what I shall choose I wot not. For I am in a strait betwixt two, having a desire to depart, and to be with Christ; which is far better: Nevertheless to abide in the flesh is more needful for you. And having this confidence, I know that I shall abide and continue with you all for your furtherance and joy of faith.
— **PHILIPPIANS 1:21-25**

Paul is talking here about physical death. Of course, the *real* Paul, the inner man, is not going to die. He's going to go on living either way: departing and being with Christ, *or* abiding in the flesh.

Paul said he hadn't *decided* yet. "I'm in a strait," he said, "between the two. I want to go on and be with Christ, which is far better." (If Paul had just said it would be better, that would have been wonderful, but he said it's even better than better!) Then he said, "Yet I know to abide in the flesh is more needful for you." If Paul was present in the flesh, he could teach and minister to these people. That was more needful for them.

Notice that *Paul* is making the choice. He didn't say, "I'm going to leave it up to God, and whatever God chooses, I will accept."

We have more to do with deciding to live or die than we have thought!

Confession: *The real me is an eternal spirit being.*

JUNE 9

THREE DIMENSIONS OF MAN

And the very God of peace sanctify you wholly; and I pray God your whole spirit and soul and body be preserved blameless unto the coming of our Lord Jesus Christ. — 1 THESSALONIANS 5:23

It will help your spiritual growth immeasurably to know the difference between your *spirit* and your *soul*.

Many people believe that "spirit" and "soul" are the same thing. Even preachers believe this! They preach about the soul as if it were the spirit.

But they can't be the same thing. It would be just as scriptural to say that the body and the soul are the same, as it would be to say that the spirit and the soul are the same. But Hebrews 4:12 says that by the Word of God, soul and spirit can be divided.

To help you understand the three dimensions of man, go through this process of elimination:

(1) With my *body* I contact the *physical* realm.

(2) With my *spirit* I contact the *spiritual* realm.

(3) With my *soul* I contact the *intellectual* and *emotional* realms.

Man is a spirit. The *spirit* is the part of man that knows God. Man possesses a *soul* — the intellect, the sensibilities, the will. And man lives in a *body*.

Confession: *I am a son of God. I am a child of God. With my spirit I contact my Father in the spiritual realm.*

JUNE 10

Heart Hunger

And Jesus said unto them, I am the bread of life: he that cometh to me shall never hunger; and he that believeth on me shall never thirst.
— JOHN 6:35

Before Adam sinned, he walked and talked with God. Adam had fellowship with God.

But when Adam fell, his spirit became estranged, or separated, from God.

Since that day, in the life of every person born into this world, there is a heart hunger — a spirit hunger.

This heart hunger causes men to seek something to satisfy it. Some look to worldly possessions. Some look to false religions of this world. Yet nothing can satisfy this heart hunger but God.

Although this heart hunger may have driven a man to all kinds of things, it ends when he finds Jesus Christ. When he becomes acquainted with the Lord Jesus Christ and receives eternal life and is born again, he becomes the child of God. Man then has a relationship with God! He can fellowship with God! His heart hunger is satisfied!

Confession: *I come to Jesus. Therefore, I shall never hunger. I believe on Jesus. Therefore, I shall never thirst. I am related to God. He is my Father. I have fellowship with Him. My heart is satisfied!*

JUNE 11

GIFT OF GOD

For the wages of sin is death; but the gift of God is eternal life through Jesus Christ our Lord. — ROMANS 6:23

God contacts men through their *spirits*.

When the Word of God is preached to a sinner who has never heard the Gospel and conviction comes upon him, it's not a physical feeling — neither is it a mental something, because he may not even understand it — but it's down deep on the inside. The Spirit of God through the Word of God is contacting the spirit of that sinner!

When that man responds to the call of God and the Gospel message, his spirit is born again. His spirit is recreated by receiving *eternal life.*

Receiving eternal life is the most miraculous event in life. It's called the New Birth. It's called the new creation. It is, in reality, God imparting His very nature, substance, and being to our human spirits.

It is described in Second Corinthians 5:17 and 18.

The New Birth is God actually giving spiritual birth to a man. And this instantaneous New Birth takes place, not in the body, not in the soul, but in the spirit of man! The spirit of man becomes a brand-new, miracle creation in God!

Confession: *I am a brand-new, miracle creation in Christ. God gave me the gift of eternal life. He imparted to my spirit His very nature, substance, and being. Residing in my own spirit is everything I'll ever need to put me over in life.*

JUNE 12

SAVING YOUR SOUL

Of his own will begat he us with the word of truth, that we should be a kind of firstfruits of his creatures. . . . Wherefore lay apart all filthiness and superfluity of naughtiness, and receive with meekness the engrafted word, which is able to save your souls. — JAMES 1:18,21

What about our *souls*? Aren't our souls saved when we're born again? No. There are many Christians who have been saved and filled with the Holy Spirit for years whose souls are not saved yet!

Some have lived and died without their souls being saved. Did they go to Heaven? Certainly. They were children of God, and their spirits were born of God.

The soul, you see, is not born again. The saving of the soul is a *process*.

The Epistle of James was written not to sinners, but to Christians. And James was telling us that our souls are not saved yet. James 1:21 bothered me for some time, until I found out the difference between the spirit and the soul.

A man's *spirit* — the innermost man — receives eternal life and is born again. But his intellect and his emotions — which constitute his *soul* — still have to be dealt with. They must be renewed.

Confession: *I am a spirit. I have a soul. I live in a body. "I" am begotten of God by the Word of truth. "I" am born again. Now I receive with meekness the engrafted Word which contains the power to save the soul which I possess. My intellect is being renewed with the Word of God.*

JUNE 13

Restoring the Soul

He restoreth my soul . . . . — PSALM 23:3

I beseech you therefore, brethren, by the mercies of God, that ye present your bodies a living sacrifice, holy, acceptable unto God, which is your reasonable service. And be not conformed to this world: but be ye transformed by the renewing of your mind, that ye may prove what is that good, and acceptable, and perfect, will of God.
— ROMANS 12:1,2

Writing to born-again, Spirit-filled Christians in Romans 12, Paul tells them to do something with their bodies and their minds. Man's spirit is born again at the New Birth, but he still has the same body and the same soul. He is to present his *body* to God, and he is to see to it that his *mind* is renewed.

The Hebrew word translated "restoreth" in Psalm 23 and the Greek word translated "renewed" in Romans 12:2 have just about the same meaning. For example, a valuable, antique chair which looks like a wreck can be *restored*. Afterwards it's still the same chair, but it has been *renewed*. A man's *spirit* is never restored; it's *born again*, or *recreated*. But his *soul* is restored when his mind becomes renewed with the Word of God.

The greatest need of the Church today is for believers to have their minds renewed with the Word of God. It is the Word of God that restores souls, renews souls, and saves souls!

Confession: *I see to it daily that my mind is renewed with the Word of God. Therefore, I am not conformed to this world. My mind is renewed to think like God thinks.*

JUNE 14

WHY DID JESUS COME?

The thief cometh not, but for to steal, and to kill, and to destroy: I am come that they might have life, and that they might have it more abundantly. — JOHN 10:10

Why did Jesus come?

Did Jesus come to give us some creed to live by? Did He come to give us a code of ethics — a list of "do's and don'ts" — to straighten us out? Did He come to start a new religion, or to found a new church?

No! Jesus came for one purpose: That we might have *life*, and that we might have it *more abundantly*!

This word "life" is the biggest word of the Gospel. Man needed life, because he was spiritually dead. Spiritual death, which is the nature of the devil, was imparted to man at the fall of man, when Adam sinned. The eradication of this devil-nature is what God has worked toward in all the ages. It was the reason why Jesus came to the earth. Jesus stated, *". . . I am come that they might have life . . . ."*

The only thing that will meet man's need is the nature of God: eternal life. Nothing can take its place.

When a person receives eternal life, he receives the nature of God, the life of God, into himself. This is that divine act that changes a man from the family of Satan to the family of God instantly.

Confession: *The life of God has been imparted to my spirit. I am alive unto God. The life of God — the nature of God — is imparted to my spirit. I will let the life and nature of God that's in me, dominate me.*

JUNE 15

DIVINE NATURE

Whereby are given unto us exceeding great and precious promises: that by these ye might be partakers of the divine nature, having escaped the corruption that is in the world through lust. — 2 PETER 1:4

When you became a child of God, God imparted His own nature — eternal life — to you. This life, this nature, this being, this substance of God, instantly changed your spirit.

You passed from spiritual death — the realm of Satan — into life, which is the realm of God (1 John 3:14). You passed from the dominion of Satan into the dominion of Christ.

When you received eternal life, the satanic nature passed out of you. The corruption from which you have escaped is spiritual death, the satanic nature (2 Peter 1:4).

The satanic nature passed out of you, not theoretically, but actually. Second Corinthians 5:17 states, "*. . . old things are passed away . . . .*" And God's nature came into you.

Now you are a partaker of God's divine nature — the nature of God — the life of God!

Confession: God's life is in me. God's nature is in me. God's ability is in me. God's wisdom is in me. For me to fail, God would have to fail. And God can never fail! I am a partaker of His divine nature.

JUNE 16

ZOE

For as the Father hath life [zoe] *in himself; so hath he given to the Son to have life* [zoe] *in himself.* — JOHN 5:26

The Greek word translated "life" in our text today is *zoe*. It is pronounced zō-ā.

Reading through the *King James Version*, or any English translation, when you see the word "life," you might think it's always talking about the same thing, but it isn't. Three other Greek words in the New Testament are translated as "life." Briefly, these words and their meanings are: *psuche*, natural life, or human life; *bios*, manner of life; and *anastrophe*, behavior.

Zoe means eternal life or God's life. It is God's nature. It is life as God has it — that which the Father has in Himself — and that which the Incarnate Son has in Himself. It is called *eternal life, everlasting life,* and sometimes just *life* in the Word of God.

No matter what "manner of life" or "behavior" you have, it won't do you any good unless you have *zoe*! And that's what Jesus came to bring you!

Confession: *For as the Father hath zoe in Himself, so hath He given to the Son to have zoe in Himself. Jesus said, "I am come that you might have zoe, and that you might have it more abundantly." I have zoe in myself. And I have it more abundantly!*

JUNE 17

HELPING OTHERS TO LIFE

And many other signs truly did Jesus in the presence of his disciples, which are not written in this book: But these are written, that ye might believe that Jesus is the Christ, the Son of God; and that believing ye might have life [zoe] through his name. — JOHN 20:30,31

Jesus did many things that are not recorded in John's Gospel, or in the other Gospels. But the things that are recorded in the Gospels are recorded for a purpose. What is this purpose? *". . . That ye might believe that Jesus is the Christ, the Son of God; and that believing ye might have zoe through his name."*

The object is that we might receive eternal life!

As a Christian, you need to know how to help others receive eternal life. The first step is to get them to read or hear what is written in the Gospels so they may know that Jesus is the Christ, the Son of God, and that as the Son of God, He has made spiritual life available to spiritually dead men.

John 3:15 and 16 shows us how: *"That whosoever believeth in him [Jesus] should not perish, but have eternal life [zoe]. For God so loved the world, that he gave his only begotten Son, that whosoever believeth in him should not perish, but have everlasting life [zoe]."*

Confession: *I believe that Jesus is the Christ, the Son of God. And, believing, I received zoe through His Name. I shall never perish. I have zoe. I have the life of God — I have the nature of God — abiding in me.*

JUNE 18

WHAT TO BELIEVE

For I delivered unto you first of all that which I also received, how that Christ died for our sins according to the scriptures; And that he was buried, and that he rose again the third day according to the scriptures.
— 1 CORINTHIANS 15:3,4

I read some time ago about a so-called minister of the Gospel who was a man of some acclaim. Some reporters interviewed him when he arrived in a large city about an article he had written. In the article, he had stated, "There is some question as to whether Jesus ever rose from the dead. And it doesn't really make any difference whether He did or not."

It makes all the difference in the world!

It makes the difference between spiritual life and spiritual death — because that's the way you receive eternal life. That's the way you are born again — by believing that Jesus Christ is the Son of God, that He died for your sins according to the Scriptures, and that He arose from the dead!

Confession: *I believe that Jesus Christ is the Son of God. I believe that He died for my sins according to the Scriptures. I believe that He was raised from the dead for my justification; that is, that I might be set right with God. I believe in my heart that I am the righteousness of God. I am made right with God through what Jesus did.*

JUNE 19

Receive Him

But as many as received him [Jesus Christ], *to them gave he power* [the right] *to become the sons of God, even to them that believe on his name.* — JOHN 1:12

Receiving Jesus Christ is an act of the will. So man acts on the Word of God by an act of his will. Man knows he is without a Savior, without an approach to God, without eternal life, so he can look up to God and pray, in essence:

Father, I come to You in the Name of the Lord Jesus Christ. I know You will not turn me away, or cast me out, because You said in Your Word, ". . . him that cometh to me I will in no wise cast out." I believe in my heart that Jesus Christ is the Son of God. I believe that He died for my sins, according to the Scriptures. I believe that He was raised from the dead for my justification, according to the Scriptures. "Justification" means that I might be set right with God. I believe that because of His death, burial, and resurrection, I am set right with God. So I receive Jesus as my Savior, and I confess Him as my Lord. Your Word says, "Whosoever shall call upon the name of the Lord shall be saved." I am calling on You now, so I know I am saved. And You said, "If thou shalt believe in thine heart that God hath raised him from the dead, thou shalt be saved." I'm confessing that with my mouth. I believe it in my heart. So I am saved. You said, ". . . with the heart man believeth unto righteousness." And with my heart I believe that I am made right with God. And You said, ". . . with the mouth confession is made unto salvation." So with my mouth I confess, I am saved! Thank You, Lord!

JUNE 20

HATH

Verily, verily, I say unto you, He that heareth my word, and believeth on him that sent me, HATH everlasting life [zoe], and shall not come into condemnation; but is passed from death unto life. — JOHN 5:24

Hath! You've got eternal life *now!* You're not going to get it when you get to Heaven; you've got *zoe* now!

But if you don't know about that *zoe* life — if you don't know what it is, or how to walk in the light of it — you'll never be able to enjoy the realities of it.

You can have something in the natural and not know you have it, and it won't do you any good. For example, sometime before Christmas of 1947, I decided to put away a little money for my wife's gift. I started by putting a $20 bill in the secret compartment of my billfold. Then I forgot all about it. A few weeks later, I ran out of gas. I didn't have any money to buy any gas, so I had to call one of the deacons of the church to come and get me. Sometime later I was going through the billfold and found that $20. Now, you couldn't really say I didn't have the money when I ran out of gas. I had it, but I didn't know it, so it didn't do me any good.

God gave us His Word so we could find out what we have — eternal life — and then walk in the light of it.

Confession: *I will learn to walk in the light of what I have — eternal life.*

JUNE 21

CHANGE

For in Christ Jesus neither circumcision availeth any thing, nor uncircumcision, but a new creature. — GALATIANS 6:15

For neither is circumcision [now] of any importance, nor uncircumcision, but [only] a new creation [the result of a new birth and a new nature in Christ Jesus, the Messiah]. — GALATIANS 6:15 *(Amplified)*

The first thing *zoe* does in a man is to change his nature. It changes his spirit. *Zoe* makes him a new creature. All things become new in his inward man, or spirit.

What this new man, or new creature, must do now is allow his inward man to dominate him. When we believers allow our spirits to dominate us, we permit the life of God in us to dominate us.

People are able to see the effects of this life of God within us. They see changes in a person's habits, conduct, speech, and so forth. Criminals become law-abiding citizens. Thieves become honest. Drunkards become sober. Prostitutes become moral. No case is incurable!

With this life (*zoe*) that comes into man, there comes a new kind of love (*agape*). And when the believer allows it to dominate him, it will destroy the cause of friction in homes: It will eliminate selfishness.

Confession: *I am a new creature. The life and nature of God has been imparted to my spirit. God is love. I will let His life dominate me. I will let His love dominate me.*

JUNE 22

DEVELOPMENT

In him [Jesus] *was life* [zoe]; *and the life* [zoe] *was the light of men.*
— JOHN 1:4

The life that came into you at the New Birth can affect your mental processes by governing your thinking and your intellect.

It certainly did mine. I received eternal life as a teenage boy on the bed of sickness, April 22, 1933. Then on August 8, 1934, I was healed by the power of God through faith and prayer.

After my healing, I returned to high school. During the sixteen months I had been bedfast, I missed one school year. And in the two years of high school I had completed before, I had been a "D" student.

At that tine, I didn't have a Greek concordance, so I didn't know about *zoe*. But I had my Bible, and the Spirit of God led me. Every day as I went to school I would say this:

"In Him was life, and the life was the light of men. That life is in me. The life of God is in me. That life is the light. (I knew light stood for development.) That life is developing me. That life is developing my spirit. That life is developing my mentality. I've got God in me. I've got God's wisdom in me. I've got God's life in me. I've got God's power in me."

Confession: *(Make your own confession today based on John 1:4, and confess the life of God within you as your light.)*

JUNE 23

HEART PURPOSE

But Daniel purposed in his heart that he would not defile himself with the portion of the king's meat, nor with the wine which he drank: therefore he requested of the prince of the eunuchs that he might not defile himself. — DANIEL 1:8

I had two favorite scriptures I either read or quoted to the Lord and on which I based my confession every morning as I walked to school. The first was John 1:4. The second was Daniel chapter 1.

Read Daniel chapter 1 and see how Daniel and the three Hebrew children, although they were captives, were chosen as students in the king's college.

The Bible says that Daniel "purposed in his heart." I used this phrase with the Lord. I knew that even though I wasn't living under the Old Covenant, there still was a principle here I could abide by.

You see, the Jews weren't supposed to eat certain meats, but that's not so with us. The Word of God says under the New Covenant, "*. . . every creature of God is good, and nothing to be refused, if it be received with thanksgiving: For it is sanctified by the word of God and prayer*" (1 Tim. 4:4,5).

So I acted upon the same principle Daniel did. I said this to the Lord every morning: "I purpose in my heart to walk in the light of life."

Confession: *I purpose in my heart to walk in the light of life. I purpose to walk in the light of the life of God in me.*

JUNE 24

FAVOR

Now God had brought Daniel into favour and tender love with the prince of the eunuchs. — DANIEL 1:9

I didn't know anything about confession of faith when I was first saved as a teenager. But somehow my spirit impelled me to say these things. Second Corinthians 5:17 was a favorite scripture of mine. I would tell everyone I met, "I'm a new creature!" They'd reply, "What's that?" And I would start preaching on it. Before I knew it, I'd have a crowd gathered around me right there on the street!

Every morning, as I walked to school, I made my confessions based on John 1:4 and Daniel chapter 1. Sometimes a bunch of us students took up the whole street as we walked along. They thought I was crazy, but I'd explain it to them as we walked along.

I would say, "Now, you see Daniel had favor with the prince of eunuchs (or, as we would call him in modern times, the dean of the college). And it was God who gave Daniel favor with him."

Then I would say to God, "God, give me favor with every teacher. Thank You for it. It is mine."

Confession: *God, give me favor with* [your teacher, your mate, your business associates, etc.]. *Thank You for it. Favor is mine.*

JUNE 25

KNOWLEDGE AND SKILL

As for these four children, God gave them knowledge and skill in all learning and wisdom: and Daniel had understanding in all visions and dreams. — DANIEL 1:17

". . . God gave them knowledge and skill. . . ."

God gave Daniel and the other three Hebrew children, knowledge and all skill.

Eternal life is the nature of God. You've got God's nature in you. Know that! Believe that! Confess that! Then that nature will begin to dominate you!

Learn to walk in the light of life. Learn to put that life into practice in your being. Walking in the light of that life will enhance your entire personality, and will increase your intelligence.

Confession: *I am a new creation. I am born again. I am a new creature. I have the life and nature of God in my spirit. That life is the light of men. I purpose to walk in the light of life. God's life is in me. God's knowledge is in me. God's skill is in me. God's ability is in me. God's wisdom is in me. He is instructing me. He is leading me. I am a child of God. The Spirit of God in me is leading me. I'll follow His leading. I'll walk in the light of life.*

177

JUNE 26

TEN TIMES BETTER

Now at the end of the days that the king had said he should bring them in [three years later] . . . the king communed with them; and among them all was found NONE like Daniel, Hananiah, Mishael, and Azariah: therefore stood they before the king. And in ALL matters of wisdom and understanding, that the king inquired of them, he found them TEN TIMES BETTER than all the magicians and astrologers that were in all his realm. — DANIEL 1:18-20

Each day I said, "God, give me favor with every teacher. Thank You for it. It is mine. Now impart to me — because I have the life and nature of God in me — knowledge and skill in all learning and wisdom that I may be ten times better . . ."

Now, I'm not bragging on me; I'm bragging on what God gave me. Because although I had been a "D" student before my sickness, after being born again and healed, I was the only student in my classes who made a straight "A" report card.

I could take a history book — and they tested me on this — read a chapter I'd never read before, put the book down, and recite it word for word. Now, I couldn't do that because I had developed my memory. I didn't know a thing in the world about memorization. I was able to do that because I looked to my spirit.

Most believers have never developed their spirits as they could have. They have just never really walked in the light of what they've had all the time.

Confession: *I purpose to develop my spirit. I purpose to walk in the light of life.*

JUNE 27

MIRACLE LIFE

For ye were sometimes darkness, but now are ye light in the Lord: walk as children of light. — EPHESIANS 5:8

The greatest miracle I've seen of eternal life affecting mentality was in a girl I'll call Mary. Mary had spent seven years in the first grade without even learning to write her name. The authorities asked her parents to take her out of school when she was fourteen years old.

As an eighteen-year-old, she behaved like a two-year-old. If she happened not to be sitting with her mother in the service, she would crawl or slide under the pews, or else she would lift up her skirt and step over them, to get where her mother was.

179

Then one night, during an evangelistic revival meeting, Mary came to the altar. There she received eternal life — the nature of God. A drastic change occurred instantly. The very next night she sat in the service and behaved like any eighteen-year-old young lady. She had fixed her hair and dressed up. Her mentality seemed to have increased overnight.

Soon afterwards, she went away to visit relatives, and there she met and married a neighboring farm boy. Many years later, I learned that after the accidental death of her husband, she had become a prosperous businesswoman who was her own financier and contractor on a housing addition she was building in her city!

Confession: *I walk as a child of light in the Lord. I walk in the light of life.*

JUNE 28

WALKING IN THE LIGHT OF LIFE

Then spake Jesus again unto them, saying, I am the light of the world: he that followeth me shall not walk in darkness, but shall have the light of life. — JOHN 8:12

I began to see some truths about eternal life before our children were born. And I believed by the grace of God that I could walk in the light of eternal life. (If God tells me in His Word I can, then I can.) I knew walking in the light of eternal life would affect my children, and so I could predict how they would turn out. I also predicted how some of the babies born in our church around the same time would turn out. I could do that because I knew what sort of light their parents were walking in and how that would affect the children. I was right one hundred percent of the time.

People can have eternal life, but if they don't walk in the light of it, developing themselves — if they don't take advantage of that life and nature — things won't turn out right in their lives. We *have* eternal life, but we have to *appropriate* it. We have to walk in the light of it.

Children should have the privilege of being born into homes where eternal life and the love of God are present. I've observed how children whose parents have this life *and walk in the light of it* respond to religious training. Such children have a fineness of spirit others do not have. They are easier to discipline, and they have keener intellects. Teenagers who receive eternal life and allow that life to dominate them are more mentally efficient afterwards than they were before they were saved.

Confession: *God's life is in me. That life is in the light, and it affects my development. I walk in the light of it. It affects my home!*

JUNE 29

MADE MANIFEST

Always bearing about in the body the dying of the Lord Jesus, that the life [zoe] *also of Jesus might be made manifest in our body. For we which live are alway delivered unto death for Jesus' sake, that the life* [zoe] *also of Jesus might be made manifest in our mortal flesh.*
— 2 CORINTHIANS 4:10,11

Paul is talking about *zoe* being manifested in our mortal bodies. But he's not talking about the resurrection of the body, for "mortal" means *subject to death*. When we're raised up, we'll have an immortal body.

No, Paul is talking about having this *zoe* life of God which came into our spirits at the New Birth manifested during *this* life — in our death-doomed mortal flesh!

I am convinced that if we learn how to walk in the light of life, and let that life which came into us at our New Birth dominate us, there is no reason at all why we can't live to a great age, if Jesus tarries His coming. I know the outward man is decaying, but the *zoe* life of God can be made manifest in our mortal flesh!

Confession: *Thank You, Father, that the life that is in my spirit can also quicken my mortal body. It can make my body full of life, health, and healing. Because in the great plan of redemption, which You planned and sent the Lord Jesus Christ to consummate, there is not only the rebirth of my spirit, but there is also healing for my physical being. "Himself took my infirmities and bare my sicknesses." What Jesus bore, I need not bear. By Jesus' stripes I am healed. I am made whole — spiritually, physically, and mentally. According to the Word of God, I am healed! I am whole!*

JUNE 30

CONDUCTOR OF LIFE

. . . God hath given to us eternal life, and this life is in his Son. He that hath the Son hath life . . . . — 1 JOHN 5:11,12

Jesus said, *"Go ye into all the world, and preach the gospel to every creature. . . . And these signs shall follow them that believe . . ."* (Mark 16:15,17). One of these signs Jesus said would follow believers — not the Early Church, not apostles, not pastors, not preachers, but believers — is, *". . . they shall lay hands on the sick, and they shall recover"* (Mark 16:18).

Why? Because the life of God is in believers!

Sometimes people are specially anointed to minister healing, but that isn't what Mark 16 is talking about! Every born-again believer has the life of God, the nature of God, the God-kind of life, in him — and by the laying on of hands, that life can be imparted into the physical bodies of others!

That's why you should lay hands on the sick. When you lay hands on them, that life of God in you is conducted through your hands to others. Often, you'll be conscious of that life flowing right out of you into them. You've got the *life* of God in you! You've got the *nature* of God in you! God's a healing God. Put God's power to work! That's how God works — through your own hands. God's not here on earth in Person, but He is *in you* by His Spirit!

Confession: *I am a believing one. I have the life of God in me. And God is a healing God. I lay hands on the sick, and they recover.*

JULY 1

THE LORDSHIP OF JESUS

Therefore we are buried with him by baptism into death: that like as Christ was raised up from the dead by the glory of the Father, even so we also should walk in newness of life. — ROMANS 6:4

Some translations of Romans 10:9 read, ". . . if thou shalt confess with thy mouth Jesus as Lord, and shalt believe in thy heart . . . thou shalt be saved." That means you must confess Jesus as your Lord and acknowledge His lordship over your life in order to be saved.

The reason for this is obvious. We've been the servants and the subjects — as well as the children — of Satan, the enemy of God. We have belonged to the kingdom of the devil. Now we want to leave that kingdom and become "naturalized citizens" of God's Kingdom. But before we can do this, we must swear allegiance to the new fatherland, so to speak. We must make an absolute, unconditional break with our old fatherland. So, the Bible says, we must confess Jesus Christ as Lord. He is the new Ruler of our intellectual life as well as our heart, or spiritual life.

Some want to have Jesus as *Savior*, but not as *Lord*. They want Him as their Savior from hell, but they don't want Him as their Lord and Ruler on earth. You can't really have one without the other.

Confession: *I walk in the newness of life. Jesus Christ is my Savior. Jesus is my Lord. Lord Jesus, I live in Your Kingdom now, and I acknowledge Your lordship over my life. I want to have Your will and Your way in every area of my life.*

JULY 2

THE LORD CHRIST

And whatsoever ye do, do it heartily, as to the Lord, and not unto men; Knowing that of the Lord ye shall receive the reward of the inheritance: for ye serve the Lord Christ. — COLOSSIANS 3:23,24

When Jesus becomes your Lord, He will want to have something to say about the kind of books you read — about the amusements you enjoy — about the governing of your physical body.

If Jesus is your Lord, He will want to have something to say about your finances — how you make your money — and how you use your money.

If Jesus is your Lord, He will want to have something to say about your marriage — about your children — about your home. He will want to dictate to you regarding your vocation in life and where you live.

Yes, Jesus will want to enter every area of your life, if He's your Lord. I want Him to be my Lord, don't you? That's what makes the Christian life blessed. The lordship of Jesus strips life of its weakness, frailty, and human guidance. It lifts life out of the realm of the natural and into the supernatural.

Confession: *Lord Jesus, I want You to have Your way in every area of my life. I want You to have Your say-so in every area of my life — in the books I read, in the company I keep, in the amusements I enjoy, in my companions, in my marriage, in my home, in my finances, and in the way I spend my time.*

JULY 3

The Living Word

For there are three that bear record in heaven, the Father, the Word, and the Holy Ghost: and these three are one. — 1 JOHN 5:7

In the beginning was the Word, and the Word was with God, and the Word was God. . . . And the Word was made flesh, and dwelt among us . . . . — JOHN 1:1,14

How can I make Jesus Lord of my life?

Jesus is the Living Word. And God has given us the written Word to unveil the Living Word to us.

Give the Word of God — primarily the New Testament — first place in your life. By doing so, you are putting Jesus first!

Let the Word of God govern your life. Let this Word be the Lord of your life. Let the Word dominate you. By doing so, you are really allowing Jesus to lord it over you — because Jesus and His Word are One.

We are living in an age when we need to get serious about spiritual matters, and we need to learn *what the Bible has to say* about love, life, home, marriage, and children.

Let the Word of God be your guide in life. When you do, you are making Jesus the Lord of your life. Then His written Word becomes the Lord of your life.

Confession: *Lord Jesus, You are the Lord of my life. I allow Your Word to dominate me. I allow Your Word to have dominion over me; therefore, YOU are lording it over me. You are dominating me. You are the Lord of my life!*

JULY 4

LAMP OF THE LORD

The spirit of man is the candle of the Lord, searching all the inward parts of the belly. **— PROVERBS 20:27**

One translation of this verse reads, "The spirit of man is the *lamp* of the Lord." To put it into modern speech, you would say, "The spirit of man is the *light bulb* of the Lord."

What this scripture means is that God will enlighten us — He will guide us — through our human spirits.

However, Christians seem to seek guidance in every other way except the way God said it is going to come! They judge how God is leading by what their physical senses tell them; but nowhere does the Bible say that God will guide us through our physical bodies! They look at things from a mental standpoint; but nowhere in the Bible does God declare that He will guide us through our mentality, our intellect, or our minds!

God said that it is the spirit of man that is the candle of the Lord. So God *will* guide us through our spirits. God will guide you through *your* human spirit.

Confession: *I am a spirit. I have a soul. I live in a physical body. My spirit is the candle of the Lord. God my Father is enlightening me through my spirit. God is guiding me through my spirit.*

JULY 5

LED BY THE SPIRIT

For as many as are led by the Spirit of God, they are the sons of God.
— ROMANS 8:14

The sons of God can expect to be led by the Spirit of God.

Believers can expect to be led, or guided, by the Holy Spirit. Jesus, referring to the time when the Holy Spirit would come, said, "He will guide you." So we don't have to look to man for guidance — that's unscriptural. All of God's children have the Spirit of God within and can expect to be guided by Him.

In February 1959, Jesus appeared to me in an open vision. I heard His footsteps coming into my hospital room. He sat on a chair by my bed and talked to me for an hour and a half about the ministry of a prophet. One of the things He said was, "The prophet's ministry is not set in the Church to guide members and tell them what to do. Under the Old Covenant, people would go to the prophet to seek advice, or direction, or guidance, because he had the Spirit of God and they didn't. No one under the Old Covenant, except the king, the priest, and the prophet, had the Holy Spirit upon them. The people knew nothing about the Spirit's leading. But under the New Covenant it does not say, 'As many as are led by the prophets, they are the sons of God.' It says, 'As many as are led by the Spirit of God, they are the sons of God.'"

Confession: *I am a child of God. I can expect to be led by the Spirit of God. He is leading me now.*

JULY 6

BORN OF THE SPIRIT

That which is born of the flesh is flesh; and that which is born of the Spirit is spirit. Marvel not that I said unto thee, Ye must be born again.
— JOHN 3:6,7

Under the New Covenant, every child of God has the Spirit of God. First, they are *born* of the Spirit. Then they can be *filled* with the Spirit. And they can expect to be *led* by the Spirit.

Born of the Spirit. The spirit of man is the part of man which is born again. The Christian's spirit has the life and nature of God in it. The inward man is born of God's Spirit and has the Spirit of God in him.

Filled with that Spirit. The born-again Christian can be *filled* with that same Spirit which he already has in him. And when he is filled with that Spirit, there will be an overflowing of that Spirit. He will speak with other tongues as the Holy Spirit gives him utterance (Acts 2:4).

Led by the Spirit. "For as many as are led by the Spirit of God, they are the sons of God." Even the born-again one who has not been filled with the Spirit, has the Spirit of God abiding in him — and he can expect to be led and guided by the Holy Spirit.

Confession: *I am a child of God. I am born of the Spirit of God. The Spirit of God leads me. He is leading me now. The Holy Spirit will rise big in me. He will give illumination to my mind. He will give direction to my spirit. I am being led by the Spirit of God.*

JULY 7

A WELL OF WATER

Jesus answered and said unto her, If thou knewest the gift of God, and who it is that saith to thee, Give me to drink; thou wouldest have asked of him, and he would have given thee living water. The woman saith unto him, Sir, thou hast nothing to draw with, and the well is deep: from whence then hast thou that living water? . . . Jesus answered and said unto her, Whosoever drinketh of this water shall thirst again: But whosoever drinketh of the water that I shall give him shall never thirst; but the water that I shall give him shall be in him a well of water springing up into everlasting life. — JOHN 4:10,11,13,14

Bible scholars know that water is a type of the Holy Spirit.

Jesus Himself used water as a type of the Spirit. When Jesus told the woman at the well of Samaria that He was the Giver of living water, she got it confused with the water in the well — natural water.

Then Jesus said, ". . . *the water that I shall give . . . shall be . . . a well of water springing up into everlasting life.*"

He was talking about the New Birth, the well of living water within the believer.

Confession: *I have drunk the living water, and I thirst no more. I am born of the Spirit of God. God's Spirit is in me. A well of water is in me springing up into everlasting life.*

JULY 8

RIVERS OF LIVING WATER

In the last day, that great day of the feast, Jesus stood and cried, saying, If any man thirst, let him come unto me, and drink. He that believeth on me, as the scripture hath said, out of his belly shall flow rivers of living water. (But this spake he of the Spirit, which they that believe on him should receive: for the Holy Ghost was not yet given; because that Jesus was not yet glorified.) — JOHN 7:37-39

Jesus used water as a type of the Holy Spirit.

Notice that there are two different experiences referred to in our texts for yesterday and today. One, the New Birth, is a *well of water* in you, springing up into everlasting life. The other, the infilling of the Holy Spirit, is *rivers*. Not just one river — but rivers.

The water in the well (salvation) is for one purpose: It blesses you. It is for your benefit. But the rivers (the infilling of the Holy Spirit) flow out of you to bless someone else. The purpose of being filled with the Holy Spirit is so that you might be a blessing to others.

Some people say, "If you are born of the Spirit, you have the Spirit, and that's all there is to it." But, no, just because you've had one drink of water is no sign that you're full of water. There is an experience subsequent to the New Birth of being filled with the Holy Spirit — and as a result of being filled, rivers of living water flow out of the belly (the spirit).

Confession: *I am filled with the Spirit of God. Rivers of living water flow from my innermost being.*

JULY 9

My Spirit Prayeth

For if I pray in an unknown tongue, my spirit prayeth, but my understanding is unfruitful. — 1 CORINTHIANS 14:14

God is a Spirit. Man is a spirit. God contacts us and deals with us through our spirits. He leads us through our spirits. He does not communicate directly through our minds, because the Holy Spirit does not dwell in our minds. And God does not contact us through our bodies either.

It should be comparatively easy for Spirit-filled believers to locate the human spirit. Those tongues come from your spirit, down on the inside of you. You speak the words out physically — but they don't come out of the physical senses. You yield your tongue to your own spirit, and the Holy Spirit in your spirit gives you the utterance.

The tongues don't come out of your mind or your soul. When you pray in tongues, your mind, your understanding, is unfruitful. Your understanding doesn't know what you're saying.

When you pray in tongues, the words come out of your innermost being — your spirit. *All the leadings I've ever gotten, have come out of my spirit.* And most have come when I was praying in other tongues — when my spirit was active and in contact with God.

Confession: *When I pray in tongues, my spirit prays. My spirit is active and in contact with God. The Holy Spirit in my spirit gives me the utterance.*

JULY 10

LOOK INSIDE

What is it then? I will pray with the spirit, and I will pray with the understanding also: I will sing with the spirit, and I will sing with the understanding also. — 1 CORINTHIANS 14:15

In every crisis of life, I've learned to look to my spirit inside of me. I've learned to pray in other tongues. And while I'm praying in other tongues, guidance comes up from inside of me, because *my spirit is active when I pray in tongues.* My mind is not active then; my spirit is active. And *it is through my spirit that God gives me guidance.*

Sometimes while I'm praying in tongues privately, I'll interpret what I've said; and through the interpretation, I'll get guidance. But this doesn't happen most of the time.

Most of the time, while I'm just praying in tongues, from somewhere way down deep inside, the knowledge of what God wants me to do will rise up in me. (It's difficult to explain spiritual things in natural ways, but I can sense something rising up within me.) It begins to take shape and form, and although I can't always put it into words (because my understanding has nothing to do with it), I know exactly on the inside of me what direction I'm to take.

Confession: *I listen to my heart. I look to my spirit inside me. I am spirit-conscious, because the Holy Spirit indwells my spirit. He gives direction to my spirit. He guides me through my spirit.*

JULY 11

Beareth Witness

The Spirit itself beareth witness with our spirit, that we are the children of God. — ROMANS 8:16

God is going to guide us. God is going to lead us. We have scripture that says so: *"For as many as are led by the Spirit of God, they are the sons of God"* (Rom. 8:14).

How does God lead?

Romans 8:16 gives us a clue: *"The Spirit itself* [Himself] *beareth witness with our spirit, that we are the children of God."*

You don't know you are a child of God because someone prophesies that you are. You don't know you are a child of God because someone says they feel like you are. That's not how you know these things. You are not a child of God because you had a vision. (You might, or you might not have a vision, but that's not what makes you a child of God.)

How, then, does the Bible say we *know* we are the children of God?

God's Spirit *"bears witness"* with our spirit. Sometimes you can't explain exactly *how* you know, but you just *know* it down on the inside of you. You have an *inward witness* that you are a child of God.

That's the number one way God leads His children — through the inward witness!

Confession: *I am born of the Spirit of God. God's Spirit bears witness with my spirit that I am a child of God. The Spirit of God leads me. He is leading me now.*

JULY 12

NUMBER ONE: INWARD WITNESS

He that believeth on the Son of God hath the witness in himself. . . .
— 1 JOHN 5:10

The way God confirms the most important thing that can ever happen to you, is also the way God leads His children: by the inward witness.

The most important aspect of your life — becoming a child of God — is confirmed to you by God's Spirit bearing witness with your spirit, that you have been born again (Rom. 8:16). This will help you understand that the number one way God leads His children is through the inward witness.

That is almost always the way I am led. Yes, I've had revelations, and I've had God lead me in other ways, too. But most of the time, I am led by the inward witness.

And you can be too!

Confession: *I am a child of God. I have been born again. I am born of the Spirit of God. God's Spirit bears witness with my spirit that I am a child of God. As many as are led by the Spirit of God, they are the sons of God. I am a child of God; therefore, the Spirit of God leads me. He is leading me now. I trust Him, the Greater One. He will rise up big in me. He will give illumination to my mind. He will give direction to my spirit, for I am a child of God. I am being led by the Spirit of God. And the Spirit of God leads me, first of all, through that wonderful inward witness.*

JULY 13

SUPERNATURAL GUIDANCE

. . . I will pray the Father, and he shall give you another Comforter, that he may abide with you for ever; Even the Spirit of truth; whom the world cannot receive, because it seeth him not, neither knoweth him: but ye know him; for he dwelleth with you, and shall be in you.

— JOHN 14:16,17

The inward witness is just as supernatural as guidance through visions, angels, and so on. It is not as *spectacular*, but it is just as *supernatural*.

Many people are looking for the spectacular, and they miss the supernatural that's right there all the time!

Let me go back to what Jesus said to me when He appeared to me in an open vision in February 1959 in El Paso, Texas. I heard footsteps coming down the hospital corridor, so I looked up to see who it was. When I saw Jesus standing in the doorway, it seemed like the hair on my neck and head stood straight up. Goose pimples popped out all over my body. Jesus was wearing a white robe and Roman sandals. He was about 5'11" tall and weighed about 180 pounds. He pulled up a chair and sat by my bed. During the hour and a half that He talked to me, He told me, "The number one way I lead all My children is through the inward witness."

Confession: *God's Holy Spirit is in me. He is in me to help me, to lead me, and to guide me. First, the Holy Spirit bears witness with my spirit that I am a child of God, then He bears witness with my spirit in all other aspects of my life.*

JULY 14

Stop Light

Howbeit when he, the Spirit of truth, is come, he will guide you into all truth . . . .
— JOHN 16:13

For the three days prior to my vision of the Lord, I had been trying to write a letter to a pastor, confirming a date I was to hold for him. I'd get half a page written to him and then I'd tear it up and throw it in the wastebasket. The second and third days I did the same thing.

As the Lord sat by my bedside, He said, "I'm going to show you how the inward witness works so you won't make the same mistakes you've made in the past. You see Me now sitting here talking to you. This is the prophet's ministry in manifestation — and a manifestation of discerning of spirits [discerning of spirits is seeing into the spirit realm]. You hear Me talking to you. And I am bringing you, through the vision, a word of knowledge and a word of wisdom. I'm telling you not to go to that church. The pastor wouldn't accept the way you minister. But I'm never again going to lead you this way. [And He hasn't.] From now on, I'm going to lead you by that inward witness you've had all the time. You had a check, a hesitancy, on the inside. And that is the way I'm going to lead you."

This inward check is like a stop sign. It's like a red light — way down on the inside.

Confession: *The Spirit of truth is come. He indwells me. He guides me. He is guiding me now.*

JULY 15

GREEN LIGHT

Thus saith the Lord, thy Redeemer, the Holy One of Israel; I am the Lord thy God which teacheth thee to profit, which leadeth thee by the way that thou shouldest go. — ISAIAH 48:17

A pastor once asked me, "Brother Hagin, do you ever go to small churches?" I replied, "Yes, I'll go anywhere the Lord says to go." Then the pastor told me about his church and said, "If God ever speaks to you about it, we want you to come." But I just dismissed his invitation.

However, several months later when I was praying about something else, this conversation came back to me. Then every day it kept coming back. Finally, after about the fourth day, I said, "Lord, do You want me to go to that church?" And the more I'd pray about it, the better I'd feel on the inside of me about accepting that invitation. (This wasn't a physical feeling — but one I recognized in my spirit.)

Sitting by my bedside, Jesus referred to this. "The more you thought about it, the better you felt about it," He reminded me. "You had a *velvety-like* feeling in your spirit. That's the green light. That's the go-ahead signal. That's the witness of the Spirit to go. Now you see Me, and I'm telling you to go to that church. But I'm never going to lead you to go anywhere again like this. From now on, I'm going to lead you like I do every Christian — by the inward witness."

Confession: *The Lord leads me in the way I should go. He leads me by the inward witness.*

JULY 16

Abundant Provision

. . . Let them say continually, Let the Lord be magnified, which hath pleasure in the prosperity of his servant. — PSALM 35:27

Here's something else the Lord said to me during the vision I had in February 1959. It was not just for my benefit, but for yours too.

He said, "If you will learn to follow that inward witness in all areas of your life, I will make you rich. I will guide you in all the affairs of life — financial as well as spiritual. I'm not opposed to my children being rich. I am opposed to their being covetous." (Some people think the Lord is interested only in their spiritual life — nothing else — but He's interested in everything we're interested in.)

The Lord has done for me exactly what He said He would do — He has made me rich. Am I a millionaire? No. That's not what the word "rich" means. "Rich" means a full supply. It means an abundant provision. I've got more than a *full supply*. I've got more than an abundant provision. It's because I learned to follow the leading of the Holy Spirit — and this guidance came to me by the inward witness.

God will make you rich, too, if you'll learn to listen to the inward witness! Jesus said to me in that vision, "Now you go teach My people how to be led by My Spirit."

Confession: *The Spirit of God is leading me in all the affairs of life. He is leading me in spiritual matters. He is leading me in financial matters. And I am listening to the inward witness.*

JULY 17

Light My Candle

For thou wilt light my candle: the Lord my God will enlighten my darkness. — **PSALM 18:28**

Sometimes even though the inward witness is there, people don't recognize it.

For example, I would be praying in tongues about the Sunday morning services in the church I was pastoring, and a burden for that church I had previously pastored, would rise up in me.

(Remember, when we pray in tongues, our spirit prays — and the spirit of man is the candle of the Lord.) That kept happening. After about thirty days, I said, "Lord, are You talking to me about going back there? If so, talk to my wife about it too."

One morning I said to Oretha, "Honey, if the Lord says anything to you, let me know." Then I waited another thirty days before I asked her, "Has the Lord been talking to you?"

She said, "If He has, I don't know it."

I got a little more specific about it. "Has the Lord said anything to you about going back to _____?"

"Oh," she said. "I thought that was just me."

Let's analyze that statement. When she said "me," if she meant the flesh, that wouldn't be right. But if she meant the real "me" — the man on the inside, which is the candle of the Lord — then it wasn't just her. *It was the Lord lighting the candle!*

Confession: *The Lord my God lights my candle. He enlightens me.*

JULY 18

ON THE INSIDE

I will instruct thee and teach thee in the way which thou shalt go: I will guide thee with mine eye. Be ye not as the horse, or as the mule, which have no understanding: whose mouth must be held in with bit and bridle . . . .
— PSALM 32:8,9

I knew by the inward witness that I should go back to that church. And I knew my wife also had the inward witness to go back. But I still wanted the Lord to move in some "supernatural" way to confirm it. (I was only twenty-three years old at the time.) I wanted God to give me a word, tongues and interpretation, prophecy — or maybe even write up in the sky, "GO TO THAT PLACE!"

So I fasted and prayed three days. The third day I was on my knees, bawling, squalling, and begging, because I didn't know any better, "Ohh, dear God . . ."

And God said to me — for He leads by an inward *voice* as well as by an inward *witness* — "Get up from there and quit acting like that!"

I got up! But I said, "Lord, if You would just give me a supernatural sign, I'd feel better about going back to that church."

He replied, "You have all I'm going to give you! You don't need any sign. You don't need any writing in the sky. You don't need tongues and interpretation, or prophecy. You know on the inside what to do. *Now do it!*"

Confession: *The eyes of my understanding are being enlightened. I know on the inside what to do. God leads me by that wonderful inward witness. And I listen to it!*

JULY 19

INSIDE SIGNALS

Who hath put wisdom in the inward parts? or who hath given under-standing to the heart? — JOB 38:36

God led us to move to Tulsa, Oklahoma, by an inward witness in the late 1960s. Our home had been in Garland, Texas, a suburb of Dallas, for seventeen years. And we had no plans to move. In fact, since our ministry was growing, I had it all planned just how we would turn our entire house into an office (we were operating the ministry out of our den and garage), and even how we could build additional facilities on our property, if necessary.

x

201

Then we went to Tulsa on business. A friend, in whose home we were staying, said to me, "Brother Hagin, you need to move to Tulsa. And I've got just the place for you! Brother T. L. Osborn's old office building is for sale, and they've asked me to sell it. Come on, I want to show it to you." (Several people had tried to buy it, but the deals always fell through, so the building was still empty.)

I wasn't much interested, to tell the truth. But I thought, *Just out of respect for my friend, I'll go.*

The minute I walked into that building, it was just like someone had rung a bell or set off a buzzer on the inside of me. Sometimes the inward witness is like that. A buzzer went off in my spirit — right down in my belly. It's difficult to describe, but you just *know* it was inside, in your spirit. This was God confirming that He wanted this building for my ministry.

Confession: *The Holy Spirit dwells in my spirit. Wisdom is in my inward parts. Understanding is in my heart. And I listen to my heart.*

JULY 20

KNOW-SO SALVATION

No man hath seen God at any time. If we love one another, God dwelleth in us, and his love is perfected in us. Hereby know we that we dwell in him, and he in us, because he hath given us of his Spirit.

— 1 JOHN 4:12,13

I was born again as a teenager on the bed of sickness on April 22, 1933. Since that day, the thought has never occurred to me that I might not be saved.

Even as a young Christian, I would run into people who would say, "You're not saved, because you don't belong to our church." Or those who would argue, "You're not saved, because you haven't been baptized our way." And many others.

But none of it disturbed me. I laughed at it — *because I had the inward witness.* Romans 8:16 says, *"The Spirit itself* [Himself] *beareth witness with our spirit, that we are the children of God."* And I had the love: *"We know that we have passed from death unto life, because we love . . ."* (1 John 3:14).

I had the witness — and I had the love. That's why I never doubted my salvation. I walked in love to the best of my ability, and I enjoyed the witness of God's Spirit on the inside.

Confession: *I have the witness. The Spirit Himself bears witness with my spirit that I am the child of God. I have the love. I know that I have passed from death unto life. God dwells in me. His love is perfected in me. I know I dwell in Him, and He dwells in me, because He has given me of His Spirit.*

JULY 21

CHRISTIAN EQUIPMENT

But ye have an unction from the Holy One, and ye know all things.
— 1 JOHN 2:20

Even as a newborn babe in Christ, still bedfast, I would know things by an inward witness.

For example, my mother said to me one day, "Son, I hate to bother you, but something is wrong with Dub." Dub, my older brother, had gone to the Rio Grande Valley to look for work. (He was seventeen at the time.) Those were Depression days. Momma was a Christian, although not a Spirit-filled one, and she just had a witness of uneasiness and trouble in her spirit. "I don't know what it is," she said. "He may be in jail or something."

"Momma," I said, "I've known that for several days. But Dub's not in jail. His physical life was in danger, but I've already prayed, and he'll make it. Dub's all right. His life will be spared."

Three nights later, Dub came in. He hadn't found work, so he had decided to ride the freight trains home. A lot of people were "riding the rails" in those days. However, a railroad detective found Dub, knocked him in the head, and threw him off a train going 50-60 miles per hour. Dub slid on his back across the coal cinders that had fallen alongside the tracks. It's a wonder he didn't break his back — and he would have, if we hadn't known about it by an inward witness and prayed. We knew it because we were Christians.

Confession: *I have an unction from the Holy One, and I know all things.*

JULY 22

LEARN TO LISTEN

Howbeit when he, the Spirit of truth, is come . . . he will shew you things to come.
— JOHN 16:13

A minister friend of mine had three serious automobile accidents in less than ten years. People were killed in these accidents. His wife was almost killed, and the minister himself was seriously injured. Both he and his wife were healed by the hand of God. When he heard me teaching along these lines of listening to your spirit, the inward witness, he said, "Brother Hagin, every one of those accidents could have been avoided if I had listened to that inward intuition."

Yet people will argue, "I just don't know why those accidents happened to a good Christian. He's a preacher."

Well, he had to learn to listen to his spirit just like you had to learn to listen to yours.

People want to blame God and say that God did these things. But as this preacher told me, "If I had listened to the inward intuition I had that something was about to happen, I would have waited and prayed. Instead, I said, 'I'm busy. I don't have time to pray.'"

Many times, if we had waited on God when we had that inward witness, God would have shown us things, and we could have avoided problems. But let's not moan and groan about our past failures. Let's take advantage of our present opportunities, and make sure that we follow our inward witness in the future. Let's learn to develop our spirit — and learn to listen to it, and then obey it.

Confession: *I am becoming spirit-conscious. I am developing my spirit. And I am listening to it!*

JULY 23

WHERE HE IS

Jesus answered and said unto him, If a man love me, he will keep my words: and my Father will love him, and we will come unto him, and make our abode with him. — JOHN 14:23

As Jesus goes on teaching in John chapter 14, He begins to talk about the Holy Spirit coming to us: Jesus and the Father, in the Person of the Holy Spirit, come to abide in us.

At present, Jesus literally — with His resurrected body — is seated at the right hand of the Father. Yet the Bible talks about "Christ in you, the hope of glory." You see, the reason why *Christ* is in us is because the *Holy Spirit* is in us.

The Holy Spirit said through Paul, *"Know ye not that ye are the temple of God, and that the Spirit of God dwelleth in you?"* (1 Cor. 3:16).

And in Second Corinthians 6:16 we read, *". . . for ye are the temple of the living God; as God hath said, I will dwell in them, and walk in them; and I will be their God, and they shall be my people."*

We've never plumbed the depths of what this is really saying: *God is dwelling in us!*

Therefore, if God is dwelling in us, then that is where God is going to speak to us — *where He is* — in our hearts, or our spirits. God communicates with us through our spirits. Our spirits pick things up from the Holy Spirit and then passes them on to our mind by an inward intuition, or inward witness.

Confession: (*Make your confession from John 14:23, First Corinthians 3:16, and Second Corinthians 6:16.*)

JULY 24

NUMBER TWO: THE INWARD VOICE

I say the truth in Christ, I lie not, my conscience also bearing me witness in the Holy Ghost.
— ROMANS 9:1

The number one way the Holy Spirit guides us is through the *inward witness*. The number two way is through the *inward voice*.

The inward man has a voice just as the outward man has a voice. We call the voice of the inward man "conscience." Sometimes it is also called intuition, inner guidance, or "the still, small voice." It is *not* the voice of the Spirit of God speaking to us, because when the Holy Spirit speaks, His voice is more authoritative. The still, small voice is the voice of our own spirit. Yet our spirit picks it up from the Holy Spirit who lives inside us.

For example, I relate in the devotion of July 19 how a "buzzer" seemed to go off inside me as I stepped inside that building that was for sale in Tulsa. I knew on the inside — *This is it!* But I didn't want to listen. When my wife asked about it later, I said, "No, we'll just stay where we are." But when we went to bed that night, I couldn't get to sleep. My conscience was hurting. My spirit knew I hadn't listened to it.

So I said, "Lord, in the natural, I don't want to move to Tulsa. But if that's what You want, I won't stand in Your way." Suddenly, on the inside of me, that still, small voice said, "I'm going to give you that building. You watch Me." And God did just that!

Confession: *I listen to the voice of my spirit. And I obey it!*

JULY 25

CONSCIENCE

. . . While as the first tabernacle was yet standing: Which was a figure for the time then present, in which were offered both gifts and sacrifices, that could not make him that did the service perfect, as pertaining to the conscience. . . . How much more shall the blood of Christ, who through the eternal Spirit offered himself without spot to God, purge your conscience from dead works to serve the living God?
— HEBREWS 9:8,9,14

Is your conscious a safe guide?

Yes it is, if your spirit has become a new man in Christ. Remember Second Corinthians 5:17: *"Therefore if any man be in Christ, he is a new creature: old things are passed away; behold, all things are become new."* That's talking about the inward man, the spirit of man. Your conscious is the voice of your spirit speaking to you. If your spirit is a new man in Christ, with the life and nature of God in it, then it is a safe guide.

A person who has never been born again could not follow the voice of his spirit, or conscience, because his unregenerate spirit would have the nature of the devil in it. His conscience would permit him to do anything.

When you have the life and nature of God in you, your conscience will not permit you to do just anything. When you are a born-again Christian, the Spirit of God is living and abiding in your spirit!

Confession: *I am a new man in Christ, with the life and nature of God abiding in my spirit. Therefore, my conscience is a safe guide.*

JULY 26

OBEYING CONSCIENCE

And Paul, earnestly beholding the council, said, Men and brethren, I have lived in all good conscience before God until this day.
— ACTS 23:1

It is interesting to go through the Epistles that Paul wrote to the Church and see what he said about his conscience. He always obeyed his conscience.

Once I heard some preachers questioning one of the top evangelists in the world. They asked him, "We know God called and anointed you to stand in this ministry — but is there something that *you* do from the natural standpoint that contributes to the success of your ministry more than any other thing?"

I listened intently to hear what he had to say. I knew he was a man of prayer, and prayer is important, but he didn't mention prayer.

He answered, "Of course, God called me to be an evangelist. But you are asking what has contributed to my success from *my* standpoint. And the one thing I do that has contributed to my success more than anything else is: *I always instantly obey my deepest premonitions.*"

In other words, what this evangelist was saying was, "I always obey what my spirit tells me — what I get right down on the inside of me."

Confession: *The Holy Spirit is in my spirit. He communicates with me through my spirit. My spirit has a voice. I obey what my spirit tells me — what I get down on the inside of me.*

JULY 27

WHEN YOU MISS IT

For if our heart condemn us, God is greater than our heart, and knoweth all things. Beloved, if our heart condemn us not, then have we confidence toward God. — 1 JOHN 3:20,21

If you're a Christian, does the Holy Spirit condemn you if you do wrong?

No. It is *your spirit* that condemns you. This is something we need to learn. We haven't learned it yet, because we've been taught wrong.

The Holy Spirit will not condemn you. Why? Because God won't condemn you. Study what Paul wrote in Romans 8. He asked, "Who is it that condemns? Does God condemn? No, it is God who *justifies.*"

Jesus said that the only sin the Holy Spirit will convict the world of is the sin of rejecting Jesus (John 16:7-9).

I've found that even when I've missed it, the Holy Spirit in me is the One who shows me the way out. He comforts me. He helps me. He doesn't condemn me.

So it is your conscience, the voice of your spirit, that condemns you when you miss it.

It is your spirit that knows the very moment when you have done wrong.

Confession: *My spirit is born of God. My spirit is fed on God's Word. My spirit is indwelled by the Holy Spirit. Therefore, it is a safe guide. When my spirit warns me of wrong, I obey it instantly. For if my heart condemns me not, then I have confidence toward God.*

JULY 28

INSIDE HELP

And herein do I exercise myself, to have always a conscience void of offence toward God, and toward men.   — ACTS 24:16

Soon after I was saved and healed, I returned to high school. Now, I don't know how it happened exactly — none of my family cursed — but we had a neighbor who could "cuss" up a storm, and I guess I picked it up from him. So at school one day, I said to one of the boys, "Hell, no . . ."

The minute I said it — and I didn't know a thing about the Spirit-filled life — in my heart I said, "Oh, dear God, forgive me!"

What condemned me? The Holy Spirit? No. It was my own spirit. This new creature, this new creation, this new man, doesn't talk that way.

Now, the flesh may want to continue doing some things it used to do, or talking like it used to talk, but you have to "crucify" the flesh. And a good way to crucify the flesh is to bring any problems right out into the open immediately.

That's what I did when I realized I had cussed. I didn't wait until I was "moved" to repent; I immediately asked the Lord to forgive me. The young man I had said it to had walked away. I found him and asked him to forgive me. He said he hadn't even noticed what I'd said; he was used to people talking that way. But I wanted to get things right with him and with God.

Confession: *I am a new creature in Christ. I talk like a new creature. I think like a new creature. I act like a new creature. My spirit leads me to do so.*

JULY 29

TENDER

Speaking lies in hypocrisy; having their conscience seared with a hot iron. — 1 TIMOTHY 4:2

Keep a tender conscience — don't violate it — because it is your conscience, the voice of your spirit, that relates to your mind what the spirit of God is saying to you down inside. If you don't keep a tender conscience, spiritual things will not be clear to you.

During the mid-'30s, I pastored a country church and usually spent Sunday nights in the home of a dear old gentleman who was about eighty-nine years old. He and I didn't get up as early as the rest of his family on this farm, so we had breakfast together about 8 o'clock.

He'd have one of those old-fashioned coffee pots sitting on the woodstove with the coffee just boiling in it. I've seen him pour that boiling coffee into a mug, hold it up to his mouth, and drink the whole cup of boiling coffee in one gulp. The first time I saw him do it, I felt like *I* was burning all the way down!

How could he do that? I certainly couldn't do it. My mouth and throat are so tender, one teaspoon of boiling coffee would have burned me. He couldn't do it either, to begin with. But through the years, drinking boiling coffee had seared this man's lips, mouth, and throat, until it was easy for him to drink the whole cup of boiling coffee in one gulp.

The same thing can happen spiritually. Keep a tender conscience. Stop the minute you miss it and your conscience condemns you. Say, "Lord, forgive me. I missed it." Or if you need to, tell someone you have wronged, "I did wrong. Please forgive me."

Confession: *I keep my conscience tender.*

JULY 30

THE DOMINANT ONE

. . . Walk in the Spirit, and ye shall not fulfil the lust of the flesh.
— GALATIANS 5:16

I learned early in my Christian life to let my spirit, my inward man, dominate my outward man. So even as a teenage boy standing alone without the fellowship of other teenagers who believed like I did, I didn't have the problems some do.

If there was anyone in my Sunday school class who was saved besides me, I didn't know it. They would cuss, drink, attend worldly dances, and they were all mixed up with one another in sexual activities. They'd say to me, "Why don't you do those things?"

First, my conscience wouldn't allow me to do those things. Also, I'd reply to them, "I'm a new creature." And they would ask, "What's a new creature?" (That pretty well proved they weren't new creatures!)

You don't need to be preached to about do's and don'ts; just let your spirit dominate you. God will enlighten you through your spirit. Let the new man on the inside be the dominant one.

Don't let your body dominate you. Your body will want to keep on doing the things it's been doing, because your body hasn't been born again yet. Instead, walk by your spirit.

Confession: *I walk by my spirit. I let my spirit dominate me. I let the new man on the inside be the dominant one. Therefore, I do not fulfill the lust of the flesh. I am not body-ruled; I am spirit-ruled.*

JULY 31

SPIRIT WALK

There is therefore now no condemnation to them which are in Christ Jesus, who walk not after the flesh, but after the Spirit.

— ROMANS 8:1

Conscience is the voice of the *human spirit*.

Reason is the voice of the *soul*, or the *mind*.

Feeling is the voice of the *body*.

The Holy Spirit does not bear witness with our reasoning. The Holy Spirit does not bear witness with our feelings. The Holy Spirit bears witness with our *spirits*.

I'm very careful about using the word "feeling." When we sense the Presence of God in a service, people often say, "I felt it." But we really don't *feel it physically* so much as we *sense it spiritually*. So I am careful to differentiate between the two, because people slip into the feeling realm so easily. Then, when they feel good, they say, "Glory to God! Hallelujah! I'm saved! I'm filled with the Spirit! Everything is fine!" But when they feel bad, they get a long face and they say, "I've lost it all. I don't feel like I did, so I must be backslidden."

If we go by feelings, we'll get into trouble. That's why so many Christians are up and down, in and out. (I call them yo-yo Christians.) They don't walk by their spirits. They don't walk in faith. They go by their feelings.

Confession: *I walk not after the flesh, but after the spirit. I don't follow feelings. I don't follow reason. I follow the voice of my spirit, my conscience!*

AUGUST 1

MOUNTAINS AND VALLEYS

Now thanks be unto God, which always causeth us to triumph in Christ . . . . — 2 CORINTHIANS 2:14

I hear people talk about being in the valley, and then on the mountain, and then back in the valley again. To tell the truth about it, I don't know what they're talking about. I've been saved since 1933, and I've never been anywhere but on the mountaintop!

You don't have to get down in the valley. People talk about their "valley experiences." I've never had any valley experiences. Oh, yes, there have been tests and trials — but I was on top of the mountain, shouting my way through it all, living above it. Praise God!

You see, those who say they're in the valleys are looking at life from the natural standpoint — from the physical. *They are trying to get a spiritual answer from the physical* — and you just can't do that.

Years ago, when I came among Pentecostal people after having been a Baptist, I'd hear them talk about "going through the valley." And when I didn't know what they were talking about, they'd look at me and say, "Your time's a-coming!" Thank God, it never has arrived!

No! Get off the negative and get on the positive side of life — and you won't have any valleys. You'll always be on the mountaintop!

Confession: *Thanks be to God, who ALWAYS causes me to triumph in Christ! I ALWAYS triumph! I live on the mountaintop!*

AUGUST 2

STIRRED UP

Wherefore I put thee in remembrance that thou stir up the gift of God, which is in thee . . . . — 2 TIMOTHY 1:6

A woman got us out of bed at 2 o'clock one morning, crying, "If I could just get back to where I was with God." I assumed she had committed some terrible sin, so I said, "Kneel down here and tell the Lord about it. He will forgive you."

She said, "I have searched my heart and as far as I know, I haven't done anything wrong." I said, "Then what makes you think you have to get back to God?" "Well," she said, "I just don't *feel* like I used to."

I was visibly aggravated with her. I told her if I went by my feelings right then, she'd have to pray for *me*! But I showed her what to do: I told her to watch and listen as I prayed.

Then I said, "Dear Lord, I'm so glad I'm a child of God. I'm so glad I've been born again. I don't feel anything, but that doesn't have anything to do with it. My inward man is a new man. I want to thank You that I'm filled with the Holy Spirit. God the Father, God the Son, and God the Holy Spirit reside in me. I want to thank You for that . . ."

I didn't feel anything at the time, but I confessed it anyway, because that's what the Word says. When I did, on the inside of me, something bubbled up.

"The expression on your face changed. Your face lit up," the woman said. "Yes," I said, "it was in me all the time. I just stirred up what is in me."

Confession: *I stir up what is in me!*

AUGUST 3

Faith — Not Sight

For we walk by faith, not by sight.   — 2 CORINTHIANS 5:7

Smith Wigglesworth said something that blessed me when I first read it way back in the late thirties, because it was so in line with my own experience. He said:

> "I am not moved by what I feel.
> I am not moved by what I see.
> I am moved only by what I believe."

Then he went on to say:

> "I can't understand God by feelings.
> I can't understand the Lord Jesus Christ by feelings.
> I understand God by what the Word says about Him.
> I understand the Lord Jesus Christ by what the Word
> says about Him. He is everything the Word says He is."

You will not be able to understand yourself by feelings. Instead, understand yourself as a born again, Spirit-filled Christian, by what the Word of God says about you.

And when you read what the Word says about you, whether you feel like it or not, say, "Yes, that's me. I have that. The Word says I have that. I can do what the Word says I can do. I am what the Word says I am."

As you do this, you will begin to develop spiritually.

Confession: *I walk by faith and not by sight. (Now make Wigglesworth's confession, your confession.)*

AUGUST 4

EXAMINE YOUR LEADING

Knowing this first, that no prophecy of the scripture is of any private interpretation. For the prophecy came not in old time by the will of man: but holy men of God spake as they were moved by the Holy Ghost. — 2 PETER 1:20,21

The Word and the Spirit agree.

How can you tell if it is the Spirit of God? If it is in line with the Word, then it is of the Spirit. If it is not in line with the Word, then it is not the Spirit.

I've had people tell me God was leading them to do something, and when I heard what it was, I said, "No, that's not the Spirit of God."

This is an extreme case, but it's true. A man told me he thought the Spirit of God was leading him and another woman to leave their spouses and marry one another. No! That is out of line with the Word! The Holy Spirit does not break up homes.

The Spirit and the Word agree! The Bible is inspired by the Spirit of God.

Examine your leading in the light of the Word.

Confession: *I am led by the Spirit of God. I examine my leading in the light of His Word, because the Word and the Spirit agree.*

AUGUST 5

DIRECTION

Trust in the Lord with all thine heart; and lean not unto thine own understanding. In all thy ways acknowledge him, and he shall direct thy paths. — **PROVERBS 3:5,6**

It is not for us to tell the Lord how to lead us. We are to let Him lead us any way He wants to!

But it is for us to find out from the Word of God how He does lead. And He leads, first of all, by the inward witness.

We can also see in the Book of Acts and elsewhere how at times some believers received guidance through a vision; others received guidance from an angel who appeared to them and told them certain things. Such phenomena, however, didn't happen every day in these people's lives. They occurred once or twice in the entire lifetime of some of them. So that's *not* the ordinary way God leads — but He can if He wants to.

Often God is trying to bear witness with our spirit — trying to guide us — but we won't listen, because we want something *spectacular*, such as a vision, or an angel. But we must remember that *anything God does is supernatural!*

Confession: *I trust in the Lord with all my heart. And I lean not to my own understanding. In all my ways I acknowledge Him, and He directs my paths.*

AUGUST 6

FLEECES?

A new heart also will I give you, and a new spirit will I put within you: and I will take away the stony heart out of your flesh, and I will give you an heart of flesh. And I will put my spirit within you . . . .
— EZEKIEL 36:26,27

To receive guidance, some people put out what they call a "fleece" before the Lord. The New Testament, however, does not say, "As many as are led by *fleeces*, they are the sons of God."

"Yes," someone may say, "but Gideon put out a fleece back in the Old Testament."

Why go back under the Old Covenant? We've got something better under the New Covenant. The Old Covenant was for spiritually dead people. I'm not spiritually dead — I'm alive! I've got the Spirit of God in me!

Remember, Gideon was not a prophet, priest, or king. Only men who stood in those three offices, under the Old Covenant, were anointed by the Spirit of God. The Spirit of God was not personally present with the rest of the people. That is why every male had to present himself once a year at the Temple in Jerusalem.

The Shekinah glory — the Presence of God — was kept shut up in the Holy of Holies. But when Jesus died on Calvary, the curtain that blocked the way into the Holy of Holies was ripped in two from top to bottom. God moved out — and He has never dwelled in an earth-made house since! He dwells in us!

Confession: *God's Spirit dwells in me! He is the Greater One, and He dwells in me!*

AUGUST 7

His Will

. . . That ye might be filled with the knowledge of his will in all wisdom and spiritual understanding; That ye might walk worthy of the Lord unto all pleasing, being fruitful in every good work, and increasing in the knowledge of God. — COLOSSIANS 1:9,10

It is dangerous for Spirit-filled Christians living under the New Covenant to put out fleeces. This fleece business is in the realm where Satan is god (2 Cor. 4:4).

When people pray, "God, if You want me to do this, then have this happen," that's a fleece. And Satan can move in the sense realm. But God has a better way of leading His children than by this hit-and-miss method of fleeces!

It was only after I came over into Pentecostal circles that I heard about fleeces. While I was pastoring one church, the board of another church asked me to try out to be their pastor. I preached for them, and driving back home, I put out a fleece.

I said, "Lord, I'm going to put out a fleece. Here it is: If that church elects me one hundred percent — if I get all the votes — I'm going to accept it as Your will."

They elected me one hundred percent. I moved there, and I got fleeced! And they got fleeced. Both of us missed God one hundred percent! As I look back, I realize that I had a check in my spirit all the time, but I didn't listen.

Confession: *I pray that I might be filled with the knowledge of God's will in all wisdom and spiritual understanding; that I might walk worthy of the Lord unto all pleasing, fruitful in every good work; and increasing in the knowledge of God.*

AUGUST 8

YOUR OWN WORDS

. . . He that sweareth to his own hurt, and changeth not.
                                                    — PSALM 15:4

Even though I missed God's perfect will by putting out a fleece, I stayed with that church one year, because I had promised them I would. I toughed it out. I'm a man of my word.

One of the characteristics of a spiritual pilgrim is that he "sweareth to his own hurt, and changeth not." In other words, he keeps his word.

If you don't learn to be a person of your word, your faith will never amount to anything. Why? Because to get faith to work for you, you have to believe in your words as well as believe in your heart: *". . . whosoever shall SAY . . . and shall not doubt in his heart, but shall believe that those things which he SAITH shall come to pass; he shall have whatsoever he SAITH"* (Mark 11:23). The things that you say are your words. And you're certainly not going to believe your word will come to pass when you know you're not a person of your word!

I'm going to keep my word. If I don't, it will affect my whole spiritual life. I tell the truth every time. I won't tell someone I'm glad to see them if I'm not. I find some way to say something without violating my conscience. I won't lie, because it would affect my faith.

"But sometimes when you lie, it just means that you're being nice," someone will argue. No, it's not. It's being devilish.

Confession: *I am a person of my word!*

AUGUST 9

WAITING ON GOD

But they that wait upon the Lord shall renew their strength; they shall mount up with wings as eagles; they shall run, and not be weary; and they shall walk, and not faint. — ISAIAH 40:31

Except for that one time when I got fleeced, I never missed it when I made a change in churches or ministry.

"What did you go by — a fleece?"

No, I went by what the inward witness said. If I had to, I would wait awhile before God. If I had to, I would wait all night long or I might fast a day or so — not that fasting will change God. It won't.

God never changes. He's the same *before* I fast, *while* I fast, and *after* I fast. But fasting changes *me*. The time I would have spent eating, I prayed and waited on God. I would spend more time in the Word. Then my spirit man would become dominant.

So I waited until I knew on the inside of me what God wanted me to do. And I never got fleeced again.

Confession: *My spirit is the candle of the Lord. He guides me. He enlightens me. He leads me through my spirit. He leads, first of all, by the inward witness. He also leads by the still, small voice. He is leading. He is guiding. He is directing. I am Spirit-led, Spirit-taught, and Spirit-guided.*

AUGUST 10

WHAT MY HEART SAYS

But thou shalt remember the Lord thy God: for it is he that giveth thee power to get wealth .... — DEUTERONOMY 8:18

I knew a man down in East Texas whose family was so poor that he didn't have a pair of shoes until he was twelve years old. He had only a fifth grade education. But way back when money was money, he had two million dollars. He made his money in investments.

Two people who had been frequent guests in his home told me that he had said, "In many years of investing, I've never lost a dime."

Here's how he did it. He told my friend, "When someone comes with an idea and wants me to invest in something, my first reaction is mental. So I have a big closet I go into and pray about it. *I wait long enough to hear what my spirit says.*

"My head may say, 'You'd be a fool to invest in that,' but if my heart says, 'Go ahead,' I do. Or, my head may say, 'You'd better get in on this one,' while my heart tells me, 'Don't do it.' So I don't. *I don't pay any attention to my head.* I just get in that closet and wait — all night sometimes. And sometimes I'm in and out of it for three days, just praying and reading my Bible, getting quiet so I can hear what my heart says."

Confession: *The Holy Spirit guides me in all the affairs of life. And I listen to what my heart says!*

223

AUGUST 11

PROPHETS

But this shall be the covenant that I will make with the house of Israel; After those days, saith the Lord, I will put my law in their inward parts, and write it in their hearts; and will be their God, and they shall be my people. — **JEREMIAH 31:33**

When Jesus appeared to me and told me to teach His people how to be led by the Spirit, He stated, "I didn't set prophets in the Church to guide people. The New Testament does not say, 'As many as are led by prophets, they are the sons of God.'

"New Testament believers," Jesus told me, "should not seek guidance through prophets. The prophets of the Old and the New Testaments are similar in some ways. Both see and know things supernaturally. But in the Old Testament, the people did not have the Spirit of God in them, or on them. They had a promise of the New Birth, but they didn't have it. So, if they were to be led by the Spirit, they had to go to someone who was anointed with the Spirit. But under the New Covenant, every believer has the Spirit of God. They don't have to go to anyone to seek guidance. The only thing the prophet's ministry may do in this area under the New Covenant, is to confirm something someone already has."

And if it doesn't confirm something you already have in your spirit, forget it!

Confession: *For as many as are led by the Spirit of God, they are the sons of God. God leads me!*

AUGUST 12

BORN OF GOD

Whosoever is born of God doth not commit sin; for his seed remaineth in him: and he cannot sin, because he is born of God. — 1 JOHN 3:9

People sometimes ask me, "How can I tell whether it is my own spirit or the Holy Spirit telling me to do something? It may just be me wanting to do it."

When you say "me," what are you talking about? If it is the real you — the man on the inside that's a new creature, with the life and nature of God in him, indwelt by the Holy Spirit — then it is right. If you mean "me," talking about the flesh, that's a different thing entirely. Learn to differentiate between the two.

A Christian's inward man isn't the one who wants to do wrong. If the inward man wants to do wrong, that person has never been born again.

First John 3:9 has bothered some Christians. They have made mistakes and failed, and they've thought, *If I were born of God, according to the Bible I wouldn't sin.* But this verse is talking about the inward man who doesn't sin.

I've done things that were wrong, but my inward man didn't do them. In fact, he didn't agree with me when I did them. He tried to get me not to do them. Physically, we are born of human parents, and we partake of their human nature. Spiritually, we are born of God, and we partake of His nature. And it is not God's nature to do wrong. Therefore, let your spirit dominate your flesh.

Confession: *I am born of God. My spirit has the life and nature of God, and its desires are right desires.*

AUGUST 13

EDIFICATION, EXHORTATION, COMFORT

But he that prophesieth speaketh unto men to edification, and exhortation, and comfort. — 1 CORINTHIANS 14:3

The following is a word of prophecy that came during a seminar I taught on being led by the Spirit:

Look inside, inside your spirit. For your spirit is the candle, the lamp of the Lord, searching all the inward parts of the belly. And so ye shall know, and ye shall walk in the light of that which ye know. No one will be able to gainsay thee, for thou wilt say, "There is light in my dwelling. I am the temple of the Holy Spirit. He dwells in me. He enlightens my spirit. Yea, I walk in that witness that's within my spirit. I do that which I know by an inward intuition. I follow that deep premonition in my innermost being. And so I am being led by the Spirit. I am rejoicing and I'm glad. Yea, I sound forth His praises evermore. I look to that which in me does reside. For residing in me is the potential of all that God has and is. All the attributes of even the Father God Himself reside within my spirit, and are potentially mine. For He has declared, 'I will walk in them. I'll live in them. I'll be their God. They will be My people.' My God is not in a far-off distant land, out of reach and not at hand. My God sits not on a pedestal; nor can He be seen with the physical, or touched with the hand. My God is a Spirit who resides in man!"

AUGUST 14

THE VOICE OF THE HOLY SPIRIT

While Peter thought on the vision, the Spirit said unto him, Behold, three men seek thee. — ACTS 10:19

God leads by an inward witness. He leads by what we call the still, small voice — the voice of our own spirits. And he also leads by the Voice of the Spirit of God speaking to us. This is more authoritative than the still, small voice. When this Voice speaks, it is so real, you may look around to see who said it — even though it comes from inside you! There have been times I've heard the Voice of the Spirit and to me it was audible, although others near me didn't hear it. It must have seemed audible to the child Samuel, too, yet Eli the prophet didn't hear it.

However, this isn't the ordinary way God leads. I have found in all my years of ministry that every time God has spoken in a spectacular way, such as in an audible voice (at least to me it was audible), there was rough sailing ahead. And if He hadn't spoken so spectacularly, I wouldn't have stayed steady.

The Bible tells us there are many voices in the world, and none of them without significance. However, this isn't a matter of listening to voices. Be careful about following anything without first examining it in the light of the Word. Don't pray to hear something. If God speaks to us, all right. If God doesn't speak to us, we have His Word, and we can walk in the light of it.

Confession: *I walk in the light of God's Word!*

AUGUST 15

PERCEPTION

Now when much time was spent, and when sailing was now dangerous, because the fast was now already past, Paul admonished them, And said unto them, Sirs, I perceive that this voyage will be with hurt and much damage, not only of the lading and ship, but also of our lives.
— ACTS 27:9,10

Paul didn't say, "I've got a revelation," or "the Lord told me," or "the Lord revealed it to me." He said, "I perceive." This was just an inward witness that he had. He perceived something spiritually.

A family of seven went out to eat. The children's food had already arrived at the table when the father suddenly said, "Let's rush home. I just have a perception that we should go." When they arrived, they found that a fire had started in their house. They were able to put it out. If we would become more spirit-conscious, many things could be averted.

"Well, God did that. He had some purpose in it," people will say. No, we miss it because we don't listen. If the sailors had listened to Paul, they could have saved the ship and all the merchandise.

God is not an enemy of man; He is trying to help us. He is not working *against* us; He is working *for* us.

Confession: *The Spirit of the Lord is in me to help me. He is working for me. I perceive His direction and His help spiritually. I am spirit-conscious.*

AUGUST 16

HIS GUIDING WORD

Thy word is a lamp unto my feet, and a light unto my path.
— **PSALM 119:105**

Don't seek guidance when the Bible has already told you what to do. Just go ahead and do it!

The Bible tells you how to act under every circumstance in life.

It tells the husband how to treat his wife.

It tells the wife how to treat her husband.

It tells parents how to treat their children.

It tells children how to respond to their parents.

It tells all of us to walk in divine love. Divine love seeks not its own. It's not out for what "I" can get, but what "I" can give.

We have God's Word, and we can walk in the light of it. I go as much by what God *doesn't* say to me by the Spirit as by what He *does* say. If He doesn't say anything, I just keep going in the direction I have been going. I just keep doing what I have been doing. I know God will tell me when to change. If He doesn't give me new directions, I don't worry about it. I don't "seek" anything. I just keep going.

229

Confession: *Lord, Your Word is a lamp unto my feet. It is a light unto my path.*

AUGUST 17

GUARDIAN ANGELS

Take heed that ye despise not one of these little ones; for I say unto you, That in heaven their angels do always behold the face of my Father which is in heaven. — MATTHEW 18:10

Years ago, a group of us were ministering to the Lord in prayer, such as is described in Acts 13:1 and 2. I had just gotten up off my knees and had sat down on the platform by a folding chair, still praying in other tongues, when suddenly Jesus stood right in front of me! And standing right behind Jesus, about two feet to Jesus' right and three feet behind Him was a large angel! The angel must have been eight feet tall — a big fellow.

Jesus talked to me about some things (and everything He said later came to pass). When He finished what He was telling me, I asked Him, "Who is that fellow? What does he represent?"

Jesus answered, "That's your angel."

I said, "My angel?"

"Yes," He said. "You remember when I was on earth I said of little children that their angel is ever before My Father's face. *You don't lose your angel just because you grow up.*"

Isn't that comforting? Everywhere I go, I've got that big fellow following me around!

Confession: *According to Hebrews 1:14, angels are sent forth to minister FOR those who are the heirs of salvation. I am an heir of salvation. My angel is sent forth to minister for me.*

AUGUST 18

GUIDANCE BY ANGELS

Are they [angels] *not all ministering spirits, sent forth to minister for them who shall be heirs of salvation?* — HEBREWS 1:14

Even as Jesus talked with me, I would glance at the angel. When I did, I could see he would start to say something.

Jesus said, "He's got a message for you."

I said to Jesus, "You're talking to me. Why don't You give me the message? Besides, the Word says, 'As many as are led by the Spirit of God, they are the sons of God.' I've got the Holy Ghost; why couldn't He talk to me?"

Jesus had mercy and was patient. He said, "Did you read in My Word where the angel of the Lord told Philip to go down the way unto Gaza? Wasn't that guidance? Didn't an angel give Cornelius directions?" Then He gave me several more New Testament illustrations of angels giving guidance.

Finally I said, "That's enough. I'll listen."

The angel started by saying, "I am sent from the Presence of Almighty God to tell you . . . (and he spoke to me about a certain direction I was to take). You'll have four thousand dollars in your hands by December 1 [this was 1963] to get you headed in this direction. For I've sent my angels out to cause the money to come."

On that date, I had exactly four thousand dollars to the penny, just as he said I would. That was the beginning of this ministry.

Confession: *I am an heir of salvation. My angel is sent forth to minister for me!*

AUGUST 19

CHARGED TO KEEP

For he [God] shall give his angels charge over thee, to keep thee in all thy ways. — **PSALM 91:11**

I heard a pioneer Pentecostal missionary tell this experience. A neighboring tribe kidnapped a little girl from the tribe where he was a missionary. The people in her tribe knew that if they didn't recover her before nightfall, they would never see her again.

So the missionary and a native interpreter made their way through the jungle to the kidnappers' village. They took trinkets and bargained with the chief for the child's return, but night overtook them. Because they couldn't travel at night in the jungle, they were forced to stay at the kidnappers' village. Sleeping on the floor of a thatched hut, they were awakened by the sound of drums. The interpreter said that the drums meant they were to be killed: The chief had decided to kill them and keep both the trinkets and the girl. Then they heard the hostile natives coming for them.

The missionary and the interpreter knelt down, prayed, and committed themselves to God. Then the missionary said, "Let's not wait for them. Let's go out. I'll go first."

He stepped outside with his eyes shut and waited for what seemed to be an eternity. One slash of their knives could cut off his head. But instead he heard moaning and groaning. He looked, and every native was on his face on the ground.

"They are calling you 'god,'" the interpreter said. "They say that when you stepped outside, two giants in white stepped out with you, holding great swords in either hand."

Confession: *God has given His angels charge over me to protect me in all my ways.*

AUGUST 20

COUNSEL WITHIN

Counsel in the heart of man is like deep water; but a man of understanding will draw it out. — PROVERBS 20:5

Although God does lead through visions and other supernatural manifestations, I would encourage you *not* to seek a vision.

Do not seek visions or similar experiences. Why? Because you might get beyond the Word, where the devil can deceive you. (*See* Second Corinthians 11:14.)

Sometimes we would prefer to have a more direct word of guidance. But we don't always get it. So don't try to manufacture one if it doesn't happen. Nowhere does the Bible say that believers sought these experiences, or that they were seeking visions when they came. The visions just happened without people seeking for them.

Be content if all you ever have is the inward witness. Be content to follow that witness. But educate, train, and develop your human spirit to the point where that witness becomes more and more real to you.

Then, if God sees fit to give you supernatural visitations and manifestations, just thank Him for them.

Confession: *I will educate, train, and develop my human spirit so that the inward witness will become more and more real to me.*

AUGUST 21

ABOVE ONLY

The Lord shall open unto thee his good treasure, the heaven to give the rain unto thy land in his season, and to bless all the work of thine hand: and thou shalt lend unto many nations, and thou shalt not borrow. And the Lord shall make thee the head, and not the tail; and thou shalt be above only, and thou shalt not be beneath . . . .

— DEUTERONOMY 28:12,13

234

The reason why Christians continually make mistakes and fail is because their spirits, which should guide them, are kept locked away in prison, so to speak. Even in our churches, the intellect has taken the throne.

Any person who shuts his spirit away and never listens to it becomes crippled in life. He becomes an easy prey to selfish and designing people.

But the person who listens to his spirit is the one who climbs to the top.

Before I began to learn in 1959 how to follow the inward witness, it cost me financially. I had to borrow money to get out of a financial hole. Yet God had said I would have money to loan if I would follow the inward witness. But when I began to follow it, I started rising to the top. And I've been rising ever since.

Confession: (*Make your own confession from today's scripture.*)

AUGUST 22

SPIRIT GROWTH

That we henceforth be no more children, tossed to and fro, and carried about with every wind of doctrine, by the sleight of men, and cunning craftiness, whereby they lie in wait to deceive; But speaking the truth in love, may grow up into him in all things, which is the head, even Christ. — EPHESIANS 4:14,15

If it is true that the spirit of man is the candle of the Lord, and if it is also true that God will enlighten and guide us through our spirits — and it is — then that part of us needs to grow. The spirit of man needs to be developed so it can be a safer guide.

Your spirit can be educated and trained, just as your mind can be educated.

And your spirit can be built up in strength, just as your body can be built up in strength.

I am well convinced that if you will follow the steps I will give over the next few days, you can train your spirit to the point where eventually you will always get an instant "yes" or "no" on the inside, even in the minor details of life.

You must realize this, though: You didn't start the first grade one day and graduate from high school the next day. It took time to develop your mentality. It also will take time to train, educate, and develop your spirit.

Confession: *I will take the time to train, educate, and develop my spirit. My spirit is growing!*

AUGUST 23

MEDITATING IN THE WORD

This book of the law shall not depart out of thy mouth; but thou shalt meditate therein day and night, that thou mayest observe to do according to all that is written therein: for then thou shalt make thy way prosperous, and then thou shalt have good success. — JOSHUA 1:8

How can your spirit be educated and trained? How can your spirit be built up in strength? There are four steps: (1) Meditating in the Word; (2) Practicing the Word; (3) Giving the Word first place; and (4) Obeying your spirit. We will study these four steps in coming days.

What God said to Joshua will work for everyone. If God didn't want Joshua to be prosperous, why did He tell him how to prosper? If God didn't want Joshua to be successful, why did He tell him how to have good success? But God wanted Joshua to be prosperous and successful. And He wants *you* to be prosperous and successful too! Furthermore, God has given us directions in today's text.

Paraphrasing this truth into New Testament language, God simply said, "The Word of God [particularly the New Covenant or New Testament] shall not depart out of your mouth. But meditate therein day and night . . . for then you shall make your way prosperous, and you shall have good success in life."

Confession: *The Word of God shall not depart out of my mouth. I shall meditate therein day and night. Therefore, I shall make my way prosperous, and I shall have good success in life!*

AUGUST 24

DAY AND NIGHT

But his delight is in the law of the Lord; and in his law doth he medi-
tate day and night. And he shall be like a tree planted by the rivers of
water, that bringeth forth his fruit in his season; his leaf also shall not
wither; and whatsoever he doeth shall prosper. — PSALM 1:2,3

If you ever want to do anything great in life — if you ever want to amount to anything in life — take time to meditate in the Word of God. Start out with at least ten or fifteen minutes a day, and build up.

For many years, I held two services a day while in the traveling ministry. And in earlier years of field ministry, I would teach in the mornings, pray aloud all afternoon, and preach and minister at night. Because I ate only one meal a day during my meetings, I would grow weak expending all this physical energy.

Then the Lord spoke to me. He said, "Don't spend all that time praying and wearing yourself out for the night service. Lie on the bed and meditate." When I began to do that, my spiritual growth was greater than ever before.

Well, that's what God promised: *". . . for then thou shalt make thy way prosperous, and then thou shalt have good success"* (Joshua 1:8). I wanted to prosper and have good success in the ministry. But this works whether you are in the ministry, raise cows, or sell automobiles!

Confession: *I take time every day to meditate in God's Word!*

AUGUST 25

MY MEDITATION

O how love I thy law! it is my meditation all the day.
— PSALM 119:97

A minister told me how he'd been trying to make a success of his church. If he heard of a pastor who was doing well, he would visit him and see what kind of program he had. Then he would try to put that man's program into action in his church — but it never worked. And he'd fly all over the country doing this.

Then the pastor decided he would meditate in the Word the way he'd heard me teach. So he took a little time out each morning to meditate on the Word. He told me that after thirty days of meditating on the Word, one Sunday they had a landslide response. More people were saved than in the previous two or three years; his people were revived — and he began to have good success.

The ministry was this pastor's life. That's where he needed to have good success. Your life calling may be different. But it is certainly true that your way can also be prosperous, and you can have good success. Take time to meditate in the Word. Shut yourself in alone with your spirit. Shut the world out.

Confession: *I will meditate in God's Word. I will observe to do what His Word teaches. My way shall be prosperous. I shall have good success in life. I shall know how to deal wisely in the affairs of life. For the Word of God says so.*

AUGUST 26

PRACTICING THE WORD

But be ye doers of the word, and not hearers only, deceiving your own selves. — JAMES 1:22

Your spirit can be developed by four things. We have just examined the first: *meditation*. Now we will look at the second: *practicing the Word*. Practicing the Word means being a doer of the Word.

There are *talkers* about the Word. And even *rejoicers* about the Word. But we don't have many *doers* of the Word.

Begin to practice being a doer of the Word. Under all circumstances, do what the Word of God tells you to do.

Some think that being a doer of the Word is simply keeping the Ten Commandments. No, that's not what James 1:22 means. After all, under the New Covenant, we have only one commandment — the commandment of love. If you love someone, you won't steal from him. You won't lie about him. Paul said that love is the fulfilling of the law. If you walk in love, you won't break any law that was given to curb sin. So, if you're a doer of the Word, you will walk in love.

But being a doer of the Word for New Covenant Christians means doing primarily what is written in the Epistles. Those are the letters written to the Church. They belong to us, and we are to do them.

Confession: *I am a doer of the Word, not just a hearer only!*

AUGUST 27

REFUSING TO FRET

Be careful for nothing; but in every thing by prayer and supplication with thanksgiving let your requests be made known unto God.
— **PHILIPPIANS 4:6**

The *Amplified* translation of this verse begins, "Do not fret or have any anxiety about anything . . . ."

Christians usually practice only part of this verse — the part that says to pray. But if we practice that part and not the part about not having anxiety, we're not practicing the Word. We're not being a doer of the Word.

First, God's Word says, "Do not fret . . . ." If you're going to fret and be anxious, it won't do you any good to make requests. Your prayers will not work.

I read a story years ago about a man, his wife, and grown son, who were in a field chopping cotton. The son wasn't quite right mentally. Storm clouds appeared, and it began to thunder, but the old man wanted to continue working. Then the lightning became bad. The family began to run for shelter. When it looked as though they weren't going to make it, the parents fell to their knees and began to pray. "Come on, Ma and Pa," the boy cried. "A scared prayer ain't no account."

There's much truth to that. That's what the Spirit of God is saying through Paul. So, when you pray, *"Be careful for nothing . . . ."*

Confession: *I do not fret or have any anxiety about anything.*

AUGUST 28

DOING PHILIPPIANS 4:6

Do not fret or have any anxiety about anything, but in every circumstance and in everything, by prayer and petition (definite requests), with thanksgiving, continue to make your wants known to God.
— PHILIPPIANS 4:6 *(Amplified)*

A minister once came to me for advice. There were many storms in his life, and I felt sorry for him. He couldn't eat or sleep.

Just to sympathize with him wasn't enough, so I had to read Philippians 4:6. "But everyone doesn't have the faith you have," he told me. "Yes, but they have the same Bible," I replied, "and it's a matter of practicing the Word."

Then I showed him how to practice the Word: I read a verse aloud and then told the Lord, "Your Word is true, and I believe it." When I first started practicing this verse, I believed I could make my requests known to God, but it was hard for me to believe I could keep from fretting. However, God won't ask us to do something we can't do. So when God said not to fret, this means we can keep from fretting.

So I say aloud, "I refuse to fret or have any anxiety about anything." Then I bring my requests to the Lord and thank Him for them. This quiets the troubled spirit the devil tried to make me have. If the devil tries to get me to worry again, I simply go back, reread this verse, and keep claiming it.

Confession: *I am a doer of Philippians 4:6!*

AUGUST 29

DOING PHILIPPIANS 4:7,8

And the peace of God, which passeth all understanding, shall keep your hearts and minds through Christ Jesus. Finally, brethren, whatsoever things are true, whatsoever things are honest, whatsoever things are just, whatsoever things are pure, whatsoever things are lovely, whatsoever things are of good report; if there be any virtue, and if there be any praise, think on these things. — **PHILIPPIANS 4:7,8**

Many people want what verse 7 talks about, but they don't want to do what verse 6 says to do in order to get it. In order to get what verse 7 says, you have to practice verse 6, which we studied yesterday.

People who worry and fret, continually think on the wrong side of life. They continually talk unbelief. If something isn't true, honest, just, pure, lovely, and of a good report, then don't think about it. Make it meet all these qualifications. Some things you hear may be true, but they may not be pure and lovely — so don't think about them. To do so is to give place to the devil, who is always seeking to enter your thought life. That's why the Bible says, "Think on these things."

Meditate and feed on the letters written to the Church. Through them, God speaks to His Church.

Confession: *I do not fret or have any anxiety about anything. Therefore, the peace of God keeps my heart and mind through Christ Jesus. I think on those things that are true, honest, just, pure, lovely, and of a good report!*

AUGUST 30

GIVING THE WORD FIRST PLACE

Thy testimonies also are my delight and my counsellors.
— PSALM 119:24

When the crises or tests come, too many Christians say, "What are we going to do now?"

The crises of life come to us all. But if you are Word-oriented, the first thing you will think about is, "What does *the Word* say about it?"

I pastored nearly twelve years, and I found that churches have problems just like families do. They have discipline problems, financial problems, and so forth.

I never discussed church problems with the people, because the more you talk about problems, the bigger they seem to get. But sometimes my deacon board would talk about church problems, and sure enough, the more they talked about them, the bigger the problems seemed to get. Then one of the deacons would look at me and say, "Oh, Brother Hagin, what in the world are we going to do?"

I'd smile and say, *"We're just going to act like the Bible is true!"*

Making that little statement would cause those deacons to sigh with relief. "It *is* true, isn't it," they'd say. "Sure it is," I'd say.

It's amazing how things would straighten out when we acted like the Bible is true!

Confession: *Lord, thy testimonies are my counselors. I put them first. I put God's Word first. I act like it's so.*

AUGUST 31

OBEYING YOUR SPIRIT

All scripture is given by inspiration of God, and is profitable for doctrine, for reproof, for correction, for instruction in righteousness: That the man of God may be perfect, throughly furnished unto all good works. — 2 TIMOTHY 3:16,17

Did you notice that meditating in the Word, practicing the Word, and giving the Word first place — the first three steps in training the human spirit — come *before* obeying your spirit?

If your spirit has had the privilege of meditating in the Word, of practicing the Word, of putting the Word first, then your spirit is an authoritative guide.

In the process of time, if you will follow the four steps we have just studied, you can know the will of God even in all the minor details of your life!

But for this to happen, God's Word, not human reasoning, must dominate your thinking. The Word has been given to us by the Holy Spirit. *If the Word is dominating us, then the Holy Spirit is dominating our thinking!*

The written Word was given to us to develop, shape, form, and fit our spirit nature — and nothing but the Word will accomplish this. Reading about the Word won't do it. That's the reason why God wants us to meditate in His Word.

Confession: *God's Word is good. I meditate in God's Word. I observe to do what His Word teaches. My way shall be prosperous. I shall have good success in life!*

SEPTEMBER 1

ALIVE

For the word of God is quick, and powerful, and sharper than any twoedged sword, piercing even to the dividing asunder of soul and spirit, and of the joints and marrow, and is a discerner of the thoughts and intents of the heart. — HEBREWS 4:12

To be strong in faith, the first thing you must settle on is the integrity of the Word of God.

You must know that the Bible is exactly what it declares itself to be — God's Word — a revelation from God to us! It is God speaking to us now! It is not only a book of the past and the future; it is a book for now. It is a God-breathed, God-indwelt, God-inspired message.

Moffatt's translation of Hebrew 4:12 reads, "For the Logos [Word] of God is a living thing . . . ." Quick! Alive! Living! But it will come alive to you only as you accept it and act upon it.

I've always maintained the following attitude toward the Word of God, and have acted upon it accordingly: *The Word is just as though the Lord Jesus Christ were here in person speaking to me.*

Confession: *God's Word is alive. It is alive in me. God speaks to me through His Word. He gives me revelation through His Word. I accept His Word as though the Lord Jesus Christ Himself were here in person speaking to me. And I act upon it accordingly.*

SEPTEMBER 2

SETTLED

For what if some did not believe? shall their unbelief make the faith of God without effect? God forbid: yea, let God be true, but every man a liar . . . . — ROMANS 3:3,4

To establish a firm foundation for your faith, I suggest you adopt the following motto which I wrote in red ink in the flyleaf of my Bible many years ago.

> The Bible says it.
> I believe it.
> And that settles it.

Determine to always do these two things: (1) Accept God's Word for what it says, and (2) Walk in the light of what the Word says. Don't try to get around certain things or explain them away. Don't try to read things into the Word just because you want to believe those things that way. Study the Word — and accept it just as it is written.

For example, the denomination I was reared in didn't teach faith and healing. I was bedfast sixteen months as a teenager, and five doctors said I had to die. But I turned to the Word of God, and the more I studied, the more I saw that the Word is true. I declared, "I am going to walk in the light of what the Word says, regardless of church teaching, because the Word is God speaking to me today." When I settled that issue in my mind, sixty percent of the battle was won: I was on the road to divine healing.

Confession: *God's Word is true. I believe God. I walk in the light of what the Word says, because the Word of God is God speaking to me today.*

SEPTEMBER 3

PERFORMANCE

Then said Jehovah . . . I watch over my word to perform it.
— JEREMIAH 1:12 (ASV)

In all probability, you have faith in your employer. You believe what he says, and you act on it. If he promises to raise your salary, you don't question him.

Also, you and your word are one. You are behind your word and your promises. If your word is no good, then you are not good.

But God's Word is more reliable than the word of a man! God's Word and God are one. If God's Word is no good and it cannot be relied upon, then God is no good, and He cannot be relied upon.

But God *can* be relied upon! He stands behind His Word! He stands behind every Word He promises!

You come to know Jesus through the Word of God. Jesus introduces you to God the Father. Then you begin to act upon God's Word. You test it. After a time of acting upon what God says in His Word, it becomes as natural to you as acting upon the word of the man for whom you are working.

Confession: *I believe God. I act upon His Word. Then He watches over His Word to perform it in my life.*

SEPTEMBER 4

THE WORD

So then faith cometh by hearing, and hearing by the word of God.
— ROMANS 10:17

"I just don't have any faith," some Christians say. "I've prayed and fasted for faith, but I just don't have any."

Asking for faith will never produce faith. Why not? Because faith doesn't come by *asking*; faith comes by *hearing*. By hearing what? The Word of God!

Having to encourage Christians to have faith means that the Word of God has lost its reality in their lives. None of the New Testament Epistles encourage believers to have faith. Why not? Because the Epistles were written to the Church. And its individual members are actually born into the family of God. Believers have received the Holy Spirit as their Teacher, Guide, and Comforter. And the measure of their faith will be the measure of their knowledge of the Father — and their knowledge of their privileges.

Simply study the Bible and get acquainted with your Heavenly Father. Walk in the closest possible fellowship with Him. Become familiar with your privileges as His child.

As you become one with the Word, and the Word becomes one with you, you will become mighty in faith.

Confession: *As I study the Word of God, I am becoming one with it. I am feeding upon it; I am hearing it; and faith is coming to me.*

SEPTEMBER 5

THE WITNESS

If we receive the witness of men, the witness of God is greater. . . . And this is the record, that God hath given to us eternal life, and this life is in his Son. He that hath the Son hath life . . . . — 1 JOHN 5:9,11,12

Faith in God is simply faith in His Word.

Study God's Word with this determination: *I will find out what God says and agree with it.* You can't expect the things of God to work for you if you take sides *against* His Word. This may mean unlearning certain "religious" ideas. Too often we've been religiously brainwashed, instead of scripturally taught.

Find out what God says in His Word regarding: (1) What God has made available for us in His plan of redemption; (2) What the Father is to you; (3) What Jesus is doing for you now at the right hand of the Father; and (4) What the Holy Spirit is doing in you.

Then find out from His Word what God thinks about the following: (1) *What* He says you are in Christ; (2) *Who* you are in Christ; (3) What you *have* because you're in Christ.

Even though it may not seem real in your life, start confessing, "Yes, that's mine, according to God's Word." You will then find that faith's confession creates reality.

Confession: *I agree with the witness of God. What He says I am, I am. What He says I have, I have.*

SEPTEMBER 6

REDEEMED

In whom [Jesus Christ] *we have redemption through his blood* . . . .
— **EPHESIANS 1:7**

Webster defines the word "redeem" as (1) *To buy back*; (2) *To free from captivity by payment of ransom.*

To walk in the highest kind of faith, you must know the reality of your redemption in Christ not as a doctrine, a philosophy, or a creed, but as an actual redemption out of the authority of Satan.

When Adam fell, mankind went into captivity.

But God had a plan — a great plan of redemption! And He sent the Lord Jesus Christ to consummate it. (Webster defines "consummate" as *complete in every detail: perfect.*)

Now God's Word tells us, *"In whom* [Jesus Christ] *we have redemption* . . . ."* How thankful we can be that we're not trying to *get* redeemed. We already *have* redemption! We are redeemed and delivered *now* from the authority of darkness; from the power of Satan!

Confession: *I am redeemed! In Christ I have redemption! Through His blood I have redemption! I'm not trying to get it; it's mine. I have it now! Jesus bought me back. Jesus freed me from captivity by the payment of a ransom — His own life!*

SEPTEMBER 7

TRANSLATED

Giving thanks unto the Father, which hath made us meet [able] to be partakers of the inheritance of the saints in light: Who hath delivered us from the power [authority] of darkness, and hath translated us into the kingdom of his dear Son: In whom we have redemption through his blood . . . . — COLOSSIANS 1:12-14

Darkness is the kingdom of Satan. And in that word "darkness" is everything Satan is.

Light is the Kingdom of God.

By means of the New Birth, you were translated out of the kingdom of darkness — and into the Kingdom of God's dear Son, the Kingdom of God, and the kingdom of light.

Our Heavenly Father has fitted His children (or made them "meet") to partake of an inheritance — "the inheritance of the saints *in light*"! Part of your inheritance is that God has delivered you out of Satan's authority of darkness, and He has now translated you into the kingdom of His dear Son!

God *has* made you meet — He *has* delivered you — He *has* translated you. Thank God, you can partake of your inheritance *now*. Don't relegate it to the future.

Confession: *Thank You, Father. You have made me able to partake of my inheritance now. I am redeemed. I am delivered from the authority of Satan now. I am translated into the kingdom of Your dear Son now. I am a citizen of the kingdom of light. I live in the light. I walk in the light. I am a saint in the light!*

SEPTEMBER 8

OVERCOMER

And they overcame him by the blood of the Lamb, and by the word of their testimony . . . . — **REVELATION 12:11**

Because Satan is the god of this world (2 Cor. 4:4), he will try to exercise authority over you in this life. He will try to dominate you. He will try to keep you from walking in your redemptive rights.

But you can overcome the devil every time, no matter what the test. You can overcome him because of the blood of the Lamb and the word of your testimony!

You simply have to know what the blood has bought for you: deliverance from the power (authority) of darkness (Satan), and translation (by virtue of the New Birth) into the kingdom of light. Then you have to add your testimony to that knowledge.

Stand your ground. Confess what the blood of the Lamb has wrought. Thank God, there is power in the blood! But the power in the blood won't just work automatically — you have to add your testimony to it.

Confession: *I am an overcomer. I overcome the devil in every confrontation; he never overcomes me. I overcome him by the blood of the Lamb, and by the word of my testimony.*

SEPTEMBER 9

DOMINION

... He [God] raised him [Christ] *from the dead, and set him at his own right hand in the heavenly places, Far above all principality, and power, and might, and dominion, and every name that is named, not only in this world, but also in that which is to come: And hath put all things under his feet, and gave him to be the head over all things to the church, Which is his body, the fulness of him that filleth all in all.*
— **EPHESIANS 1:20-23**

Once we are new creatures in Christ Jesus, Satan's dominion over us ended. Jesus is the Lord and Head of this new Body — the Church.

We are the Body. Christ is the Head. The Church is the Body. Christ is the Head.

The whole Body of believers — all the born-again ones — are new creatures in Christ Jesus. Then each of us individually is a new creature, too, because all of us are members of that Body.

Satan has no right to rule over the Body of Christ — and he has no right to rule over us individually either.

Christ is the Head of the Body. He is the One who is to rule and dominate the Body of Christ. Satan has lost his dominion over our spirits, our bodies, our minds, our finances, and the circumstances of our lives, because God has put *all things* under Christ's feet.

Confession: *God has put all things under Christ's feet. I am a member of the Body of Christ. The feet are in the Body, so Satan is under my feet!*

SEPTEMBER 10

CUSTODIAN

What? know ye not that your body is the temple of the Holy Ghost which is in you, which ye have of God, and ye are not your own? For ye are bought with a price: therefore glorify God in your body, and in your spirit, which are God's. — 1 CORINTHIANS 6:19,20

Some have said, "Brother Hagin, our spirits belong to the Lord all right, but our bodies haven't been redeemed yet. So we have to go on suffering sickness and disease in the physical realm."

But in the text above, God's Word tells us that not only your spirit, but your body as well, is bought with a price. Therefore, we are told, *". . . glorify God in your body . . . ."*

Does God get glory out of the devil dominating us physically? Does God get glory when the temple of the Holy Spirit is being defaced with disease? No, certainly not.

Why does God permit it, then? Because you are the custodian of your body, the temple of God's spirit. God said to *you* to do something about your body.

Learn to stand against anything that attacks your body just as quickly as you stand against whatever attacks your spirit. Simply say, "Satan, you don't have any right to put that on my body. My body belongs to God."

Confession: *My body is the temple of God. I will be a good custodian. I will glorify God in my body.*

SEPTEMBER 11

PURCHASED

Do you not know that your body is the temple (the very sanctuary) of the Holy Spirit Who lives within you, Whom you have received [as a Gift] from God? You are not your own, You were bought with a price [purchased with a preciousness and paid for, made His own]. So then, honor God and bring glory to Him in your body.

— 1 CORINTHIANS 6:19,20 (*Amplified*)

I like the way I saw a missionary, who had returned from the field, minister to the sick.

Ministering to one woman, he prayed first: "Father, this woman is Your child. She belongs to You. It's not right for the devil to dominate her. You laid her sickness and disease on Jesus, for it is written, '. . .*Himself took our infirmities, and bare our sicknesses*'" (Matt. 8:17).

Then the missionary talked to the devil: "Satan, this woman's body is a temple of the Holy Ghost. It belongs to God, and you have no right to trespass on God's property. Remove yourself from God's property!"

Then he talked to the woman: "Satan has oppressed your body with sickness, but God has made provision for your deliverance. Your body is a temple of the Holy Ghost, and you are commanded to glorify God in your body. Can God be glorified in your body by the devil dominating it? No. Therefore, stand against this sickness with me. We *demand* that Satan stop trespassing on God's property!"

Confession: *I will honor God and bring glory to Him in my body.*

SEPTEMBER 12

NO TRESPASSING!

Leave no [such] room or foothold for the devil [give no opportunity to him]. — EPHESIANS 4:27 (*Amplified*)

I remember reading in *Reader's Digest* about a lovely little patch of grass that people were prone to cut across. So the gardener built a small fence around this beautiful square of grass — just some small stakes and string. But people persisted in stepping over the string and walking across the grass. So the gardener painted a crude sign:

> Gentlemen *will not*,
> and others *must not*,
> trespass on this property!

That gave me the idea of putting up a sign on my body. You can't see it, because it's in the spirit. But the devil can see it. My sign says:

> NO TRESPASSING!
> DEVIL, THIS MEANS YOU!

I did that by faith. I've had that sign up for years now, and the devil doesn't trespass on God's property — my body.

As the custodian of your body, it's your job to see to it that Satan does not trespass on God's property.

Confession: *As a custodian of God's property, I do not allow trespassers. I leave no room, nor do I even give a foothold for the devil. I allow him no opportunity.*

SEPTEMBER 13

NEW CREATION

Therefore if any man be in Christ, he is a new creature [creation]*: old things are passed away; behold, all things are become new.*
— 2 CORINTHIANS 5:17

I'm glad I'm a new creature. I was only fifteen when I was born again, but I remember exactly what happened. Something took place inside of me. It seemed as if a two-ton load rolled off my chest. Not only did something depart *from* me — but something came *into* me!

The moment you accepted Jesus Christ as your Savior and confessed Him as your Lord (Rom. 10:9,10), you, too, were recreated. At that moment, the redemption which Jesus provided two thousand years ago became a reality to you. At that instant, the very life and nature of God were imparted to your spirit. You were recreated — born again!

The New Birth is not an experience. It is not a religion. It is not joining a church. *It is the re-birth of your spirit.*

When you were born again, old things passed away. In the sight of God, all sin and all of your past life were blotted out. All you had been — spiritually speaking — was blotted out. It ceased to exist. And you became a new man in Christ Jesus. God sees nothing in your life before the moment you were born again!

All things inside you became new. Your spirit was recreated. You passed from death unto life (1 John 3:14)!

257

Confession: *I am a new creature in Christ. I am a new creation. I am recreated. The life and nature of God are within me. I have passed from death unto life! I am a new creature!*

SEPTEMBER 14

FAMILY

But as many as received him, to them gave he power to become the sons of God, even to them that believe on his name: Which were born, not of blood, nor of the will of the flesh, nor of the will of man, but of God. — JOHN 1:12,13

No truth in all the Bible is as far reaching as the blessed fact that when we are born again we come into the family of God! God the Father is our Father!

He cares for us! He is interested in us — each of us individually — not just as a group, or a body, or a church. He is interested in each of His children, and He loves each of us with the same love.

However, our Heavenly Father is not the Father of everyone, as some supposed. Jesus said to some very religious people, *"Ye are of your father the devil . . ."* (John 8:44). Yes, God is the Creator of all mankind, but a man must be born again to become His child. He is *God* to the world, but *Father* only to the new creation man.

God is your very own Father. You are His very own child. And since He is your Father, you can be assured that He will take a father's place and perform a father's part. You can be certain that as your Heavenly Father, God loves you, and He will take care of you.

Confession: *I am born of God. I am born into God's family. God the Father is my Father. I am His very own child. He is my very own Father. He loves me. He provides for me. He takes care of me.*

SEPTEMBER 15

LOVED

I [Jesus] in them [believers], and thou [God the Father] in me, that they may be made perfect in one; and that the world may know that thou hast sent me, and hast loved them, as thou hast loved me.

— JOHN 17:23

When you know — really know — that God is your very own Father and you are His very own child, this knowledge will have the following effect on you: *You will have as much freedom and fellowship with the Father as Jesus had in His earth walk,* because God the Father loves you even as He loved Jesus! John 17:23 says so: *". . . and hast loved them, as thou hast loved me."*

"I just can't believe that God loves me as much as He loved Jesus," some may say.

Thank God, I can! I believe it, because the Bible says it, and that settles it!

You and I can say with Jesus *". . . I am not alone, because the Father is with me"* (John 16:32). Because if God loves me as He loved Jesus — and He does — then He is with me as He was with Jesus. I am never afraid, just as Jesus was never afraid. There is nothing to fear. What can man do to the man or woman whom God loves and protects!

Confession: *God the Father is my very own Father. I am His very own child. And He loves me in my earth walk just as much as He loved Jesus in His earth walk. I can fellowship with Him just as Jesus did. I am free from fear just as Jesus was, for I am not alone. My Father is with me.*

SEPTEMBER 16

BORN AGAIN

Being born again, not of corruptible seed, but of incorruptible, by the word of God, which liveth and abideth for ever. — 1 PETER 1:23

We are begotten of God.

We are born of God.

We are children of God.

We are heirs of God.

We are joint-heirs ("joint" means *equal*) with Jesus (Rom. 8:17).

In declaring this, we do not magnify ourselves. We magnify God and what He has done for us through the Lord Jesus Christ. We do not make ourselves new creatures. God made us new creatures. He is the Author and Finisher of our faith.

We are new creatures created by God in Christ Jesus!

Confession: *I am begotten of God. I am born of God. I am born of incorruptible seed by the living Word of God. I was born into the spiritual realm, given eternal life, and made a branch of the vine through the incorruptible Word of God.*

SEPTEMBER 17

HIS WORKMANSHIP

For we are his workmanship, created in Christ Jesus unto good works,
which God hath before ordained that we should walk in them.
— EPHESIANS 2:10

We believers didn't make ourselves who and what we are — God did.
So be careful about passing judgment on God's creation.

Christians who think they are being humble, sometimes say, "I'm so
unworthy." But God didn't make any unworthy new creations. I'm not
unworthy, and you're not unworthy either. To say that you are unworthy is not humility — it is ignorance of the Word of God, and it gives
place to the devil to dominate you.

We are God's workmanship! When you belittle yourself, you are actually complaining about what God has done. You're belittling His workmanship.

"Created in Christ Jesus," our scripture says. Quit looking at yourself
from the natural standpoint. Look at yourself *in Jesus.* You'll look
much better. You see, God the Father doesn't see you like anyone else
sees you. He sees you in *Christ!*

Confession: *I am God's workmanship. He made me a new creation. He*
created me in Christ Jesus. I see myself as God sees me. I see myself in
Christ.

SEPTEMBER 18

BLOTTED OUT

I, even I, am he that blotteth out thy transgressions for mine own sake, and will not remember thy sins. — ISAIAH 43:25

"I guess I'm just paying for the life I lived before I got saved," a minister who was having a hard time once said to me.

Many Christians, like that minister, are defeated, permitting things to take place in their lives, because they think that's the way it has to be. They don't know the difference between *repentance* and *doing penance*. They try to do penance for their past life. But in reality, since they repented of their sins, God has no knowledge that they've ever done anything wrong!

"I blotted out your transgression," God said, "for My own sake." God didn't do it for *your* sake, but for *His own* sake. "I will not remember your sins," He promised. If God doesn't remember them, why should you? You shouldn't!

When you were born again, you were redeemed from the penalty of sin. If you had to go on paying for your wrongdoing, you'd have to go to hell when you died, because that's part of the penalty too. However, thank God, we are redeemed not only from the *power* of sin, but also from the *penalty* of sin. Jesus took our place. He suffered the penalty of sin.

Confession: *When I repented, my Heavenly Father blotted out my transgressions. He does not remember my sins. Therefore, I won't remember them either. And I won't remind Him of them.*

SEPTEMBER 19

New Creation Facts

Be ye not unequally yoked together with unbelievers: for what fellowship hath righteousness with unrighteousness? and what communion hath light with darkness? And what concord hath Christ with Belial? or what part hath he that believeth with an infidel? And what agreement hath the temple of God with idols? for ye are the temple of the living God; as God hath said, I will dwell in them, and walk in them; and I will be their God, and they shall be my people.

— 2 CORINTHIANS 6:14-16

In order to have strong faith, you must see yourself as God sees you — and you must say about yourself what God says about you.

In the scripture quoted above, believers are called *believers*, and unbelievers are called *unbelievers*. So you can call yourself a believer.

Believers are called *righteousness*, and unbelievers are called *unrighteousness*. Have you ever called yourself *righteousness*? That's what the Bible calls you, so you are.

Believers are called *light*, and unbelievers are called *darkness*.

"And what concord hath Christ with Belial?" here the Church is identified with Christ. Christ is the Head, and we are the Body. Your head doesn't go by one name and your body by another, does it? The Church is identified with Christ — we are the Body of Christ. Think about it. Let it soak in. What a basis for faith!

Confession: *Because I am in Christ — I am a believer. I am righteousness. I am light. I am one who believes. I am the temple of God.*

SEPTEMBER 20

GOD, OUR RIGHTEOUSNESS

Even the righteousness of God which is by faith of Jesus Christ unto all and upon all them that believe . . . .   — ROMANS 3:22

To be a complete overcomer — to walk in the highest kind of faith — you must know the reality of your own righteousness in Christ.

Read Romans 3:21-26. Mark these scriptures in your Bible. Think on them — feed on them — until they become a part of your inner-consciousness.

If your Bible is a *King James Version*, keep in mind that the same Greek word which is translated in verse 26 as "just" (and other forms thereof) can also be translated "righteous." So you may substitute the word "righteous" for "just." Many translations read this way.

For example, *Young's Literal Translation of the Bible* translates Romans 3:26 this way, "for the shewing forth of His [God's] righteousness in the present time, for His being righteous, and declaring him righteous who is of the faith of Jesus."

What do these scriptures tell us? That God Himself is righteous. And that God has declared us to be righteous because we have believed in Jesus.

Confession: *God the Father declared Himself righteous through Jesus Christ. And God the Father — my very own Father — declares me righteous, for I believe in Jesus. Therefore, I am righteous. I am a recipient of the righteousness of God.*

SEPTEMBER 21

RIGHT STANDING

For if by one man's offence death reigned by one; much more they which receive abundance of grace and of the gift of righteousness shall reign in life by one, Jesus Christ. — ROMANS 5:17

For with the heart man believeth unto righteousness . . . . — ROMANS 10:10

Most people think righteousness is a state of spiritual development which you grow into by right living. The Bible teaches right living — but right living itself will never make you righteous. (If it would, you wouldn't need Jesus.)

Righteousness means rightness, or right standing with God.

Righteousness is a gift. A gift is something you receive now — whole and complete. A fruit, on the other hand, is a state of spiritual development — something which grows and develops. Thank God, *we can grow spiritually — but we cannot grow in righteousness*. In fact, you won't be any more righteous when you get to Heaven than you are right now.

How did you get to be righteous? You were born that way! Righteousness comes through the New Birth. With your heart you believed unto righteousness. When you were born again, you received the life and nature of God the Father (John 5:24,26; 2 Peter 1:4). God's nature makes you righteous!

Confession: *I have righteousness. It was given to me. I believed unto righteousness and I received it at my New Birth. I have right standing with God. I am righteous.*

SEPTEMBER 22

THE RIGHTEOUSNESS OF GOD

For he hath made him to be sin for us, who knew no sin; that we might be made the righteousness of God in him. — 2 CORINTHIANS 5:21

"For he hath made him to be sin for us, who knew no sin . . . ."

I've tested people by reading this portion of Scripture and then I've asked them, "How many of you believe that's true?" They all lifted their hands. Then I would read the last part of the same verse, *". . . that we might be made the righteousness of God in him."*

And then I would say to them, "Therefore, we — you and I — are the righteousness of God in Christ. How many of you believe that's true?"

Most of the time I couldn't get half of the crowd to lift their hands on the last part. And yet, if the first part of that verse is true, then the last part must be true too!

God made a provision for us that belongs to us. We need to realize that it is ours!

Confession: *Jesus became sin for me that I might become the righteousness of God in Him. I am the righteousness of God in Christ. God provided righteousness for me. Righteousness is mine. I have it now! I am righteous now.*

SEPTEMBER 23

REIGNING IN RIGHTEOUSNESS

For if because of one man's trespass (lapse, offense) death reigned through that one, much more surely will those who receive [God's] overflowing grace (unmerited favor) and the free gift of righteousness [putting them into right standing with Himself] reign as kings in life through the one Man Jesus Christ (the Messiah, the Anointed One).
— **ROMANS 5:17** (*Amplified*)

One of our greatest problems is relegating everything to the future. Think about the songs we sing: "When we all get to Heaven . . ." Thank God we are going to get there, but we don't have to wait until we get there to enjoy God's blessings. We can have them *now*!

Yes, we will reign with Christ *then*. But we don't have to wait until then! When does our text say we will reign as kings? Now! In life! In *this* life! How? By Jesus Christ!

Paul used this illustration of reigning as kings because in the day in which he lived, they had kings. Each king reigned over his own particular domain. His word was the final authority. What he said went! He ruled. He reigned.

The Word says that we reign in life by Christ Jesus. Why? Because we have been made the righteousness of God in Christ.

Confession: *Because I have received the free gift of righteousness, which puts me into right standing with God, I reign in life through the One, Jesus Christ. I reign as a righteous king in my domain. What I say goes!*

SEPTEMBER 24

EFFECTUAL PRAYER

. . . The effectual fervent prayer of a righteous man availeth much.
— JAMES 5:16

Jesus who is righteous became your Righteousness (1 Cor. 1:30). Your standing with God is secure. Therefore, you can stand in the Presence of God as though you had never done wrong! As though you had never sinned! Without a sense of condemnation, and without a spiritual inferiority complex! No wonder Hebrews 4:16 says, *"Let us therefore come BOLDLY unto the throne of grace, that we may obtain mercy, and find grace to help in time of need."*

When you know these powerful spiritual truths, you won't have to run around to get someone else to do your praying for you. You'll know that God the Father will hear you as quickly as He hears any other believer. Why? Because you have just as good a standing with God as any other Christian has. God doesn't love one member of His Body more than another.

People sometimes think, *If I could just get So-and-so to pray, his prayer would work. He's a real man of God.* No, that Christian may have learned how to take advantage of what belongs to him a little better than you have, but he's not any more righteous than you are. And God won't hear him pray any quicker than He will hear you pray.

Confession: *I am the righteousness of God in Christ. Because I am righteous. God hears me when I pray. And my prayers avail much.*

SEPTEMBER 25

PROVISION

If we confess our sins, he is faithful and just to forgive us our sins, and to cleanse us from all unrighteousness. — 1 JOHN 1:9

Someone once asked me, "I can see from the Scriptures that we've received remission from our past sins; that we've received the gift of righteousness; and that we've been made righteous new creatures. But what about those sins I've committed since I've become a Christian?"

Thank God for His provision — First John 1:9! This verse isn't for sinners — it's for Christians! First John is written for Christians (1 John 2:1,2).

When a man sins, he is under condemnation. He loses his sense of righteousness. But when he confesses to the Lord, "I have sinned; I have failed You. Forgive me, Lord, in Jesus' Name." The Lord does two things:

1. He forgives him

2. He cleanses him

What does God cleanse him from? All unrighteousness!

Unrighteousness is simply the word righteousness with the prefix "un" attached to it. When we are cleansed from *un*righteousness, or *non*-righteousness, then we are righteous again! Praise the Lord!

Confession: *Thank You, Father, for Your provision of First John 1:9. Thank You for Your faithfulness in forgiving and cleansing me from all unrighteousness, that I may continually have right standing in Your sight.*

SEPTEMBER 26

RECEIVING THE HOLY SPIRIT

And they were all filled with the Holy Ghost . . . .   — ACTS 2:4

. . . They sent unto them Peter and John: Who, when they were come down, prayed for them, that they might receive the Holy Ghost.
                                                            — ACTS 8:14,15

. . . Have ye received the Holy Ghost since ye believed? . . .
                                                            — ACTS 19:2

In New Testament times, it was the exception for believers not to have received the indwelling of the Holy Spirit, with the supernatural sign and initial evidence of speaking in tongues. The Epistles were written to believers who knew Jesus as Savior and who had been filled with the Holy Spirit.

Thank God, the Holy Spirit is in us too. But too often people who have been born again and then filled with the Spirit just think of themselves as having received a blessing or some kind of experience — and they miss entirely what the Word of God teaches! *A Divine Personality actually comes to live in us! God Himself in the Person of the Holy Spirit indwells us!*

Confession: *God Himself in the Person of the Holy Spirit indwells me. The Creator dwells in me. God lives in me.*

SEPTEMBER 27

GOD-INSIDE

Do you not discern and understand that you [the whole church at Corinth] are God's temple (His sanctuary), and that God's Spirit has His permanent dwelling in you [to be at home in you, collectively as a church and also individually]?

— 1 CORINTHIANS 3:16 *(Amplified)*

God Himself, after He makes us new creatures, actually makes our bodies His home. No longer does He dwell in an earth-made Holy of Holies. God says, *"What? know ye not that your body is the temple of the Holy Ghost which is in you? . . . "* (1 Cor. 6:19).

We need to become mindful that we are the temple of the Holy Spirit — we have God inside of us!

Chiseled on the front of a beautiful church in Texas is an Old Testament scripture declaring that the building was the temple of God. I get provoked every time I drive by. Why? Because these people have a lie right on the front of their church building!

To say that a church building is the house of God because He dwells there, is incorrect. God doesn't dwell in a church building. If we mean that a church building is the house of God because it has been dedicated to God, that *is* correct. But we must be careful not to confuse spiritual things with natural things. Therefore, we must be careful to state spiritual things as they really are.

Your *body* is the house or temple of God — not the building where you worship. Remembering this fact will help you in your obedience and in your faith.

Confession: *My body is the temple of God. God has His permanent dwelling in me. God is at home in me.*

SEPTEMBER 28

THE GREATER ONE WITHIN

Ye are of God, little children, and have overcome them: because greater is he that is in you, than he that is in the world. — 1 JOHN 4:4

It should be common practice for you to say in every crisis of life: *"I am a victor. I am more than a conqueror. The Creator dwells in me. The Greater One lives in me. He can put me over. The Greater One will make me a success. I can't fail."*

272

That's not bragging on you; it's bragging on the Greater One who is in you. And it will put Him to work for you!

If you're a born-again, Spirit-filled believer, you have in you, ready for your use, everything you will ever need to put you over. The divine potential of all the power that there is, indwells you!

If you will believe the Bible and begin to confess what it says, the Greater One will rise up in you and give illumination to your mind, direction to your spirit, health to your body, and help in every aspect of life.

Confession: *Greater is He who is in me than he that is in the world. The Greater One is greater than the devil, greater than disease, greater than poverty, greater than death, greater than all the power of the enemy. And He lives in me! The Greater One can make me a success. I cannot fail!*

SEPTEMBER 29

ABILITY

. . . For ye are the temple of the living God; as God hath said, I will dwell in them, and walk in them; and I will be their God, and they shall be my people. — 2 CORINTHIANS 6:16

Few Christians seem to be conscious of the fact that God lives in them. They couldn't be and still talk the way they do.

What do I mean? When a need arises in their life, some Christians are quick to say, "No, I can't do that." Why? Because they're trusting in themselves, or the flesh, to put them over. They know they don't have the ability in themselves to do it.

But if we are conscious that God is in us, then we know He has the ability to do *anything*. So we can stop saying, "I can't," and we can begin saying with confidence, "I *can* — because I'm trusting God! I *can* — because God is in me! I *can* — because greater is He that is in me than he that is in the world!"

No matter what you face — and you may be facing seemingly impossible obstacles in your life — you can say, "God will put me over! He'll make me a success! The Greater One indwells me!"

That's scriptural believing. That's faith talking. And it will put the Greater One to work for you!

Confession: *The Spirit of God indwells me. I trust the Indwelling One. He has the ability. I can do all things — because the Spirit of God is in me. I can — because He has all ability.*

SEPTEMBER 30

HELPER

And I will ask the Father, and He will give you another Comforter (Counselor, Helper, Intercessor, Advocate, Strengthener, and Standby), that He may remain with you forever. — JOHN 14:16 (*Amplified*)

It is sad to realize that some Christians ignore the Holy Spirit who is indwelling within them. I believe they mistakenly think He will come in, take control of their lives, and make them do whatever needs to be done automatically with no effort on their part — but He won't. Demons do that. They are the ones that make people do things which the people don't want to do. Demons drive, force, and control people.

The Holy Spirit, on the other hand, is a Gentleman. He will never force you to do anything against your will. In the Scriptures we see that the Holy Spirit leads, guides, prompts, and urges. He may give you a gentle "push," but He will never *force* you to act.

Some complain, "Why doesn't God do this or that?" The Holy Spirit won't do anything until you put Him to work for you! He is sent to be your Helper. He is not sent to do the job for you, but to *help you* do it.

When you know the Holy Spirit is in you, then you can act on God's Word intelligently, and the Holy Spirit will work through you. Begin to talk in line with today's confession, and you will find that He who indwells you will become more real to you.

Confession: *The Greater One is in me. I'm depending on Him. He will live big in me. He will help me. The Greater One will put me over. He will make me a success!*

OCTOBER 1

THE SAME SPIRIT

But if the Spirit of him that raised up Jesus from the dead dwell in you, he that raised up Christ from the dead shall also quicken your mortal bodies by his Spirit that dwelleth in you. — **ROMANS 8:11**

The term "mortal bodies" in this text does not refer to our resurrected bodies in the *future*; it refers to our mortal bodies *now*! ("Mortal" means *death-doomed*.) Our bodies will not be mortal in the grave. They are mortal *now*. The Spirit will not dwell in them then. The Spirit of God dwells in them *now*. Now is when we need our mortal bodies quickened by God's Spirit which indwells us.

One of the reasons for the Holy Spirit's indwelling our mortal bodies is to heal us of the diseases which are continually trying to attach themselves to us.

Healing is part of God's plan or covenant for us today. Healing is part of His provision for His children — His Body — upon the earth.

If we could understand God's plan of healing as we ought to understand it, the sick would simply be healed the moment sickness tried to touch them!

Confession: *The same Spirit that raised Christ from the dead dwells in me. He lives in me. He quickens my mortal body. He heals my mortal body.*

OCTOBER 2

HIS PERMANENT HOME

May He grant you out of the rich treasury of His glory to be strength-ened and reinforced with mighty power in the inner man by the [Holy] Spirit [Himself indwelling your innermost being and personality]. May Christ through your faith [actually] dwell (settle down, abide, make His permanent home) in your hearts . . . .

— **EPHESIANS 3:16,17** *(Amplified)*

How does Christ actually dwell, settle down, and make His permanent home in your heart? *Through your faith.*

That's what God wants to do: Make His permanent home in your heart! But that's what Christians haven't allowed Him to do! (Remember: This scripture was written to born-again, Spirit-filled Christians.)

Christians sing, "Come by here, Lord, come by here," implying that the Lord's not here — but *if* we could just get Him to come by, He might do something for us. And we sing, "Reach out and touch Jesus as He passes by." All of these sentiments are based on physical sense knowl-edge. I don't have to reach out and touch the Lord, because He lives in me! And we sing, "Just to have a touch, O Lord, from You." What do I want with *touches* when I've got the Holy Spirit living inside me?

Trust God who already dwells within you! Learn to become "God-inside-minded!"

Confession: *I am strengthened and reinforced with mighty power in my inner man by the Holy Spirit indwelling my innermost being. Christ actually dwells, settles down, abides, and makes His permanent home in my heart!*

OCTOBER 3

FELLOWSHIP

God is faithful, by whom ye were called unto the fellowship of his Son Jesus Christ our Lord. — 1 CORINTHIANS 1:9

The highest honor God has conferred upon you is to be a joint-fellowshipper with God the Father, His Son, and the Holy Spirit in carrying out God's plan for the redemption of the human race.

By virtue of the New Birth, you became related to the Creator of the universe! You became God's child. You have a relationship with Him. But relationship without fellowship is a lifeless thing. It's like marriage without love or fellowship.

Fellowship with God is the mother of faith. And God has called you individually into fellowship with His Son.

Confession: *God has called me into fellowship with His Son, Jesus Christ. I will walk in fellowship and communion with Jesus. I will talk with Jesus. I will work with Jesus. I am a joint-fellowshipper with God the Father, with Jesus Christ, and with the Holy Spirit in carrying out God's great plan of redemption for the human race.*

OCTOBER 4

FELLOWSHIP IN PRAYER

That which we have seen and heard declare we unto you, that ye also may have fellowship with us: and truly our fellowship is with the Father, and with his Son Jesus Christ. And these things write we unto you, that your joy may be full. . . . But if we walk in the light, as he is in the light, we have fellowship one with another, and the blood of Jesus Christ his Son cleanseth us from all sin. — 1 JOHN 1:3,4,7

If you have fellowship with God, and you're walking in the light as He is in the light, then prayer becomes one of the greatest assets you have inherited in Christ.

Prayer is joining forces with God the Father. It is fellowshipping with Him. It is carrying out His will upon the earth.

Prayer should never be a problem or a burden to you. It should be a joy! Prayer — real prayer — won't take anything *out* of you; it will always put something *into* you! Because you are fellowshipping with God when you pray.

Confession: *I have fellowshipped with my Father in prayer. And my joy is full! I fellowship with God. I commune with God — I talk with Him, and I listen to Him — that I may carry out His will upon the earth.*

OCTOBER 5

JOINING FORCES

What shall we then say to these things? If God be for us, who can be against us? He that spared not his own Son, but delivered him up for us all, how shall he not with him also freely give us all things?
— **ROMANS 8:31,32**

God and you are working together in carrying out His plan for the redemption of the world. God can't get along without you anymore than you can get along without Him. That's one reason why Jesus gave us the illustration of the vine and the branches. The vine can't bear fruit without the branches, and the branches can't live without the vine.

Our text today is a part of the conclusion of the first eight chapters of Romans. And this passage shows us the absolute oneness of the Father God with His children. It shows us the perfect fellowship and cooperation God's children enjoy with their Heavenly Father. It shows the mastery God's children have over the forces of darkness and circumstances. And God climaxes this passage with verse 37: *"Nay, in all these things we are more than conquerors through him that loved us."*

God is working actively on your behalf. He is standing up for you. He is fighting for you. He is supplying all your needs. Out of the treasury of His abundant grace, He is giving you His wisdom and His ability!

Confession: *God is for me! Who can be against me? I am one with my Father! He is active on my behalf. He supplies my needs. I fellowship and cooperate with Him!*

OCTOBER 6

SUFFICIENCY

And such trust have we through Christ to God-ward: Not that we are sufficient of ourselves to think any thing as of ourselves; but our sufficiency is of God; Who also hath made us able ministers of the new testament [New Covenant] . . . .   — 2 CORINTHIANS 3:4-6

We aren't ordinary people.

We're tied up with Omnipotence.

We're united with God Himself.

We're carrying out God's will here on the earth.

We're the channels through whom God is pouring Himself out upon the world.

It is perfectly normal, then, that God should become our sufficiency — that His ability should become our ability.

Now we can better understand First Corinthians 3:9, *"For we are labourers together with God . . . ."* That's fellowship with the Father! He supplies strength, wisdom, grace, and ability — the supernatural tools with which we work as able ministers of the New Covenant.

Confession: *My sufficiency is of God, who makes me an able minister of the New Covenant. God is my sufficiency. He is my ability. I am a laborer together with God in carrying out His will upon the earth.*

OCTOBER 7

THE NAME

. . . Jesus came and spake unto them, saying, ALL POWER [authority] *IS GIVEN UNTO ME in heaven and in earth. GO YE THEREFORE . . . .*
— MATTHEW 28:18,19

And these signs shall follow them that believe; IN MY NAME . . . .
— MARK 16:17

What effect would it have on your life if a wealthy man were to give you a legal document, telling you to use it to supply every one of your needs?

Yet we have been given something even greater than that! God has given us the power of attorney to use the Name of Jesus! And that Name has authority in this earth. The use of that Name is not a matter of faith, actually, but rather it is a matter of assuming your legal rights in Christ, taking your place as a son of God, and using what belongs to you. His Name belongs to you!

We have a right to use that Name against our enemies. We have a right to use that Name in our praise and worship. We have a right to use that Name in petitions. Praise God, that Name belongs to us!

That Name has been given to us that we might carry out the will of God the Father in this dispensation in which we live. The Early Church used this authority. They acted for Jesus in His stead. And we are to use His Name and act in His stead today!

Confession: *All authority in Heaven and earth resides in the Name of Jesus. The use of that Name and its authority have been given to me. I have a right to use the Name of Jesus!*

OCTOBER 8

THE FATHER GLORIFIED

And whatsoever ye shall ask in my name, that will I do, that the Father
may be glorified in the Son. — JOHN 14:13

What a striking promise!

When we are born into the family of God, the right and privilege to use
the Name of Jesus is given to us by the New Birth. All authority vested
in that Name is given to us so that the Father may be glorified in the Son.

The Son was an outcast on the earth. He hung naked before the world
and was crucified. But wherever the shame of the crucifixion has been
preached, the might, power, and honor of His Name also has gone —
shedding blessings upon the human race and bringing glory to God the
Father.

Jesus' Name is to take Jesus' place upon the earth. All Jesus could do
during His earth walk can now be done by every believer. Jesus is in that
Name. Jesus *is* that Name. All Jesus was — all He did — all He is — all
He will ever be — is in that Name now!

When we use Jesus' Name, we bring onto the scene the fullness of His
finished work at Calvary. By our use of that Name, the living, healing
Christ is present — to the glory of God the Father!

Confession: *I will use the Name of Jesus, as directed by His Word, to*
bring glory to God the Father.

OCTOBER 9

FAITH DEMONSTRATED

And Jesus answering saith unto them, Have faith in God.
— MARK 11:22

The margin of a good *King James* reference Bible renders today's text as, "Have the faith of God." Greek scholars tell us the literal translation of what Jesus said here is, "Have the God-kind of faith." Some modern translations also show the verse that way.

Even if you don't know anything about Greek, you can readily see that this would be a correct translation of this verse, because Jesus had just demonstrated to the disciples that He had that kind of faith: the God-kind of faith, the kind of faith that God used to create the world in the beginning.

Earlier in this chapter, Jesus had spoken to the barren fig tree. He hadn't prayed. He had simply said to that tree, "*. . . No man eat fruit of thee hereafter for ever . . .*" (v. 14).

The next morning, as Jesus and the disciples passed by the same place, they saw that the fig tree had dried up from its roots. Peter, remembering, said, "*. . . Master, behold, the fig tree which thou cursedst is withered away*" (v. 21).

Jesus answered him, "Have the God-kind of faith."

Jesus demonstrated the God-kind of faith for us. Then He told us to have it.

Confession: *I see the demonstration of the God-kind of faith by my Lord Jesus Christ. Jesus expects me to know about and to have the God-kind of faith! And I do have it!*

OCTOBER 10

FAITH DEFINED

For verily I say unto you, That whosoever shall say unto this mountain, Be thou removed, and be thou cast into the sea; and shall not doubt in his heart, but shall believe that those things which he saith shall come to pass; he shall have whatsoever he saith.

— MARK 11:23

Just after Jesus had demonstrated the God-kind of faith, He defined it. Mark 11:23 is Jesus' definition of the God-kind of faith. He described it as the kind of faith in which: (1) A person believes in his heart; (2) Then, a person says with his mouth what he believes in his heart; (3) And, it comes to pass.

God used that kind of faith to create the world in the beginning. God believed that what He said would come to pass! So He said, "Let there be an earth." And there was an earth. In fact, He created everything — the sun, the moon, the stars, the plants, and the animals — everything except man — by believing what He said would come to pass. Then God said it. And it came to pass. That is the God-kind of faith!

Confession: *"Whosever shall say . . ."* includes me. What I believe in my heart, and say with my mouth, shall come to pass. I live and operate in the God-kind of faith.

OCTOBER 11

FAITH DEALT

For I say, through the grace given unto me, to every man that is among you, not to think of himself more highly than he ought to think; but to think soberly, according as God hath dealt to every man the measure of faith. — ROMANS 12:3

"Faith — that's what I want!" many people say to me. "And I'm praying that God will give it to me."

If that's what you're doing, you're wasting your time. It would do no more good to pray that God will give you faith than it would to twiddle your thumbs and recite "Twinkle, Twinkle, Little Star." Praying for faith is lost motion and wasted time, because every believer already has a measure of the God-kind of faith. You don't have to get it. You don't have to pray for it. You don't have to fast for it. You don't have to promise to do better and be good to get it. You already have it!

In this verse in Romans, Paul wasn't writing to sinners, but to believers. He said, ". . . I say . . . to every man that is among you* [not to every man in the world], . . . *God hath dealt to every man the measure of faith.*"

All believers have faith! God gave it to them!

Confession: *God dealt to me the measure of faith. I have a measure of the God-kind of faith! God already gave it to me! I have it now!*

OCTOBER 12

SAVED THROUGH FAITH!

For by grace are ye saved through faith; and that not of yourselves: it is the gift of God. — EPHESIANS 2:8

Notice that the faith you are saved by is "not of yourselves." In other words, it's not a natural, human faith. It's the gift of God! That agrees with Romans 12:3, which states that *". . . God hath dealt to every man the measure of faith."*

Yet Christians will say, "I just don't have any faith."

I always answer by saying, "Then why don't you get saved? Saved people have faith! You can't be saved without faith."

All believers have faith. The Bible says they do! But many Christians don't realize they do — and they're not using the faith they have. By continually talking about how they don't have faith, they "take sides" against God, against the Bible, and against themselves, without recognizing what they are doing.

God's Word is God speaking. God and His Word are one: If God's Word says something, that is God saying it. And God's Word says that God has dealt to you the measure of faith. It has to be the God-kind of faith — because that's the only kind of faith God has!

Confession: *I am saved! And I was saved by grace through faith — the gift of God! I have a measure of the God-kind of faith! I have a measure of the kind of faith which created the world in the beginning! I have a measure of mountain-moving faith!*

OCTOBER 13

How Faith Comes

So then faith cometh by hearing, and hearing by the word of God.
— **ROMANS 10:17**

How does God give the sinner faith to be saved?

Let me read along with you from Romans chapter 10, which talks about salvation and about getting faith to be saved. (My comments are in brackets.)

"But what saith it? The word is nigh thee, even in thy mouth, and in thy heart: that is, the word of faith, which we preach [Notice that God's Word is called 'the word of faith.' That's because it *builds* faith. It causes faith to come into the hearts of those who are open to it.]; *That if thou shalt confess with thy mouth the Lord Jesus, and shalt believe in thine heart that God hath raised him from the dead, thou shalt be saved. For with the heart man believeth unto righteousness; and with the mouth confession is made unto salvation. . . . For whosoever shall call upon the name of the Lord shall be saved. How then shall they call on him in whom they have not believed?* [Now get this.] *and how shall they believe in him of whom they have not heard? . . . So then faith cometh by hearing, and hearing by the word of God."* Rom. 10:8-10,13,14,17).

You cannot believe without hearing. Faith comes by hearing. Hearing what? The Word of God!

Confession: *I listen to the Word of God. And faith comes to me.*

OCTOBER 14

THE WORD OF FAITH

But what saith it? The word is nigh thee, even in thy mouth, and in thy heart: that is, the word of faith, which we preach. — ROMANS 10:8

God's Word is called *"the word of faith."*

Faith is based on facts — the facts of God's Word.

Unbelief is founded on theories. This is my definition of a theory: "A theory is a supposition established upon ignorance of the subject under discussion." The reason why many churches are full of unbelief is because they've heard too much theory. The ministry has thrived on a psychology of unbelief, and the poor, dear church members are simply a product of what they have heard their ministers preach.

The best way to really help people is to tell them what the Bible says — to give them what God's Word says — not what some man says. Man can be wrong, but God can never be wrong.

No matter what the circumstances — no matter what has happened in your life — God's Word has something to say on the subject. Find out what God's Word says. Faith will come — and it will change things for you.

Confession: *The Word . . . God's Word . . . the word of faith . . . is near me. I hide it in my heart. I speak it with my mouth. It produces faith. And faith changes things.*

OCTOBER 15

THE SAME FAITH

We having the same spirit of faith, according as it is written, I believed, and therefore have I spoken; we also believe, and therefore speak.
— 2 CORINTHIANS 4:13

Paul wrote, *"We HAVING the same spirit of faith . . . ."*

He didn't say, "trying to have," or "praying for," or "hoping for"; he said, *"having"*! Having what? The same spirit of faith. And what kind of faith is that? The kind that (1) believes, and (2) therefore speaks.

Isn't that the same kind of faith Jesus is talking about in Mark 11:23? The kind that (1) believes in the heart, (2) says with the mouth, and (3) then it comes to pass?

Yes! That's the same spirit of faith! And Second Corinthians 4:13 says that we have it!

Confession: *I have the same spirit of faith. I believe and therefore I speak. I have a measure of the God-kind of faith. I have a measure of the kind of faith that created the worlds in the beginning. I have a measure of mountain-moving faith.*

OCTOBER 16

GROWING FAITH

We are bound to thank God always for you, brethren, as it is meet,
because that your faith groweth exceedingly . . . .
— **2 THESSALONIANS 1:3**

God gets all believers started off equally with *the measure* of faith after they are born again. He doesn't give one baby Christian more faith than He gives another. After we are born again, however, it is up to each one of us to develop the measure of faith that has been given to us.

Too many have done with their faith what the fellow did with his one talent: He wrapped it in a napkin, hid it, and didn't use it.

Your measure of faith can be increased — it can grow. But *you* are the one who increases it — not God!

Your measure of faith can be increased by doing these two things: (1) Feeding it on the Word of God, and (2) Exercising it by putting it into practice.

Confession: *God has given me the measure of faith. I will see to it that my faith grows exceedingly. I will feed my faith on the Word of God. I will exercise my faith — I will put it into practice. My faith is growing.*

OCTOBER 17

FAITH IS MEASURABLE

When Jesus heard it, he marvelled, and said to them that followed, Verily I say unto you, I have not found so great faith, no, not in Israel.
— MATTHEW 8:10

A centurion came to Jesus on behalf of his sick servant. When Jesus said, *". . . I will come and heal him"* (Matt. 8:7), the centurion answered, *". . . speak the word only, and my servant shall be healed"* (v. 8). Jesus said to him, *". . . Go thy way; and as thou hast believed, so be it done unto thee . . ."* (v. 13).

Turning to His disciples, Jesus said, *". . . I have not found so GREAT faith, no, not in Israel"* (v. 10). Therefore, it is possible for a person to develop great faith.

On the other hand, an example of little faith is seen when Peter began to sink after having walked on the water. Jesus chided Peter, saying, *". . . O thou of LITTLE faith, wherefore didst thou doubt?"* (Matt. 14:31).

If faith can be *great*, and faith can be *little*, then faith is *measurable*!

Here are some scriptures that prove faith is measurable: Growing faith (2 Thess. 1:3); weak faith (Rom. 4:19); strong faith (Rom. 4:20); rich faith (James 2:5); full of faith (Acts 6:5); perfect faith (James 2:22); unfeigned faith (1 Tim. 1:5); shipwrecked faith (1 Tim. 1:19); overcoming faith (1 John 5:4).

Confession: *My faith is growing. My faith is measuring up to a great faith, strong faith, rich faith, perfect faith, unfeigned faith, overcoming faith, I am full of faith!*

OCTOBER 18

FAITH FOOD

But he [Jesus] answered and said, It is written, Man shall not live by bread alone, but by every word that proceedeth out of the mouth of God. — MATTHEW 4:4

Here, Jesus is using a natural human term to convey a spiritual thought. He is saying that what bread, or food, is to the body, the Word of God is to the spirit, or heart, of man.

You can feed your spirit. You can feed your faith. God's Word is *faith food.*

Smith Wigglesworth, the great English preacher under whose ministry fourteen people were reportedly raised from the dead, is called an apostle of faith. He said, "I never consider myself thoroughly dressed unless I have my New Testament in my pocket. I would as soon go out without my shoes as without my Bible!"

In Wigglesworth's travels over the world, he stayed in many homes. People have reported that after each meal, even in restaurants, he would push back from the table, get out his Testament, and say, "We have fed the body; now let's feed the inward man." Then Wigglesworth would read something about faith, usually winding up giving a little faith message.

Confession: *I live by every Word of God. I feed my faith. I feed my inward man. I feed on faith food — God's Word!*

OCTOBER 19

A DEMAND

But without faith it is impossible to please him: for he that cometh to God must believe that he is, and that he is a rewarder of them that diligently seek him. — HEBREWS 11:6

God demands faith of us.

Now, if God demands that we have faith when it is impossible for us to have faith, then we have a right to challenge His justice. But if God places in our hands the means whereby faith can be produced, then the responsibility is up to us as to whether we have faith or not.

God has given us His Word, and He has told us that, *". . . faith cometh by hearing, and hearing by the word of God"* (Rom. 10:17).

F. F. Bosworth, an authority on healing and the author of the classic *Christ the Healer*, said, "Most Christians feed their bodies three hot meals a day, their spirits one cold snack a week, and then wonder why they are so weak in faith."

Confession: *I will please my Heavenly Father. I will walk in faith. I will feed my faith regularly on the faith food God has put into my hands.*

OCTOBER 20

EXERCISE

. . . According to your faith be it unto you.   — MATTHEW 9:29

If you eat natural food regularly and get no exercise, you'll grow fat and flabby. Likewise, if you don't exercise your faith, your "faith muscles" will be flabby.

Exercise your faith on the level where you are. Some Christians are beyond others in the development of their faith. As you feed and exercise your faith, it will grow. Remember, no one climbs a ladder by starting on the top rung!

Some people have become defeated because they tried to believe *beyond* their level of faith. They heard faith taught, and they tried to start at the top of the ladder. Because their faith wasn't at that level, faith didn't work for them, and they said, "That faith business doesn't work. I tried it, but it doesn't work."

Faith will work for you as you exercise it. After awhile you'll be able to believe God for things you never dreamed you could. According to your faith be it unto you. If your request is based on God's Word, and you believe God to do it, God will do it.

Wherever you are in faith, keep your attitude right. Keep a positive attitude — and keep the switch of faith turned on. Keep believing God and using your faith.

Confession: *According to my faith be it unto me. I am using my faith today. I am exercising my faith. I am putting my faith into practice. I see to it that my faith is always at work!*

OCTOBER 21

FAITH'S LOCATION

For with the heart man believeth . . . .   — ROMANS 10:10

. . . And shall not doubt in his heart, but shall believe . . . .
          — MARK 11:23

Faith — real faith, Bible faith, scriptural faith — is of the heart, not the head.

What does it mean to believe with the heart? What is the heart of man?

Well, it's not the physical organ that pumps blood through your body and keeps you alive. You couldn't believe with your physical heart any more than you could believe with your physical hand, eye, ear, nose, or foot!

Consider how we use the term "heart" today. When we talk about the "heart" of a tree, we mean the center, the very core, of the tree. When we talk about the "heart" of a subject, we mean the most important part of that subject; the very center of it; the main part around which the rest revolves.

Likewise, when God speaks of man's "heart," He is speaking about the main part of the man — the very center of man's being — his spirit!

Confession: *With my heart I believe God. I do not doubt in my heart. I believe in my heart.*

OCTOBER 22

THE HIDDEN MAN

But let it be the hidden man of the heart, in that which is not corrupt-
ible, even the ornament of a meek and quiet spirit, which is in the sight
of God of great price. — 1 PETER 3:4

For which cause we faint not; but though our outward man perish, yet
the inward man is renewed day by day. — 2 CORINTHIANS 4:16

Let's allow God to tell us what the heart is. In First Peter 3:4, God says
that the heart is a man — a *hidden* man.

That is, this hidden man is hidden to the physical senses. You can't see
him with your physical eye, nor feel him with your physical hand.
That's because he is not a physical being; he is the "inward man" spoken of in Second Corinthians 4:16.

These two expressions found in Scripture give us God's definition of the
human spirit: "The inward man" and "the hidden man of the heart."

Confession: *I believe God from the hidden man of my heart. I believe*
God from my inward man. I believe God from my spirit.

OCTOBER 23

SPIRIT BEING

And the very God of peace sanctify you wholly; and I pray God your whole spirit and soul and body be preserved blameless unto the coming of our Lord Jesus Christ. — 1 THESSALONIANS 5:23

You *are* a spirit.

You *have* a soul.

And you *live* in a body.

With your *spirit* you contact the spiritual world.

With your *body* you contact the physical world.

And with your *soul* you contact the intellectual world.

These are the only three realms you contact. There are no more.

Man is a spirit being who was created in the image of God, who is a Spirit. (*See* Genesis 1:26; John 4:24.)

You, too, are a spirit being. And it will help your faith to think like that, because faith is of the heart, or the spirit, or the inward man. (The terms "spirit" of man and "heart" of man are used interchangeably throughout the Bible.) Faith is not of the head. Faith is not of the body. *Faith is of the heart!*

Confession: *I am a spirit. I have a soul. And I live in a body. I am a spirit being created in the image of God. With my spirit I contact God. With my spirit I believe God!*

OCTOBER 24

HEART VS. HEAD

Trust in the Lord with all thine heart; and lean not unto thine own understanding. — PROVERBS 3:5

Your own understanding is simply your own mental processes — your own human thinking. In other words, we could read this verse, "Trust in the Lord with all thine heart; and lean not unto thine own *head.*"

Faith will work in your heart with doubt in your head! Many Christians are defeated because when a doubt enters their mind, they say, "I'm doubting." But Jesus didn't say, ". . . and shall not doubt in his *head.*" Jesus said, ". . . *and shall not doubt in his heart, but shall believe . . .*" (Mark 11:23). It's heart faith that gets the job done — not head faith.

Some of the greatest miracles that have ever happened in my life came when I began to make such faith statements as, "I believe from my heart that I receive my healing" — even though my *head* was saying, "It's not so. It's not so!" (And I was healed of two serious organic heart problems and an incurable blood disease in my almost totally paralyzed body.)

Do you ever have trouble with your head? Then just trust in the Lord with all your heart (not your head), and lean not unto your own understanding!

Confession: *I trust in the Lord with all my heart. I do not lean to my own understanding. I believe from my heart that what God's Word says is true.*

OCTOBER 25

HEAD FAITH

The other disciples therefore said unto him [Thomas], We have seen the Lord. But he said unto them, Except I shall see in his hands the print of the nails, and put my finger into the print of the nails, and thrust my hand into his side, I will not believe. And after eight days . . . came Jesus, the doors being shut, and stood in the midst, and said, Peace be unto you. Then saith he to Thomas, Reach hither thy finger, and behold my hands; and reach hither thy hand, and thrust it into my side: and BE NOT FAITHLESS, BUT BELIEVING. And Thomas answered and said unto him, My Lord and my God. Jesus saith unto him, Thomas, because thou hast seen me, thou hast believed: BLESSED ARE THEY THAT HAVE NOT SEEN, AND YET HAVE BELIEVED.
— JOHN 20:25-29

Thomas' faith was head faith. And Jesus did not commend Thomas for it. Jesus said, "You have believed because you have seen." Anyone can have that kind of faith, whether he be saint or sinner. That's head faith. Head faith is believing what your physical senses tell you.

Jesus commended heart faith. He said, *". . . blessed are they that have not seen, and yet have believed."* To believe with the heart means to believe apart from what your physical body or physical senses may indicate. The physical man believes what he sees with his physical eyes, hears with his physical ears, or feels with his physical senses. But the heart, on the other hand, believes in the Word of God regardless of what the physical senses say.

Confession: *I am not faithless; I am believing. I believe according to what God's Word says, regardless of what I see, hear, or feel.*

OCTOBER 26

HEART FAITH

Who against hope BELIEVED in hope, that he [Abraham], *might become the father of many nations, ACCORDING TO THAT WHICH WAS SPOKEN, So shall thy seed be.* — ROMANS 4:18

For God's own account of Abraham and his faith, read Romans chapter 4. Verse 18 says that Abraham believed. What did Abraham believe? He believed ". . . *according to that which was spoken . . . .*"

Abraham did not believe according to what he could *see*. Abraham did not believe according to what he could *feel*. Abraham did not believe according to what his physical senses told him. Abraham did not even believe according to what his mind told him. Abraham believed according to what was spoken by God!

Knowing this scripture has brought me through many hard places. When opposition and contradicting circumstances have said, "No, you don't have it." I've just stood my ground, I've said from my heart, "I believe according to that which is spoken."

And "that which is spoken" is God's Word!

Confession: *I believe according to that which is spoken. I believe according to that which is written. I am not moved by what I see. I am not moved by what I feel. I am moved only by what I believe!*

OCTOBER 27

AS THOUGH THEY WERE

(As it is written, I have made thee a father of many nations,) before him whom he believed, even God, who quickeneth the dead, and calleth those things which be not as though they were.— ROMANS 4:17

If Abraham believed according to what was spoken, exactly what *was* spoken? What did Abraham believe?

When Abram (as he was then called) was ninety-nine years old, the Lord said to him, *"Neither shall thy name any more be called Abram, but thy name shall be Abraham; for a father of many nations have I made thee"* (Gen. 17:5). Notice that God did not say, "I'm *going* to do it"; He said, "I *have made* thee."

When God made Abraham that promise, Abraham was childless. But Abraham was told he was not to believe he was "going to be" (future tense) a father. (Those who are always "going to" get something never get it. It is the same with the ones who say, "I'm going to get saved sometime." Or "I'm going to get my healing sometime.")

No, faith is always present tense! Abraham had to believe he "was made" the father of many nations.

For, you see, faith calleth those things which be not as though they were. That's what causes them to come into being!

Confession: *Like my Heavenly Father, I call those things which be not as though they were. And they come into being! They're mine. I have them now!*

OCTOBER 28

IMITATORS OF GOD

Therefore be imitators of God [copy Him and follow His example], as well-beloved children [imitate their father].

— EPHESIANS 5:1 (*Amplified*)

"I'm not going to believe I've got something I don't see!" one preacher said to me.

"Do you believe you have a brain?" I replied.

"Certainly," he said.

"Have you ever seen it?"

Abraham believed something he couldn't see. Thomas refused to believe something he couldn't see. Thomas' name isn't listed in the gallery of the heros of faith in Hebrews chapter 11. But Abraham's name is.

Another person once said to me, "Well, it would be all right for God to call those things which be not as though they were, because He's God. But it would be wrong for me to do that."

If it's wrong for *you* to do it, it's wrong for *God* to do it! Children of the devil act like the devil. Children of God are to act like God. God is a faith God. And we are faith children of a faith God. Because we are faith children of a faith God, we are to act in faith. And faith calls those things which be not as though they were!

Confession: *I am the faith child of a faith God. I imitate God, my Father. I follow His example as His well-beloved child. I act in faith. I call those things which be not as though they were. And they become.*

OCTOBER 29

STRONG FAITH

He [Abraham] staggered not at the promise of God through unbelief; but was strong in faith, giving glory to God; And being fully persuaded that, what he had promised, he was able also to perform.
— ROMANS 4:20,21

"I'm weak in faith," one woman said to me. "Will you pray that I'll grow stronger in faith?"

"No," I said, "I won't. To tell you the truth, you are *strong* in faith! You just don't know it. May I ask you some questions?"

"Yes, of course," she said.

"Are you fully persuaded — fully persuaded — that what God has promised He is able to perform?"

"Certainly," she said. "I know God can do anything He said He would do. And I know He will do it."

"Can you say, 'Glory to God,' and praise God for His promises?"

"Certainly, I can. I do that every day."

"Then you are strong in faith," I said, "according to Romans 4:20 and 21." Abraham was also strong in faith. What is strong faith? Giving glory to God. And being fully persuaded that what God has promised He is able also to perform. If you can meet these two requirements, then you are strong in faith too.

Confession: *I am fully persuaded that what God has promised, He is able to perform. I can give glory to God. I am strong in faith. I have the Abraham-kind of faith. I have a measure of the God-kind of faith.*

OCTOBER 30

UNFORGIVENESS

And when ye stand praying, forgive, if ye have ought against any: that your Father also which is in heaven may forgive you your trespasses.
— **MARK 11:25**

Jesus had just made those marvelous, thrilling, amazing, astounding statements recorded in Mark 11:23 and 24. (And no one has ever yet plumbed the depths of those statements.)

But at the same time — at the same scene — and with the same breath — Jesus said, *"And when ye stand praying, forgive . . . ."*

If there is an air of unforgiveness about you, your faith won't work! Your prayers won't work!

Unforgiveness is the only hindrance to faith that Jesus ever mentioned. Therefore, the subject of unforgiveness must be of primary importance. (If my prayers and my faith don't work, the area of unforgiveness would be the first place I'd examine in my life.)

However, I never permit unforgiveness about anyone to enter into my mind at all. I refuse to think about anything evil. I refuse to be resentful toward anyone. No matter what they have done to me — no matter what they have said about me — I will not permit it to affect me.

Confession: *My prayers work. My faith works. I do not permit unforgiveness into my being. I refuse to have ought against anyone.*

OCTOBER 31

FORGIVENESS

But if ye do not forgive, neither will your Father which is in heaven forgive your trespasses.   — MARK 11:26

"Brother Hagin," a woman once said, "cast this old, unforgiving spirit out of me. I've got something against a woman here at church, and I can't forgive her. I don't seem to have the ability to forgive."

I replied, "Do you ever have to forgive your husband?"

"Oh, yes. I have to forgive him, and he has to forgive me."

"I thought you said you didn't have the ability to forgive."

She laughed and said, "I can forgive, can't I?"

"Certainly," I said, "if you can forgive one person, you can forgive another."

She understood and replied, "I can forgive. I do forgive. That's it!"

And it's just that simple. Don't complicate forgiveness. Jesus said, "When ye stand praying, forgive." That means we can forgive. Jesus didn't ask us to do something we can't do.

Confession: *I can forgive. I am quick to forgive. And my Father in Heaven forgives me.*

NOVEMBER 1

HEART LOVE

. . . The love of God is shed abroad in our hearts by the Holy Ghost which is given unto us. — **ROMANS 5:5**

"I hate my mother-in-law!" a minister's wife once said to me. "I don't even know if I'm saved or not, because the Bible says, '*Whosoever hateth his brother is a murderer: and ye know that no murderer hath eternal life abiding in him*'" (1 John 3:15).

I knew this woman was saved and filled with the Holy Spirit. But I also knew that she was letting the devil dominate her through her mind and flesh.

So I said, "Look me in the eye and say out loud, 'I hate my mother-in-law.' As you're saying this, check up on the inside of you — because the love of God has been shed abroad in our *hearts*, not our *heads* — and tell me what is happening."

She did what I had asked and said, surprised, "Something is 'scratching' me down in my spirit!"

"Yes, something on the inside of you is trying to get your attention," I told her. "The love of God in your spirit wants to dominate you, but you are allowing your mind — where those thoughts have built up — to dominate you. In your heart, you actually love everyone."

"Yes, I do," she agreed. "What shall I do now?"

"Act in love. And let your heart dominate you — not your head."

Confession: *I let the love of God shed abroad in my heart by the Holy Spirit dominate me.*

NOVEMBER 2

FAITH RELEASED

For verily I say unto you, That whosoever shall SAY unto this mountain, Be thou removed, and be thou cast into the sea; and shall not doubt in his heart, but shall believe that those things which he SAITH shall come to pass; he shall have whatsoever he saith. — MARK 11:23

Years ago, after spending an entire day in a church sanctuary praying, waiting on God, and reading and meditating on His Word, I lay down on the carpeting in front of the altar. I had come to the place where my mind was quiet. About that time, the Lord spoke to me in my spirit in as clear a voice as I'd ever heard.

He said, "Did you ever notice in Mark chapter 11, verse 23, that the word 'say' is included three times in some form, and the word 'believe' is used only once?"

I arose to a seated position and replied aloud, "No, I never noticed that!" (And there's no telling how many hundreds of times I had quoted that verse.)

Then the Lord said, "My people are not missing it primarily in their believing. They are missing it in their saying. They have been taught to believe, but *faith must be released in words through your mouth. You can have what you say.*" He added, "You will have to do three times as much teaching about the saying part as the believing part to get people to see this."

Confession: *I have what I say. I release my faith in words.*

NOVEMBER 3

WHAT I SAY

For verily I say unto you, That whosoever shall say unto this mountain, Be thou removed, and be thou cast into the sea; and shall not doubt in his heart, but shall believe that those things which he saith shall come to pass; HE SHALL HAVE WHATSOEVER HE SAITH.
— MARK 11:23

Let's examine what Jesus said in today's text: *". . . and shall not doubt in his heart, but shall believe* [that is, believe in his heart] *that those things which he saith shall come to pass . . . ."* Those things that you *say* are your words — your confessions — and those words give you power over demons, disease, and circumstances.

What is it Jesus says you shall have? What you believe for? No. Many people think, *If I believe strongly enough, it will come to pass.* But at the same time, they are talking unbelief, so what they are asking for *cannot* come to pass!

Jesus did not say, "He shall have whatsoever he BELIEVETH"; He said, *". . . he shall have whatsoever he SAITH."*

For you do receive what you say. If you're not satisfied with what you have in life, then check up on what you are saying — what you are confessing. *All you have and all you are today is a result of what you believed and said yesterday!*

Confession: *I believe in my heart. I believe in my words.*

NOVEMBER 4

WORDS

Thou art snared with the words of thy mouth, thou art taken with the words of thy mouth. — PROVERBS 6:2

Many Christians blame certain things on the devil, when actually they are taken captive by the words of their own mouths. One writer expressed it this way:

> You said you could not — and the moment you said it you were whipped. You said you did not have faith — and doubt rose up like a giant and bound you. You are imprisoned with your own words. You talked failure, and failure held you in bondage.

Our words dominate us. That's what Jesus was saying in Mark 11:23: *". . . he shall have whatsoever he saith."*

Never talk failure. Never talk defeat. Never acknowledge for one moment that God's ability or power cannot put you over. If you do talk failure or defeat, you are acknowledging that God cannot and has not put you over in life.

But thank God, He *can*! And He *has*! If you will believe right and talk right, you will walk in the reality of it!

Confession: *I refuse to talk failure. I refuse to talk defeat. God puts me over in life.*

NOVEMBER 5

WHAT TO SAY

Ye are of God, little children, and have overcome them: because greater is he that is in you, than he that is in the world. — 1 JOHN 4:4

What is the Holy Spirit doing in you?

Is the Holy Spirit just a "spiritual hitchhiker?" Does He just hitchhike a ride through life with you? Is He just some excess baggage for you to carry through life?

No! The Holy Spirit lives within you to help you!

He lives within you to strengthen you!

He lives within you to comfort you!

He lives within you to put you over in life!

Make positive confessions like this instead of talking failure and doubt.

Confession: *I believe that the Greater One lives in me. I believe that He is greater than the devil. I believe that He is greater than the tests and trials I may be facing. I believe that He is greater than the storm I may be going through. I believe that He is greater than the problems that may be confronting me. I believe that He is greater than the circumstances which may appear to have me bound. I believe that the Greater One is greater than sickness and disease. I believe that the Greater One is greater than anything and everything! And the Greater One dwells in me!*

NOVEMBER 6

EVIL REPORT

. . . We be not able to go up against the people; for they are stronger than we. And they brought up an evil report of the land which they had searched unto the children of Israel, saying, The land, through which we have gone to search it, is a land that eateth up the inhabitants thereof; and all the people that we saw in it are men of a great stature . . . giants . . . and we were in our own sight as grasshoppers, and so we were in their sight. — NUMBERS 13:31-33

Israel came out of Egypt and to the border of Canaan, to a place called Kadesh-barnea. From there they sent twelve men to spy out the land of Canaan. And the Bible says that ten of those spies brought back "an evil report."

What is an evil report? It is a report of doubt. (A believer has no more business peddling doubt than he does peddling dope!)

God had already told the children of Israel that He had given them this land flowing with milk and honey. They acknowledged that it was, indeed, a land flowing with milk and honey. "BUT," they complained, "there are giants in the land, and we are not able to take it!"

The children of Israel confessed what they believed. They *believed* they couldn't succeed. Then they *said,* "We can't." And they *received* exactly what they said! Israel accepted the majority report — the evil report — and said they couldn't take the land. And Israel got exactly what they said: God did not allow that generation to take the land.

Jesus said in Mark 11:23 that you will have whatever you say.

Confession: *I refuse to be a doubt peddler. I refuse to have an evil report!*

NOVEMBER 7

A GOOD REPORT

And Caleb stilled the people before Moses, and said, Let us go up at once, and possess it; for we are well able to overcome it.
— NUMBERS 13:30

And Joshua . . . and Caleb . . . spake unto all the company of the children of Israel, saying, The land, which we passed through to search it, is an exceeding good land. If the Lord delight in us, then he will bring us into this land, and give it us; a land which floweth with milk and honey. Only rebel not ye against the Lord, neither fear ye the people of the land; for they are bread for us: their defence is departed from them, and the Lord is with us: fear them not. — NUMBERS 14:6-9

Joshua and Caleb were the two spies who had a good report. They didn't deny that giants were in Canaan; they simply added that the children of Israel would be able to overcome the giants.

"We are well able to overcome them," they said, "for the Lord is with us!" That was their good report.

Similarly, we believers must not stick our heads in the sand like ostriches and deny that problems and difficulties exist in our lives. Yes, the "giants" are there — but we are well able to overcome them, because the Lord is with us!

When you face the giants of life, don't have a negative confession. Don't talk doubt and have an evil report. *Faith always has a good report!*

Confession: *I am well able to overcome the giants in my life — because the Lord is with me! Greater is He who is in me than he who is in the world.*

NOVEMBER 8

FEELINGS

. . . For he hath said, I will never leave thee, nor forsake thee.
— HEBREWS 13:5

A woman came up to me at the close of a service where I had taught on faith. She was crying almost hysterically. She said, "Brother Hagin, pray for me!"

"What is the matter?" I asked.

"It seems like the Lord has forsaken me!"

"What awful sin have you committed to make the Lord forsake you?"

"As far as I know, I haven't done anything," she said. "It just seems like the presence of the Lord is gone from me."

"The Bible doesn't say we walk by 'seems like,'" I explained to her. "It says we walk by faith. And God's Word says that the Lord will never leave you, nor forsake you."

"I know that," she cried, "but it just seems like He has."

"You have more faith in 'seems like' than you have in the Bible."

"But I know what I feel!" she said, almost angrily.

"Yes," I said, "but I know my Jesus. Jesus said it, and I believe it. We cannot be concerned by what we feel."

If you start believing right, thinking right, and talking right, it won't be long until you'll be feeling right!

Confession: *Jesus will never leave me, nor forsake me. He said it. I believe it. And I say it.*

NOVEMBER 9

PRAYING AND SAYING

Therefore I say unto you, What things soever ye desire, when ye pray, believe that ye receive them, and ye shall have them. — MARK 11:24

Faith will work by *saying* without *praying* (notice Mark 11:23 doesn't mention praying), but faith also works by prayer.

However, when you *pray* it, you still have to *say* (or confess) it.

Let me repeat that: *Faith will work by SAYING it, or it will work by PRAYING it, but when you PRAY it, you still have to SAY it.*

Mark 11:23 and 24 brought me off a bed of sickness many years ago. After I had prayed, then I began to *say* (not think) out loud in my room, "I believe that I receive healing for my body." Then I specified each thing that was wrong with me: "I believe I receive healing for the heart condition. I believe I receive healing for this paralysis. I believe I receive healing for the incurable blood disease."

And just in case I had missed anything, I concluded, "I believe that I receive healing from the top of my head to the soles of my feet."

Within the hour every symptom of physical deficiency disappeared from my body, and I was standing on the floor beside the bed — healed!

Confession: *What things soever I desire, when I pray, I believe that I receive them. I confess what I believe. I hold fast to my confession. And I never fail to receive them.*

NOVEMBER 10

Believing First

Jesus said unto him, If thou canst believe, all things are possible to him that believeth. — MARK 9:23

There is just a shade of difference in what you *believe* when you say it, and when you pray it.

Look again at Mark 11:23 and 24. Jesus didn't say, "Just believe." He told us exactly *what* to believe. Faith by saying is: *". . . believe that those things which he saith shall come to pass . . ."* (v. 23). When you are believing that those things which you say shall come to pass, then that means they haven't come to pass yet. But keep on believing that those things you said — be sure you've said it — shall come to pass. I always keep saying right in the face of contradictory circumstances, "It shall come to pass." What will happen then? *". . . He shall have whatsoever he saith."* Sooner or later you shall have it!

Faith by praying is: *". . . when ye pray, believe that ye receive them . . ."* (v. 24). *When* you pray. Not *after* you pray. Not next week. But *when* you pray — that very moment — believe. Believe what? Believe that you receive your requests. Begin to say, "I believe that I receive." And what will happen? *". . . Ye shall have them!"*

Yes, the having will come, but the having doesn't come first. Believing comes first; then the having follows.

Confession: *I am a believer. When I pray, I believe that I receive. When I say, I believe that what I say shall come to pass.*

NOVEMBER 11

FAITH FOR FINANCES

Let us hold fast the profession [confession] *of our faith without wavering; (for he is faithful that promised).* — HEBREWS 10:23

When I've needed things in my own life, I've always stood on Mark 11:23 and said (or confessed) what I was believing God for. I've always just *said* it, and not *prayed* it.

(When another person is involved, however, what they believe can affect your prayers; especially if they are not in agreement with you.)

I haven't prayed about money for years, and I've never been without money. I always just say, "The money will come," and it comes. When I need a certain amount, I am specific in my confession: I specify the amount I need.

Once I needed $1,500 by the first of the month. So I *said* it. And I kept saying it. During times of prayer, I didn't pray it; I just said, "By the first of the month I'll have $1,500."

When the first of the month came, I had $1,500! Praise the Lord!

Confession: *I hold fast to my confession of faith without wavering. For He is faithful who promises. And I have what I say.*

NOVEMBER 12

IN ALL REALMS

Beloved, I wish above all things that thou mayest prosper and be in health, even as thy soul prospereth. — 3 JOHN 2

The Lord Himself taught me about faith for finances many years ago. I was in the field ministry then, and I had been fasting and praying several days concerning a severe shortage of finances. The Lord spoke to me, saying, "Your trouble is you aren't practicing what you preach. You preach faith, but you don't practice it."

I protested, "Why, Lord, I do!"

"Oh, you practice faith when it comes to healing, and that is commendable," He said. "You've used your faith for salvation, the baptism in the Holy Spirit, and healing. But *faith is the same in every realm.* If you needed healing, you would claim it by faith and publicly announce you were healed. You must do the same thing with finances.

"I'll tell you what to do: First, never pray about money — that is, in the sense you have been praying. What you need is on earth. I'm not going to rain money down from Heaven. It would be counterfeit, and I'm not a counterfeiter. What you need is down there. I made the earth and everything in it. And I didn't make it for the devil and his crowd. Claim whatever you need. Just say, 'Satan, take your hands off of my money.' Because Satan is the one keeping it from you, not Me."

Confession: *Jesus has redeemed me from the hand of the enemy. And in the Name of Jesus, I have authority to claim what God has provided.*

NOVEMBER 13

YOUR DESIRES

Therefore I say unto you, What things soever ye desire, when ye pray, believe that ye receive them, and ye shall have them.

— MARK 11:24

". . . What things soever ye desire . . . ."

No, not what things soever your grandpa desires. Not what things soever your aunt desires. Not what things soever your husband desires. Not what things soever your wife desires.

You *can* get your desires. However, if what you desire is not what someone else desires, you won't be able to push your desires off on them. Why? Because when someone else is involved, their will comes into play on the situation.

Your faith will always work for you in your own life. And sometimes — not always — you can make your faith work for someone else.

Confession: *My faith always works for me in my own life. By divine wisdom I will know when I can make my faith work for others.*

NOVEMBER 14

AGREEMENT

Again I say unto you, That if two of you shall agree on earth as touching any thing that they shall ask, it shall be done for them of my Father which is in heaven. — MATTHEW 18:19

You won't be able to get someone healed if you're believing that they will live, but they're believing they will die! There's no agreement there. When praying for others, it is important to get them to agree.

Usually, when someone comes to me with a prayer request, I say (if I can agree with it), "Let's join hands now and agree. Listen while I pray, and agree with my prayer. Because if we both pray at once and we don't pay attention to each other, you may be praying in one direction and I may be praying in another."

Once a woman came for prayer for a financial need. I prayed, "Father, we agree concerning the one hundred dollars this family needs by the first of next month. We agree that by the first of the month they'll have this extra one hundred dollars. You said that if two of you agree as touching anything they ask, it shall be done. We agree that it is done, and we thank You for it now, in the Name of Jesus. Amen."

I looked at the woman and asked, "Is it done?"

She started crying, "I hope it is," she said.

It wasn't. There was no agreement.

Confession: *If there are two of us . . . and we're on earth . . . and we agree as touching anything we ask in line with God's Word . . . it shall be done for us of our Father in Heaven!*

NOVEMBER 15

SPIRITUAL BABES

As newborn babes, desire the sincere milk of the word, that ye may grow thereby. — 1 PETER 2:2

Under what circumstances can you help others?

As long as people are bona fide baby Christians, you can carry them on your faith and get things for them. It's the easiest thing in the world to get a new Christian healed. And it's comparatively easy to get Christians healed who have never been taught about divine healing. But God expects a little more from people who have had time and opportunity to know about spiritual matters.

When my wife and I were married in November 1938, she was a Methodist, and she knew nothing about healing. In December, the first real Norther' blew into Texas and she got a sore throat. She said, "I'll have to go have my throat swabbed out. I'll have a bad throat all winter. I do every year."

That was a good opportunity to teach her about divine healing. Remembering Mark 11:23, I said, "No, we'll not have your throat swabbed out. This chronic sore throat will leave you and will never return."

It left. And all these years have come and gone, and she has never had a sore throat since. But I couldn't do that for her today, because she has developed her own faith, and God expects her to use it.

Confession: *I do desire the Word, that I may grow thereby — that my faith may grow thereby — so that I can help others.*

NOVEMBER 16

FAITH FOR ANOTHER

For the eyes of the Lord run to and fro throughout the whole earth, to shew himself strong in the behalf of them whose heart is perfect toward him . . . . — 2 CHRONICLES 16:9

I was told I had an emergency telephone call. My sister, Oleta, was on the line, crying hysterically. She told me her daughter's baby had been born dead. The doctor now said the baby was alive, but he couldn't live, and he wouldn't be normal if he did live, because of a lack of oxygen to his brain. The doctor told the family, "The baby's face is deformed. It would be better if you didn't see him. We'll just dispose of the body when the baby does expire."

Oleta cried, "Benny [the baby's father] wants you to pray."

I knew my family were just babies when it came to spiritual matters, and I thought about Mark 11:23, "Oleta, where is Benny?" I asked.

"Right outside the phone booth," she replied.

"Now listen — the minute you hang up, turn to Benny and *say,* 'Benny, Uncle Ken said the baby will live and not die. He will be all right.'"

"Do you think so?" Oleta asked.

"No, I don't *think so; I know so.* I've got Jesus' Word for it."

Not ten minutes later, a nurse came running out and told them, "You can see the baby! He's all right. While we were looking at him, his face filled out just like you'd blow up a balloon!"

You can't shut God out, if you'll believe Him.

Confession: *I believe God. I believe He desires to show Himself strong on my behalf.*

NOVEMBER 17

THE SENT WORD

He sent his word, and healed them . . . .   — PSALM 107:20

An unsaved uncle of mine once contacted my mother. He wanted her to get in touch with me so I would pray for his daughter, who was dying. I told Momma when he called back to tell him that I said my cousin would live and not die.

"Oh, son, have you heard from the Lord?" Momma asked. (She knew the Lord sometimes told me things.)

"Yes, I heard from the Lord. She will live and not die," I assured her.

"Praise the Lord. That's fine."

"Yes, I heard from the Lord in Mark 11:23."

"Oh," she said, her voice dropping in disappointment.

People put more emphasis on some kind of manifestation than they do the Word. Don't do that. Put the Word first.

When I told Momma again what to tell my uncle, she said, "Do you suppose it will work, Son?"

"Certainly, it will work! Will the multiplication table work? No one ever says, 'I don't know if I've got enough faith to work the multiplication table. If you'll work the multiplication table, it will work. And if you'll work Mark 11:23, it will work. It's the Word that does it.'"

That's where some miss it. They think *they're* going to have to perform. No, *God* does it. All we're to do is what the Word tells us to do.

Confession: *God's Word works. I act on it, and it works for me.*

NOVEMBER 18

GROWING UP

That we henceforth be no more children . . . . — EPHESIANS 4:14

I learned later that a few minutes after Momma told my uncle that I had said my cousin would recover, my cousin suddenly opened her eyes and was perfectly all right! She was in intensive care, with three doctors around her bed, and the head surgeon had said she'd never come out of it.

I knew she would be well all the time, because Mark 11:23 said so. Through the years, I could make the Word work *once* with each of my relatives, bringing the supernatural to them. But I could never do it again. You see, that gave them concrete evidence that the Word worked. But when they'd come back to me the second time, I couldn't carry them any longer on my faith. God expected *them* to do a little bit the next time — at least to agree with me.

You can't always make the Word work for others. It is not right to carry people spiritually all their lives any more than it is for parents to carry their children in the natural all their lives. There comes a day when they have to get out on their own. And there comes a day when God says, "Put that big young'un down and let him walk!"

Confession: *I am growing up spiritually. I am growing in faith.*

NOVEMBER 19

THANKSGIVING

Oh that men would praise the Lord for his goodness, and for his wonderful works to the children of men! And let them sacrifice the sacrifices of thanksgiving, and declare his works with rejoicing.
— PSALM 107:21,22

The forefathers of the United States set aside a day each year to offer thanks to God for His blessings on them in this new world. He had blessed them both spiritually and materially.

We should also offer thanksgiving to God for the spiritual and material blessings of life He has bestowed upon us. And we should thank God for His loving protection and care for us.

This Thanksgiving season, let's look into God's Word to see what He has to say about "the giving of thanks." We'll look into the New Testament, because we live under the New Covenant, to see what the New Covenant says we are to give thanks for.

Confession: *I praise the Lord for His goodness. I sacrifice the sacrifice of thanksgiving, and declare His works with rejoicing. I thank Him for the spiritual and material blessings in life. I thank God for His protection and care.*

NOVEMBER 20

First of All

I exhort therefore, that, first of all, supplications, prayers, interces-
sions, and giving of thanks, be made for all men; For kings, and for all
that are in authority . . . . — 1 TIMOTHY 2:1,2

When we follow the directions in God's Word and put first things first,
we get results. This is especially true in regard to Scripture. If we follow
the directions and put first things first, we can expect to receive from
God the things He has provided for us.

"First of all" means first of all.

But also notice that along with supplications, along with prayers, along
with intercessions, the Word inserts, "giving of thanks."

Lest we misunderstand exactly who he is talking about, Paul goes on to
tell us exactly who these "all men" are. "Kings" would include presi-
dents, rulers, and other leaders of nations. "All that are in authority"
would include state, county, and city leaders, etc.

If we as Christians want to please God, who will we place as number
one on our prayer and thanksgiving list? Ourselves? Our children? Our
grandchildren? Our church? No. If we want to please God, we will have
to do exactly as God said to do. We will have to pray and offer thanks
first of all for all who are in authority.

325

Confession: *Thank You, Lord, for our president. Thank You for all who*
are in authority.

NOVEMBER 21

GIVING OF THANKS

I exhort therefore, that, first of all, supplications, prayers, intercessions, and giving of thanks, be made for all men; For kings, and for all that are in authority . . . . — 1 TIMOTHY 2:1,2

The Word of God is clear on this subject. I believe many Christians have practiced this scripture to some extent, but I believe we have somewhat neglected the "giving of thanks."

326

God wants us to offer thanksgiving to Him. And we have much to thank God for!

But too many Christians are always griping and talking about what is wrong with our nation. The Bible does not tell us as Christians to do that.

Instead, as Christians we are exhorted to make supplications, prayers, intercessions, and the giving of thanks for our leaders. (It is impossible that our prayers for them would work at the same time we're criticizing them.)

Confession: *I give thanks according to God's Word for my country's leaders. I give thanks for this great country.*

NOVEMBER 22

Purpose

. . . That we may lead a quiet and peaceable life in all godliness and honesty. For this is good and acceptable in the sight of God our Saviour; Who will have all men to be saved, and to come unto the knowledge of the truth. — 1 TIMOTHY 2:2-4

God doesn't tell us to do something just to fill up space in the Bible. He has a purpose in mind. We are to pray for those in authority so that we who are Christians may lead a quiet and peaceable life. God is concerned about us, and He will work on our behalf, even when those in authority are not Christians.

God's ultimate purpose is that we be able to spread the Gospel freely. If we do not live under a stable government, the spreading of the Gospel is hindered. For example, times of political upheaval, war, travel restrictions, and other limitations hinder the spreading of the Gospel. Jesus said, *"And this gospel of the kingdom shall be preached in all the world for a witness unto all nations; and then shall the end come"* (Matt. 24:14). The devil will try his best to see that this is not accomplished. Therefore, we are exhorted to offer intercessory prayer, supplications, and the giving of thanks for those who lead our nation.

Confession: *Father, I thank You for our leaders. I thank You because You hear and answer prayer, and because You are working on my behalf.*

NOVEMBER 23

THANK YOU, FATHER

Giving thanks unto the Father, which hath made us meet to be partakers of the inheritance of the saints in light: Who hath delivered us from the power of darkness, and hath translated us into the kingdom of his dear Son: In whom we have redemption through his blood, even the forgiveness of sins. — COLOSSIANS 1:12-14

The New Covenant tells us we should be giving thanks unto the Father because He has made us able to be partakers of something. Of what? "*. . . Of the inheritance of the saints in light*"!

The Amplified Bible translates verse 13 as, "[The Father] has delivered and drawn us to Himself out of the control and the dominion of darkness . . . ."

God Himself has delivered us from the control of Satan! Satan's kingdom is the kingdom of darkness. God's kingdom is the kingdom of light. The Father has made us able to be partakers of the inheritance of the saints in light. He has delivered us out from under the control and dominion of darkness. Satan has no control over us. He cannot dominate us.

And we are told to thank God for that!

Confession: *Thank You, Father, for making me fit to be a partaker of the inheritance of the saints in light. Thank You for delivering me out of the authority of darkness. Thank You for transferring me into the kingdom of Your dear Son — the kingdom of light.*

NOVEMBER 24

CHANGING OF LORDS

For sin shall not have dominion over you: for ye are not under the law, but under grace. — ROMANS 6:14

Another translation of today's text reads, "For sin shall not lord it over you."

Sin and Satan are synonymous terms. Therefore, we could read this verse, "For Satan shall not have dominion over you," or "Satan shall not lord it over you."

The reason why Satan cannot lord it over you is found in Colossians 1:13 — the Father has delivered you out from under Satan's control and dominion.

The moment you were born again and became a new creature in Christ Jesus, Jesus became your Lord. Now He is the One who dominates you; Satan is no longer your lord. Satan can no longer lord it over you. When you were born again, Satan's dominion over you ended — and Jesus' dominion over you began!

And anything that is of Satan — sickness, disease, bad habits, or whatever — can no longer lord it over you!

Confession: *Jesus is my Lord. Thank You, Father. Thank You for delivering me from the power of Satan. Thank You because Satan can no longer lord it over me. Thank You because sickness, disease, and bad habits can no longer lord it over me. Thank You because Satan has no dominion over me!*

NOVEMBER 25

A GREAT PLAN

Christ hath redeemed us from the curse of the law, being made a curse for us: for it is written, Cursed is every one that hangeth on a tree.
— GALATIANS 3:13

Part of the inheritance that Colossians 1:12-14 tells us we should be giving thanks to the Father for, is "*. . . redemption through his blood . . .* " (v. 14).

What are we redeemed from? From the curse of the law. And what is the curse of the law? The only way to find out, is to go to the law and see what it says the curse is.

The term "the law," as found in the New Testament, refers to the first five books of the Bible, the Pentateuch. Reading there, we find that the curse, or punishment, for breaking God's law is threefold:

    1. Spiritual death (Gen. 2:17)

    2. Poverty (Deut. 28:15-68)

    3. Sickness (Deut. 28:15-68)

Galatians 3:13 tells us that Christ has redeemed us from the curse of the law, and Colossians 1:12-14 tells us to thank God for our redemption! We are to thank the Father for this great plan of redemption which He planned and sent the Lord Jesus Christ to consummate!

Confession: *Thank You, Father, for Your great plan of redemption which You planned and sent the Lord Jesus Christ to consummate! Thank You because I am redeemed from death! Thank You because I am redeemed from poverty! Thank You because I am redeemed from sickness! Thank You, Father!*

NOVEMBER 26

SPIRIT-FILLED

And be not drunk with wine, wherein is excess; but be filled with the Spirit; Speaking to yourselves in psalms and hymns and spiritual songs, singing and making melody in your heart to the Lord; Giving thanks always for all things unto God and the Father in the name of our Lord Jesus Christ. — EPHESIANS 5:18-20

"I just can't thank God like I should," some people have said.

You can if you follow Paul's admonition in Ephesians 5:18-20, "... *be filled with the Spirit* . . . ." And just after giving this admonition to these Pentecostal people, Paul gives some ways to keep filled with the Spirit: *"Speaking to yourselves in psalms and hymns and spiritual songs, singing and making melody in your heart to the Lord."*

An overflowing heart will be your testimony! Your cup will be full and running over! You will have a song in your heart!

"Giving thanks always for all things . . . ." Your heart is thankful. You give thanks for all of God's blessings. You can even give thanks for every test. You don't give thanks for what the devil has done, but you give thanks for the Word, for the opportunity to see God at work, and for the fact that you know God can make all things work together for your good.

Confession: *I keep being filled with the Holy Spirit. I speak in the Spirit. I sing in the Spirit. I make melody in my heart to the Lord. And I am thankful.*

NOVEMBER 27

GIVING THANKS WELL

Let the word of Christ dwell in you richly in all wisdom; teaching and admonishing one another in psalms and hymns and spiritual songs, singing with grace in your hearts to the Lord. And whatsoever ye do in word or deed, do all in the name of the Lord Jesus, giving thanks to God and the Father by him. — COLOSSIANS 3:16,17

In every thing give thanks: for this is the will of God in Christ Jesus concerning you. — 1 THESSALONIANS 5:18

Notice how yesterday's scripture and today's scripture are very similar.

A song in the heart and the giving of thanks simply go hand-in-hand.

And if you are filled with the Holy Spirit, you will experience this praise and this thanksgiving.

If you don't, then you're simply not filled with the Spirit. Be filled! (*See* John 7:37-39, 14:16,17; Acts 1:4,5, 2:4, 8:14-17, 10:44-46, 19:1-3,6.) Then you'll have a spirit of praise and a spirit of thanksgiving.

Confession: *I let the word of Christ dwell in me richly. I benefit from teaching and admonishing in psalms and hymns and spiritual songs. I sing with grace in my heart to the Lord. Whatever I do in word or deed, I do in the Name of the Lord Jesus. I give thanks to God the Father by Him.*

NOVEMBER 28

BE FILLED

For he that speaketh in an unknown tongue speaketh not unto men, but unto God: for no man understandeth him; howbeit in the spirit he speaketh mysteries. . . . For if I pray in an unknown tongue, my spirit prayeth, but my understanding is unfruitful. What is it then? I will pray with the spirit, and I will pray with the understanding also: I will sing with the spirit, and I will sing with the understanding also. Else when thou shalt bless with the spirit, how shall he that occupieth the room of the unlearned say Amen at thy giving of thanks, seeing he understandeth not what thou sayest? For thou verily givest thanks well, but the other is not edified. — 1 CORINTHIANS 14:2,14-17

God has given to the Church a divine, supernatural means of communication with Himself! God is a Spirit. When we speak in tongues, our spirit is in direct contact with God, who is a Spirit! We are talking to Him by a divine, supernatural means. By this means we can "*. . . bless with the spirit . . . .*" And we can "*. . . givest thanks well . . . .*"

When Paul referred to "he that occupieth the room of the unlearned," he meant those persons who are unlearned in spiritual things. If you invited me to dinner and said, "Please give thanks," and I prayed in tongues, you wouldn't know what I said. You wouldn't be edified. Therefore, Paul said it would be better to pray with the understanding in that instance.

But notice that the Word of God declares that praying in tongues is a perfect way to give thanks well!

Confession: *I shall bless God with the Spirit. I shall give thanks well.*

NOVEMBER 29

MIDNIGHT PRAISE

And at midnight Paul and Silas prayed, and sang praises unto God: and the prisoners heard them. — ACTS 16:25

Singing, praising, and thanksgiving all go together.

Paul and Silas had been beaten with many stripes, cast into prison, and their feet put in stocks. But at midnight they prayed and sang praises to God — aloud. The other prisoners heard them!

Most people in similar circumstances would have griped and complained. If they had been like some modern Christians, Silas would have said, "Paul, are you still there?" And Paul would have answered, "Where else would I be?"

Silas would have complained, "I'll tell you, my poor back is hurting so bad. I don't understand why God let this happen to us. He knows we've tried to serve Him and do our best!"

That kind of praying would have gotten Paul and Silas further in — instead of out! God didn't have them thrown in jail; the devil did. But there's truth and instruction here to help us in our midnight hour — the hour of test, of trial — when the storms of life come. That's the time to pray, praise, sing, and give thanks to God!

Confession: *I praise and thank God at all times. I never have a "poor old me" attitude. I keep an attitude of praise at all times.*

NOVEMBER 30

WORSHIP

As they ministered to the Lord, and fasted, the Holy Ghost said . . . .
— ACTS 13:2

This is the prayer of worship — ministering to the Lord.

It is true that God is concerned about us. He is interested in us, and wants to meet our needs, because He has told us to ask. But my personal observation is that too large a percentage of our praying is, "Give me, give me, give me."

We need to take time in our individual prayer lives, in our gatherings, in our churches, to wait on God and to minister to the Lord. In this kind of atmosphere God can move. As they ministered to the Lord and fasted, the Holy Ghost manifested Himself!

God made man for His own pleasure so He would have someone with whom to fellowship. He is our Father. We are born of God. No earthly parent ever enjoyed the fellowship of his children more than God enjoys the fellowship of His sons and daughters.

Take time to minister to the Lord: To pray. To wait on God. To tell Him how much you love Him. To praise Him. To thank Him for His goodness and mercy.

Confession: *(Make up your own confession. Practice today's lesson by ministering to the Lord.)*

DECEMBER 1

EL SHADDAI

And when Abram was ninety years old and nine, the Lord appeared to Abram, and said unto him, I AM THE ALMIGHTY GOD; walk before me, and be thou perfect. — **GENESIS 17:1**

The original Hebrew of this Old Testament verse reads that God said, "I am El Shaddai."

God was revealed to Israel by seven covenant names, one of which was El Shaddai — which literally means "the God who is more than enough," or "the All-Sufficient One."

It will help your faith to think of God as "the One who is more than enough!"

Throughout the Old Testament, God revealed Himself as El Shaddai — the God who is more than enough. For example, as God was bringing the children of Israel out of Egyptian bondage, Pharaoh's soldiers went after them to recapture them and make them slaves again. On one side of the children of Israel was the wilderness; on the other side, mountains. The Red Sea lay before them. They seemingly were boxed in, but they looked to God — the God who is more than enough — and He divided the sea! He congealed the depths in the heart of the sea (Exod. 15:8)! He froze the waters! The waters stood up on each side like a wall, and Israel walked across to the other side. Our God is more than enough!

Confession: *My Father is El Shaddai, the God who is more than enough. He's more than any mountain to my right. He's more than any enemy behind me. He's more than any obstacle before me. He is my very own Father. And He is El Shaddai — the God who is more than enough!*

DECEMBER 2

MORE THAN ENOUGH

And the sun stood still, and the moon stayed, until the people had avenged themselves upon their enemies . . . . — JOSHUA 10:13

We see El Shaddai with Israel in Canaan's land. (And incidentally, Canaan is not a type of Heaven. It couldn't be. In Heaven there won't be battles to fight, cities to take, or enemies or giants to overcome — they're here in this world. No, Canaan is a type of the baptism of the Holy Spirit and our rights and privileges in Christ Jesus.) When Israel ran into difficulty in Canaan, Joshua, their leader, spoke to the Lord. *And God stopped the whole universe because a man of God prayed!* God can do that — He's the God who is more than enough!

All through the Old Testament, we see El Shaddai moving in the lives of men and women, prophets, priests, and kings. But He's not just the God of *yesterday*; He's the God of *now*! He didn't identify Himself as "the God who *was* more than enough," or "the God who *will be* more than enough." Too often we relegate everything back to the *past*, saying, "Oh, it was wonderful back when God did such things," or to the *future*, saying, "When we all get to Heaven, everything will be wonderful." No, things will be different *here and now* if you will trust in this God who is more than enough!

Confession: *I believe God. I trust in God now. He is more than enough today! He is more than enough to overcome any situation I could face. He is MORE THAN ENOUGH for me.*

DECEMBER 3

HE DELIVERS

Because he [the believer] *hath set his love upon me* [God]*, therefore will I deliver him . . . .* — PSALM 91:14

"I will," or "I shall" is the strongest assertion that can be made in the English language. And in the last part of Psalm 91, there are seven things this God who is more than enough says He will do for the person who has set his love upon Him. (Thank God, I've set my love upon Him — have you?)

Notice that God didn't say, "I *may* do it," or "If I don't run out of energy, I'll do it. If My power doesn't wane, I'll do it." No! He is the All-Sufficient One, and He said, "I *will* do it."

First, God said, "I will deliver them . . . ." This God who is more than enough is a delivering God. He kept His Word with Abraham, and delivered Israel — and He's still the Deliverer today.

Our God is not the oppressor; He is the Deliverer! Acts 10:38 makes that clear. Satan is the oppressor of mankind — but Jesus is our Deliverer!

Confession: *I have set my love upon God; therefore, He delivers me. He is a delivering God. And God is more than enough. He will never run out of energy. He will never run out of power. God will do all that He has said He will do. He's the All-Sufficient One, and He WILL do it!*

DECEMBER 4

HE ANSWERS

Because he hath set his love upon me, therefore. . . . He shall call upon me, and I will answer him . . . . — PSALM 91:14,15

Call unto me, and I will answer thee, and shew thee great and mighty things, which thou knowest not. — JEREMIAH 33:3

And all things, whatsoever ye shall ask in prayer, believing, ye shall receive. — MATTHEW 21:22

Therefore I say unto you, What things soever ye desire, when ye pray, believe that ye receive them, and ye shall have them. — MARK 11:24

And in that day ye shall ask me nothing. Verily, verily, I say unto you, Whatsoever ye shall ask the Father in my name, he will give it you . . . ask, and ye shall receive, that your joy may be full.
— JOHN 16:23,24

These are by no means all of the scriptures on the subject of prayer. But these scriptures alone are enough to set our hearts on fire. They're enough to start us praying. Why? Because El Shaddai said to us, "I will answer." The Almighty God — the One who is more than enough — has promised to answer those who set their love on Him!

Confession: *I have set my love upon Almighty God; therefore, He answers me. I call upon Him, and He answers me. I ask, and He gives me. I seek, and He causes me to find. I knock, and He opens it to me. What things soever I desire, when I pray, I believe that I receive them, and God causes me to have them. Whatever I ask in Jesus' Name, Almighty God gives me. My joy is full!*

DECEMBER 5

HE'S THE WAY OUT

Because he hath set his love upon me, therefore. . . . I will be with him in trouble; I will deliver him . . . . — PSALM 91:14,15

God didn't say you weren't going to have trouble. In fact, He rather infers that you will have trouble because you're a Christian! The world will persecute you, talk about you, speak evil of you. An enemy is arrayed against you. The god of this world puts pressure on you at every turn (2 Cor. 4:4).

Some people think it's God who is putting pressure on them, but it isn't. Jesus contrasted His works and the works of the devil like this: *"The thief cometh not, but for to steal, and to kill, and to destroy: I am come that they might have life, and that they might have it more abundantly"* (John 10:10). God is not a thief. That which steals, kills, and destroys is the devil — not God.

God says in His Word, *"Many are the afflictions of the righteous: but the Lord delivereth him out of them all"* (Ps. 34:19). The word "afflictions" here means *tests* and *trials*. And that's what your troubles are. But the Lord has promised to deliver you out of how many of them: half? No! Out of them *all*! The Lord didn't just promise to be with you in trouble and then stop there. He's there to deliver you out of that trouble. And He's more than enough!

Confession: *I have set my love upon God; therefore, no matter what the test or trial, I know that El Shaddai is with me to deliver me. And He's more than enough!*

DECEMBER 6

HE HONORS

Because he hath set his love upon me, therefore . . . I will set him on high. . . . and honour him. — PSALM 91:14,15

I'd rather have God honor me than to have all the acclaim this world can offer.

The story is told that one day Napoleon was reviewing his troops when his horse began to buck. A young private stepped over, took the horse by the bridle, and quieted him down. Napoleon said, "Thank you, Captain." And the private moved into rank of a captain. But the other officers shunned this young man. They had earned their rank, but his had been granted to him. Napoleon noticed this and called for a full, gala review of his army. He sat this young man on a horse by his side, and they rode out to the parade grounds together. The other officers then began to say, "That fellow's a favorite with Napoleon." And they began to court his favor.

The world may not know it, but the time is coming when they are going to find out that we are favorites with the King of kings and Lord of lords. And they'll wish they had courted our favor. Jesus Himself said, *"To him that overcometh will I grant to sit with me in my throne, even as I also overcame, and am set down with my Father in his throne"* (Rev. 3:21). Jesus' favor far outshines any that this world can bestow.

Confession: *Because I have set my love upon God, He will set me on high. He will honor me. I am a favorite with the King of kings and Lord of lords. I am a favorite with the God who is more than enough!*

DECEMBER 7

LONG LIFE

Because he hath set his love upon me, therefore. . . . With long life will I satisfy him . . . .
          PSALM 91:14,16

"But, Brother Hagin," someone said, "I knew a minister who was a wonderful man of God, and he died at age forty-two."

That doesn't mean I have to die young. I don't know what that minister believed — but I know what I believe. And I know that the God who is more than enough said, "I will satisfy him with long life."

Someone else will say, "That just means we're going to live forever in Heaven." No, even sinners are going to live forever. They're going to live in one place, and we're going to live in another. That scripture is referring to our enjoying long life here upon this earth.

A reading of Proverbs reveals that the Word of God says that doing certain things will lengthen your life, but doing certain other things will shorten your life. Ephesians 6:1-3 tells children to honor their parents, *"That it may be well with thee, and thou mayest live long on the earth."* Peter quoted the Psalms assuring us that these promises belong to us (1 Peter 3:10; Ps. 34:12).

Our promised lifespan is seventy or eighty years (Ps. 90:10). But don't compromise. Don't settle for anything less. *And believe God for all you can!*

Confession: *Because I have set my love upon God, El Shaddai will satisfy me with long life. Unless the Lord Jesus Christ returns before I die, I will live out my years in service to God. I will live and work together with God in carrying out His will upon the earth.*

DECEMBER 8

SALVATION

Because he hath set his love upon me, therefore. . . . [will I] shew him my salvation. — PSALM 91:14,16

Although I don't agree with all Dr. C. I. Scofield's notes in his *Reference Bible*, his footnote following Romans 1:16, referring to the word "salvation," is excellent. Dr. Scofield, a Greek and Hebrew scholar, wrote:

> The Greek and Hebrew words for salvation imply the ideas of *deliverance, safety, preservation, healing,* and *soundness* [health].

El Shaddai has promised to show us deliverance, safety, preservation, healing, and health. For He has promised to show us His salvation!

Confession: *Because I have set my love upon God, the God who is more than enough has shown me His salvation. He has made known to me the Gospel of Jesus Christ, which is the power of God unto salvation (Rom. 1:16). This Gospel is the power of God unto my deliverance. It is the power of God unto my safety. It is the power of God unto my preservation. It is the power of God unto my healing. It is the power of God unto my health. And it is more than enough!*

DECEMBER 9

CROWNED WITH GLORY

When I view and consider Your heavens, the work of Your fingers, the moon and the stars, which You have ordained and established, What is man that You are mindful of him, and the son of [earthborn] man that You care for him? Yet You have made him but a little lower than God [or heavenly beings], and You have crowned him with glory and honor. You made him to have dominion over the works of Your hands . . . .
— PSALM 8:3-6 (*Amplified*)

God did not create man for death! Death, sin, sickness, hatred, revenge, and all such tragedies reflect conditions on earth that had no place in the original plan of the Creator. Man was created instead for joy, happiness, and peace!

Man was designed for eternal fellowship with God. He was created in God's very image and likeness (Gen. 1:26,27). He was created for joy, happiness, and peace. And he was created to give God pleasure (Rev. 4:11).

God gave man a place in His creation second only to Himself, with dominion as far reaching as the universe itself (Ps. 8:3-6; Gen. 1:26-28). Adam was the master of himself, of creation, and of Satan. Adam did not have to yield to sin — he had a choice.

Confession: *I will do what I was designed to do; I will fellowship with God. I will give Him pleasure. The Bible says that without faith it is impossible to please God (Heb. 11:6). So I will walk in faith. I will not be dominated by sin, sickness, fear, and doubt, or anything else that is of the devil. I choose to walk with God.*

DECEMBER 10

SHORT OF THE GLORY

For all have sinned, and come short of the glory of God.
— ROMANS 3:23

Man did the *unthinkable*! Given dominion over all the works of God's hand, Adam was originally the god of this world. But Adam *knowingly* committed high treason against God by selling out to Satan the dominion which God had originally given him. Adam's treason was done on such a legal basis that God could not annul the contract He had made with Adam, and which Adam had passed on to Satan. Hence, Satan, not Adam, became the god of this world (2 Cor. 4:4). And thus began Satan's destructive reign.

So spiritual death — which is *separation from God* — came to man. When God came down in the cool of the day to walk and talk with Adam, God called, "Adam, where art thou?" And Adam said, "I hid myself." He was separated from God!

Another aspect of spiritual death — *having Satan's nature* — also came to man. The devil became man's spiritual father. Notice Jesus said to the Pharisees, *"Ye are of your father the devil . . ."* (John 8:44). Man is spiritually a child of the devil. He partakes of his father's nature. This explains why man cannot be saved by conduct. Man cannot stand in the Presence of God as he is, having the nature of his father, the devil, in him. If man is ever saved, he must be saved by someone paying the penalty for his sins, and someone giving him a new nature.

Confession: *Thank You, Father, for my new nature. Thank You, Father, that You have made provision for me to be a "partaker of the divine nature" (2 Peter 1:4).*

DECEMBER 11

A Great Plan!

And I will put enmity between thee and the woman, and between thy seed and her seed; it shall bruise thy head, and thou shalt bruise his heel. — GENESIS 3:15

Man fell.

But God had a plan — a great plan — *redemption*! God assumed the liabilities of man's transgressions and redeemed him from Satan's dominion. God had a plan to give *life* back to man. God's plan allowed man's nature to be changed back into harmony with God's nature.

God cannot ignore man's transgressions. Justice demanded that the penalty for man's crime be paid — but man himself was unable to pay it. Therefore, because man couldn't save himself, God had to provide a Redeemer.

No sooner had man fallen under the dominion of his enemy, Satan, than God began to speak forth His plan concerning the Coming One. This One, the seed of woman (for it was prophesied that a woman would give birth to a child independent of natural generation) would break Satan's dominion over man! This One would set men free! This One would bruise the head of the serpent!

In Oriental languages, "bruising the head" means breaking the lordship of a ruler. When God spoke those words to Satan in Genesis 3:15, Satan had just come into the dominion meant to belong to man. But God spoke forth that his Wonderful Seed of woman would come to break Satan's lordship.

Confession: *Thank You, Father, for Your great plan of redemption, which You planned and sent the Lord Jesus Christ to consummate.*

DECEMBER 12

IMMANUEL

And he [Ahaz] said, Hear ye now, O house of David; Is it a small thing for you to weary men, but will ye weary my God also? Therefore the Lord himself shall give you a sign; Behold, a virgin shall conceive, and bear a son, and shall call his name Immanuel. — ISAIAH 7:13,14

God began to speak through His prophets, promising that a Redeemer would come who would break Satan's dominion and restore to man his lost dominion.

The prophet Isaiah, for example, looked down through time and pointed to a daughter of David who would give birth to that promised Redeemer 750 years later.

"The Lord Himself will give you a sign," Isaiah prophesied. "He will show you a miracle, a wonder, something out of the ordinary."

What will it be?

A virgin shall conceive, and bear a son. A virgin shall give birth to a son in a supernatural way.

His Name shall be called Immanuel — which means "God with us," or "Incarnation." Here, God suggests the union of deity and humanity.

Confession: *The Lord Himself gave a sign, a wonder. A virgin did conceive and bear a Son. His Name is called Immanuel — God with us. He came to redeem us. Thank You, Father, for Your great plan of redemption, which You planned and sent Immanuel to consummate.*

DECEMBER 13

THE SEED

. . . For the Lord hath created a new thing in the earth, A woman shall compass a man. — **JEREMIAH 31:22**

Adam was *created*. The rest of the human race was *generated* by natural processes. If Jesus had been born by natural generation, He would have been a fallen spirit.

But Romans 5:12 tells us, *"Wherefore, as by one man* [Adam] *sin entered into the world, and death by sin; and so death passed upon all men, for that all have sinned."*

Man is subject to death; to the devil. Thus, man's seed could only produce another fallen man.

Therefore, the Redeemer could not be a subject of death. The Promised Seed had to be One over whom Satan had no legal claims or authority. He had to be brought forth by a special act of divine power. He had to be conceived by the Holy Spirit!

The words God spoke through the prophet Jeremiah could be translated literally as, "A woman shall encompass a man-child." The womb of the virgin was simply the receptacle of the Holy Seed until He was brought forth.

Confession: *Thank You, Father, for Your great plan of redemption. I am so glad that You created a new thing in the earth. I am so glad that You sent forth the Holy Seed to redeem us.*

DECEMBER 14

FROM EVERLASTING

But thou, Bethlehem Ephratah, though thou be little among the thousands of Judah, yet out of thee shall he come forth unto me that is to be ruler in Israel; whose goings forth have been from of old, from everlasting. — MICAH 5:2

This remarkable prophetic utterance about One who would be born of the family of Judah to be a Ruler in Israel states that His goings forth were from of old, from everlasting. He has traveled up and down through eternity, and He has left His footprints on the ages!

Too frequently people simply look at the physical side of Jesus' birth and talk about His being born as a little babe, when actually He pre-existed with the Father from the beginning!

The Person we now know as Jesus Christ is one of the three Divine Persons of the Deity. As God, He had no beginning.

Confession: *The goings forth of Christ, my Lord, were from of old, from everlasting. As God, He had no beginning. Yet He came forth to this world to redeem me from the dominion of Satan. I can trust this Eternal One with my life.*

DECEMBER 15

FOR MEDITATION

For unto us a child is born, unto us a son is given: and the government shall be upon his shoulder: and his name shall be called Wonderful, Counsellor, The mighty God, The everlasting Father, The Prince of Peace.
— ISAIAH 9:6

Divine names and titles ascribed to Jesus prove that He is, by nature, divine and a member of the Godhead:

Emmanuel (Matt. 1:23) . . . God (John 1:1) . . . Lord (Luke 19:34) . . . Lord of All (Acts 10:36) . . . Lord of Glory (1 Cor. 2:8) . . . Wonderful, Counsellor, Mighty God, Everlasting Father, Prince of Peace (Isa. 9:6,7) . . . the Lord's Christ (Luke 2:26) . . . Son of God (Rom. 1:4) . . . His Son (John 3:16-18) . . . God's Beloved Son (Matt 3:17) . . . Only Begotten Son (John 1:18) . . . Alpha and Omega, Beginning and the End, the First and the Last (Rev. 22:13) . . . the Lord (Acts 9:17) . . . Son of the Highest (Luke 1:32) . . . Bread of God (John 6:33) . . . Holy One of God (Mark 1:24) . . . Thy Holy Child Jesus (Acts 4:30) . . . King of kings and Lord of lords (Rev. 19:16) . . . Lord and Savior (2 Peter 3:2) . . . Word of God (Rev. 19:13).

Confession: *Jesus is my Lord. My Lord is called Emmanuel . . . God . . . Lord of All . . . Lord of Glory . . . Wonderful . . . Counsellor . . . Mighty God . . . Everlasting Father . . . Prince of Peace . . . the Lord's Christ . . . Son of God . . . His Son . . . Only Begotten Son . . . Alpha and Omega . . . Beginning and the End . . . the First and the Last . . . the Lord . . . Son of the Highest . . . Bread of God . . . Holy One of God . . . the Holy Child Jesus . . . King of kings and Lord of lords . . . Lord and Savior . . . Word of God. That's who my Lord is! No wonder Satan cannot dominate me!*

DECEMBER 16

FOR FURTHER MEDITATION

For it pleased the Father that in him should all fulness dwell.
— COLOSSIANS 1:19

The Word of God plainly teaches that our Redeemer is divine.
These divine offices are ascribed to Him:

> Creator (Col. 1:16) . . . Mediator (1 Tim. 2:4,5) . . . Head of the
> Church (Col. 1:16-24) . . . Savior (2 Peter 3:2) . . . Judge (2 Tim. 4:1)
> . . . Preserver (Heb. 1:1-3) . . . Life-Giver (John 10:28) . . . Lord and
> Christ (Acts 2:36) . . . Resurrection and Life (John 11:25).

Divine character is ascribed to Christ. Ordinary men are sinners by
nature, but Christ Jesus is not an ordinary man. He is:

> Holy by Birth (Luke 1:35) . . . Righteous (Isa. 53:11) . . . Faithful (Isa.
> 11:5) . . . Truth (John 14:6) . . . Just (John 5:30) . . . Guileless (1 Peter
> 2:22) . . . Sinless (2 Cor. 5:21) . . . Spotless (1 Peter 1:19) . . . Innocent
> (Matt. 27:4) . . . Harmless (Heb. 7:26) . . . Obedient to God (Heb. 5:8-10)
> . . . Obedient to Earthly Parents (Luke 2:51) . . . Zealous (John 2:17)
> . . . Meek (Matt. 11:29) . . . Lowly in Heart (Matt. 11:29) . . . Merci-
> ful (Heb. 2:17) . . . Patient (Isa. 53:7) . . . Long-Suffering (1 Tim. 1:16)
> . . . Compassionate (Matt. 15:32) . . . Benevolent (Acts 10:38) . . . Lov-
> ing (John 15:13) . . . Self-Denying (2 Cor. 8:9) . . . Humble (Phil. 2:5-11)
> . . . Resigned (Luke 22:42) . . . Forgiving (Luke 23:34).

Confession: *Jesus Christ is worthy. Thank God for this Worthy One. Thank God for this Divine One. Thank God that One who is the Creator would come to earth from glory to be the Mediator, the Head of the Church, the Savior, the Judge, the Preserver, the Life-Giver, the Lord and Savior. And thank God, this Worthy One is my Lord.*

DECEMBER 17

HUMILITY

Who [Christ Jesus], *being in the form of God, thought it not robbery to be equal with God: But made himself of no reputation, and took upon him the form of a servant, and was made in the likeness of men: And being found in fashion as a man, he humbled himself, and became obedient unto death, even the death of the cross.*

— **PHILIPPIANS 2:6-8**

Christ has always existed in the form of God. But He emptied Himself and took the form of a bond servant, being made in the likeness of men.

This suggests a distinct operation of God totally different from natural generation: A miracle. First, God took Christ from the Godhead in Heaven — and then He placed Christ in the womb of a virgin to be united with flesh in a unique conception.

> *Wherefore when he cometh into the world, he saith, Sacrifice and offering thou wouldest not, but a body hast thou prepared me.*
> — **HEBREWS 10:5**

God prepared a body — a special body — for this Being called the Son of God. In the Incarnation, Christ became a man!

Confession: *Thank You, Jesus, for emptying Yourself and being made in the likeness of men. It was our only hope. Thank You for humbling Yourself and becoming obedient unto death; yes, even the death of the cross. And thank You, Father, for highly exalting Him, and for giving to Him the Name which is above every name. At that Name my knee does bow, and my tongue does confess that Jesus Christ is Lord, to the glory of God the Father (Phil. 2:9,10).*

DECEMBER 18

INCARNATION

In the beginning was the Word, and the Word was with God, and the Word was God. . . . And the Word was made flesh, and dwelt among us, (and we beheld his glory, the glory as of the only begotten of the Father,) full of grace and truth. — JOHN 1:1,14

Webster defines Incarnation as "The union of divinity with humanity in Jesus Christ."

Incarnation was the only solution to the human problem — the only hope for mankind to be reunited with God. *Any religion that denies the Incarnation of Jesus of Nazareth is false!*

This Eternal Being, called Emmanuel — God with us, or Jesus the Christ — is here called the Word. The Word existed in the beginning. The Word was with God — with God in fellowship, in purpose, working with Him. God made the worlds through the Word (Heb. 1:2; John 1:3).

And this Eternal Being was God! He possessed the same nature. He existed in the same form and on an equality with God (Phil. 2:6).

And this Being became flesh! The Word became a man and dwelt among us. He became human — as much a man as if He'd never been anything else, yet He did not cease to be what He had been. The Word made His home among us, and we beheld the glory of God (Col. 1:15; Heb. 1:3).

Confession: Jesus came and dwelled in flesh so that I might be eternally reunited with the Father. Jesus became like me, so that I could become like Him. I will walk in the reality of what the Incarnation made possible for me. I am reunited with my Father!

DECEMBER 19

MEDIATOR

For there is one God, and one mediator between God and men, the man Christ Jesus. — 1 TIMOTHY 2:5

Man's condition demanded an Incarnation — man had become spiritually dead with no approach to God. The Incarnation of Deity with humanity provided One who could stand as man's Mediator. Equal with God on one hand and united with man on the other, this One could assume the obligations of man's treason and satisfy the claims of Justice, thereby bridging the chasm between God and man.

God created man in His own image, just a little lower than Himself; so nearly like God that it was possible for God and man to become united for eternity in one individual! (When Christ became a man and took on a physical body in the Incarnation, He did so for eternity. Therefore, there is a God-man in Heaven today at the Father's right hand as a result of the Incarnation.) *It was possible for God and man to become united!*

God can dwell in these human bodies of ours, God can impart His *life* and *nature* to our spirits. That's what takes place at the New Birth: Spiritual death is eradicated from the spirit, and God gives man His *life!*

Confession: *Today at the right hand of the Father there is a God-man, our Mediator, Jesus Christ. Jesus bridged the gap for me. He made it possible for spiritual death to depart from my spirit, and for God's own life and nature to take its place in my spirit. Therefore, God now dwells in my spirit. God lives in me!*

354

DECEMBER 20

HE CAME TO SAVE

And she shall bring forth a son, and thou shalt call his name Jesus: for he shall save his people from their sins. — MATTHEW 1:21

The first step in redemption was Christ's identification with our humanity. This took place in His Incarnation. Christ was made flesh (John 1:14). Hebrews 2:14 says, *"Forasmuch then as the children are partakers of flesh and blood, he also himself likewise took part of the same . . . ."*

But at the time of His Incarnation, Jesus did not partake of the *nature* that reigned in the spirit of man. Had He done so then, He would have been *spiritually dead* during His earthly ministry! Then He could not have pleased the Father by doing His own will. No, His identification with the spirit nature of man didn't take place until His crucifixion.

There God actually made Jesus Christ to become sin for us (2 Cor. 5:21). Our sin nature itself was laid upon Jesus Christ until He became all that spiritual death had made man. In the mind of God, it was not Jesus Christ who hung on the cross; it was the human race who hung there. Therefore, each of us may say with Paul, "I was crucified with Christ."

Confession: *Because Jesus came to save me from my sins, I can claim Galatians 2:20, which says: "I am crucified with Christ: nevertheless I live; yet not I, but Christ liveth in me: and the life which I now live in the flesh I live by the faith of the Son of God, who loved me, and gave himself for me."*

DECEMBER 21

THAT WE MIGHT BE SONS

But when the fulness of the time was come, God sent forth his Son, made of a woman, made under the law, To redeem them that were under the law, that we might receive the adoption of sons. And because ye are sons, God hath sent forth the Spirit of his Son into your hearts, crying, Abba, Father. Wherefore thou art no more a servant, but a son; and if a son, then an heir of God through Christ. — GALATIANS 4:4-7

The object of the Incarnation was that man might be given the right to become a child of God (John 1:12).

Man could become a child of God only by receiving the nature of God; therefore, Christ came that man might receive eternal life (John 10:10; 1 John 5:11,12).

And man could receive eternal life only after he had been legally redeemed from Satan's authority (Col. 1:13,14).

Confession: *God sent forth His Son to redeem us, that we might become sons of God. I have received Christ; therefore, I have life. I am a son of God. And because I am, God has sent forth the Spirit of His Son into my heart, crying, "Abba, Father." I am no more a servant; but a son. I am an heir of God through Christ.*

DECEMBER 22

HE CAME TO DECLARE HIM

No man hath seen God at any time; the only begotten Son, which is in the bosom of the Father, he hath declared him. — JOHN 1:18

How Jesus realized and appreciated the phase of His mission on earth: Declaring the true nature of His Father!

A noted Bible scholar once said, concerning the Incarnation, "We know now that God is like this that we have seen in Jesus. He is Christ-like. And if He is, He is a good God and trustworthy. If the heart that is back of the universe is like this gentle heart that broke upon the Cross, He can have my heart without qualifications and without reservations. I know nothing higher to say of God than that He should live like Christ . . . . Strange, a man lived among us and when we think of God we think of Him in terms of this man or He is not good. We may transfer every single moral quality in Jesus to God without loss or degradation to our thought of God. On the contrary, by thinking of Him in terms of Jesus we heighten our views of God. All those who have tried to think of Him in other terms have lowered and impoverished our idea of Him."

Confession: Jesus has declared God the Father to me. I know what God is like — He's like Jesus! God is a good God — and I do trust Him.

DECEMBER 23

INCARNATE REVELATOR

Jesus saith unto him [Philip] . . . *he that hath seen me hath seen the Father . . . .*
— JOHN 14:9

Man born into a world ruled by Satan did not by nature know his Creator. Since Adam's sin — when man died *spiritually* — God and man had been spiritually separated.

Man desperately needed an Incarnation. The Incarnation of Jesus Christ — God manifested in the flesh — gave to the world the true knowledge of the nature of God.

Spiritually dead men couldn't know the nature of the Creator without a revelation from Him. God had been conceived as weird, cruel, grotesque, immoral, aloof, or perhaps, an impersonal energy, but He was never thought of as a God of love — a loving Heavenly Father.

"What's he *really* like?" people will inquire about some movie star, TV personality, politician, etc. And sometimes those close to that celebrity will attempt in an interview to tell what he is really like.

"What's God *really* like?" people want to know.

Friends, if you want to know what God is really like — *just look at Jesus!*

Confession: *I have seen Jesus in the revelation of God's Word. Therefore, I have seen the Father. I know what the Father is like. He's just like Jesus! He's a God of love. He's a Father God. And because of Jesus, He's my very own Father. I am His very own child. I'm so thankful for this great plan of redemption which included revealing my Father to the world.*

DECEMBER 24

HIS GLORY

And the Word became flesh. And pitched his tent among us, And we gazed upon his glory, — A glory . . . Full of favour and truth.
— JOHN 1:14 (*Rotherham*)

I love Rotherham's translation of John 1:14 — it is so beautiful.

We've tended to think of Christ's coming to the earth as a man only in terms of His self-denial in leaving glory, or else in terms of His suffering on this earth. But I believe it was a joy to Christ, who so loved man and so desired man's fellowship, to "pitch His tent" among us so that He might give to alienated man — who had never known his Creator — a true conception of His Heavenly Father.

It was *good tidings of great joy* which the angel proclaimed to the shepherds — and to all people everywhere. Man, separated from God for four thousand years, could now gaze upon God's glory, could now see God, could now know God as He is, and could now be reunited with Him!

> *And the angel said unto them, Fear not: for, behold, I bring you good tidings of great joy, which shall be to all people. For unto you is born this day in the city of David a Saviour, which is Christ the Lord.* — LUKE 2:10,11

The Word has become flesh!

DECEMBER 25

LOVE SENT HIS SON TO SAVE

. . . For that which is conceived in her
is of the Holy Ghost.
And she shall bring forth a son,
and thou shalt call his name JESUS:
for he shall save his people from their sins.

For God so loved the world,
that he gave his only begotten Son,
that whosoever believeth in him
should not perish,
but have everlasting life.

For God sent not his Son into the world
to condemn the world;
but that the world through him
might be saved.

— MATTHEW 1:20,21; JOHN 3:16,17

DECEMBER 26

OUR FATHER

. . . For your Father knoweth what things ye have need of, before ye ask him. After this manner therefore pray ye: Our Father . . . .
— MATTHEW 6:8,9

Although God had given to Israel as clear a revelation of Himself as it was possible to give spiritually dead men, they still didn't really know Him. They didn't recognize *God manifested in the flesh* when Jesus stood in their midst. (Under the Old Covenant, God's Presence was shut up in the Holy of Holies.)

Thus, it was into a hard, harsh atmosphere of Justice that Jesus Christ came. And the Jews of His day could not understand Him. He talked about God as His *Father.* He told of the Father's *love* and *care* for His own! It mystified them. When Jesus introduced God as a Father God of love, His words, for the most part, fell upon unresponsive ears.

Yet we must admit, as we meditate on Jesus' words about the love of God, that even born-again children of God sometimes fail to see the love side of God. Israel never grasped it. They didn't understand who it was Jesus was talking about. It was new to them. To tell the truth, it's new to most church members today! They have been taught to fear God, and to shrink from a God of Justice. They've never really seen the love side of God that Jesus came to reveal.

Confession: *I hereby make a quality decision to see and know the love side of God that Jesus came to reveal. I will meditate on Jesus' revelation of God until I really know Him as my Father God of love.*

DECEMBER 27

A FATHER'S PART

Therefore take no thought, saying, What shall we eat? or, What shall we drink? or, Wherewithal shall we be clothed? (For after all these things do the Gentiles seek:) for your heavenly Father knoweth that ye have need of all these things. But seek ye first the kingdom of God, and his righteousness; and all these things shall be ADDED unto you. Take therefore no thought for the morrow: for the morrow shall take thought for the things of itself. Sufficient unto the day is the evil thereof.
— MATTHEW 6:31-34

Added to you! Not taken away! That proves that the Father cares for His own.

Another translation reads, "Be not therefore anxious for the morrow." You see, God doesn't want His children to be anxious, or to worry. In today's passage, God is saying, "Have no worry, no fret, no anxiety. Because I am your Heavenly Father, I know you have need of these things. But seek first the Kingdom of God and His righteousness, and all these things shall be added unto you."

That's what God our Father is saying! If God is your Father, you may be assured that He will take a father's place and perform a father's part. You may be certain that if God is your Father, He loves you, and He will care for you. Praise God, I'm glad He's my Father! Is He yours?

Confession: *I do not worry about what I shall eat or drink, or what I shall wear. My Heavenly Father knows I have need of all these things. I have sought first the Kingdom of God and His righteousness, and all these things are added unto me.*

DECEMBER 28

THE FATHER'S LOVE

He that hath my commandments, and keepeth them, he it is that loveth me: and he that loveth me shall be loved of my Father, and I will love him, and will manifest myself to him. Judas saith unto him, not Iscariot, Lord, how is it that thou wilt manifest thyself unto us, and not unto the world? Jesus answered and said unto him, If a man love me, he will keep my words: and my Father will love him, and we will come unto him, and make our abode with him. — JOHN 14:21-23

Two things are emphasized in today's text:

1. Jesus said, *"He that hath my commandments, and keepeth them . . ."* Keep in mind what Jesus' commandments are. He said, *"A new commandment I give unto you, That ye love one another; as I have loved you . . ."* (John 13:34). There's no reason for you to worry about any other commandments. Walking in love sums up the whole business, because the Word of God says, *". . . love is the fulfilling of the law"* (Rom. 13:10). (If you keep Jesus' commandments, you will have fulfilled the rest of the commandments.)

2. *". . . Shall be loved of my Father . . . ."* If you walk in love, you are walking in God's realm, because God is love. God's very nature, because He is love, compels Him to care for us, protect us, and shield us!

Confession: *I have Jesus' commandments, and I keep them. I love others as God has loved me. I walk in love toward my brethren. I show my love for Jesus by keeping His love commandment. I am loved of the Father!*

DECEMBER 29

How Much More

If ye then, being evil, know how to give good gifts unto your children, how much more shall your Father which is in heaven give good things to them that ask him?   — MATTHEW 7:11

Would you, as a parent, plan, purpose, and will for your children to go through life poverty-stricken, sick, downtrodden, downcast, down-and-out, with their nose to the grindstone? No! Assuredly not!

My younger brother had a difficult time getting his education. Our father left when this brother was only six months old. He graduated from high school during the Depression by working the 11 p.m. to 7 a.m. shift at a local cotton mill and then going to school immediately after work.

In time, this brother married, had a son, and became a very successful businessman. He said to me — and I guess this has been a driving force in my brother's life — "I'd rather let my boy die now than to have it like I had it. But I'm going to see to it that he doesn't have it rough like I did."

My brother worked hard to provide a better life for his family than he had known growing up. Just looking at it from the natural standpoint, he did all this because he loved them. And that's what Jesus meant when He said that if natural men know how to give good gifts to their children, *how much more* will our loving Heavenly Father give good things to those who ask Him!

Confession: *Even good natural fathers know how to give good gifts to their children. HOW MUCH MORE will my Father in Heaven give good things to me when I ask Him?*

DECEMBER 30

HUSBANDMAN

I am the true vine, and my Father is the husbandman. — JOHN 15:1

My Heavenly Father is the Caretaker.

He is the Protector.

He is the Shield.

He is the Sustainer.

He is the Trainer.

He is the Educator.

The Greek word translated "husbandman" involves all those shades of meaning. As the husbandman trains the branches of a vine, so God trains the branches of the Body of Christ.

And remember, God is love!

Confession: *Jesus is the true vine. I am a branch. My Father is the husbandman. He is my Caretaker, my Protector, my Shield, my Sustainer, my Trainer, my Educator. I will bear much fruit!*

DECEMBER 31

LOVER

For the Father himself loveth you, because ye have loved me, and have believed that I came out from God. — JOHN 16:27

Nothing can be stronger or more comforting than the fact that the Father Himself knows you, loves you, and longs to bless you!

In fact, John 17:23 says that *God loves us as He loved Jesus.* What a staggering thought! Yet it is true! Jesus said it!

God the Father is *your* Father! He cares for you. He is interested in you individually — not just as a group, or as a body of believers, or as a church. God is interested in each of His children, and He loves each one of us with the same love.

Get acquainted with your Father through His Word. It is in His Word that you will learn about your Heavenly Father, about His love, His nature, how He cares for you, how He loves you. He is everything the Word says He is. And He will do everything the Word says He will do!

Confession: *I love Jesus, and I believe He came out from God. Therefore, the Father Himself loves me. God knows me. He cares for me. He longs to bless me. He is interested in my well-being. I get acquainted with Him through the Word. God is everything the Word says He is. He will do everything the Word says He will do.*

FAITH LIBRARY PUBLICATIONS FAVORITES

To order any of these books or for a complete listing
of our Faith Library books, audio and video tapes,
and music tapes and CDs, please call:

1-888-28-FAITH — Offer #605
(1-888-283-2484)

ANOTHER LOOK AT FAITH
Kenneth Hagin Jr. • Item #733

This book focuses on what faith is not, thus answering common misunderstandings of what it means to live by faith.

THE BELIEVER'S AUTHORITY
Kenneth E. Hagin • Item #406

Our all-time bestseller, this book provides excellent insight into the authority that rightfully belongs to every believer in Christ!

BLESSED IS . . . Untying the 'NOTS' That Hinder Your Blessing!
Kenneth Hagin Jr. • Item #736

This book creatively teaches believers from Psalm 1 what *not* to do in order to be blessed by God and receive His richest and best!

DON'T QUIT! YOUR FAITH WILL SEE YOU THROUGH
Kenneth Hagin Jr. • Item #724

Learn how you can develop faith that won't quit and come out of tests or trials victoriously.

FOLLOWING GOD'S PLAN FOR YOUR LIFE
Kenneth E. Hagin • Item #519

It's up to individual Christians to fulfill the divine purpose that God ordained for their lives before the beginning of time. This book can help believers stay on the course God has set before them!

FAITH LIBRARY PUBLICATIONS FAVORITES

GOD'S WORD: A Never-Failing Remedy

Kenneth E. Hagin • Item #526

The never-failing remedy for every adversity of life can be found in the pages of God's holy written Word! And when you act on the Word, it truly becomes a never-failing remedy!

THE HEALING ANOINTING

Kenneth E. Hagin • Item #527

This dynamic book explores the operation of God's powerful anointing in divine healing.

HEALING: Forever Settled

Kenneth Hagin Jr. • Item #723

The primary question among believers is whether it's God's will to heal people today. Healing is a forever-settled subject because God's Word is forever settled!

HOW TO LIVE WORRY-FREE

Kenneth Hagin Jr. • Item #735

Sound teaching from God's Word is combined with practical insights to illustrate the perils of worry and to help guide the believer into the peace of God.

HOW YOU CAN BE LED BY THE SPIRIT OF GOD

Kenneth E. Hagin • Item #513

These step-by-step guidelines based on the Scriptures can help Christians avoid spiritual pitfalls and follow the Spirit of God in every area of life.

IT'S YOUR MOVE!

Kenneth Hagin Jr. • Item #730

Move out of the arena of discouragement and despair and into the arena of God's blessings that are yours in Christ.

FAITH LIBRARY PUBLICATIONS FAVORITES

JESUS — NAME ABOVE ALL NAMES
Kenneth Hagin Jr. • Item #737
This exciting book discusses the redemptive realities and blessings that every believer inherits at salvation through the power of Jesus' Name.

LOVE: The Way to Victory
Kenneth E. Hagin • Item #523
By acting on the truths contained in this book, believers can turn around seemingly impossible situations in their lives — just by walking in the God-kind of love!

THE TRIUMPHANT CHURCH: Dominion Over All the Powers of Darkness
Kenneth E. Hagin • Item #520
This bestseller is a comprehensive biblical study of the origin and operation of Satan that shows believers how to enforce his defeat in their lives.

THE UNTAPPED POWER IN PRAISE
Kenneth Hagin Jr. • Item #725
The power of God is available to set believers free. This book teaches how to tap into that power through praise!

WELCOME TO GOD'S FAMILY: A FOUNDATIONAL GUIDE FOR SPIRIT-FILLED LIVING
Kenneth E. Hagin • Item #528
Increase your spiritual effectiveness by discovering what it means to be born again and how you can partake of the biblical benefits that God has provided for you as His child!

WHAT TO DO WHEN FAITH SEEMS WEAK AND VICTORY LOST
Kenneth E. Hagin • Item #501
The ten steps outlined in this book can bring any believer out of defeat into certain victory!

The Word of Faith

The Word of Faith is a full-color monthly magazine with faith-building teaching articles by Rev. Kenneth E. Hagin and Rev. Kenneth Hagin Jr.

The Word of Faith also includes encouraging true-life stories of Christians who have overcome circumstances through God's Word, plus information about the various outreaches of Kenneth Hagin Ministries and RHEMA Bible Church.

To receive a free subscription to *The Word of Faith*, call:

1-888-28-FAITH
(1-888-283-2484)

Offer #603

RHEMA
Bible Training Center

Providing Skilled Laborers for the End-Time Harvest!

Do you desire —

- to find and effectively fulfill God's plan for your life?
- to know how to "rightly divide the Word of truth"?
- to learn how to follow and flow with the Spirit of God?
- to run your God-given race with excellence and integrity?
- to become not only a laborer but a *skilled* laborer?

If so, then RHEMA Bible Training Center is here for you!

For a free video and full-color catalog, call:

1-888-28-FAITH Offer #602
(1-888-283-2484)

RHEMA Bible Training Center admits students of any race, color, or ethnic origin.

RHEMA

Correspondence Bible School

•Flexible•

Enroll anytime; choose your topic of study; study at
your own pace!

•Affordable•

Pay as you go — only $25 per lesson!
(Price subject to change without notice.)

•Profitable•

"Words cannot adequately describe the tremendous
impact RCBS has had on my life. I have learned so
much, and I am always sharing my newfound knowledge
with everyone I can. I feel like a blind person who has
just had his eyes opened!"

Louisiana

"RCBS has been a stepping-stone in my growing faith to
serve God with the authority that He has given the
Church over all the power of the enemy!"

New York

The RHEMA Correspondence Bible School is a home Bible
study course that can help you in your everyday life!

This course of study has been designed with the layman in
mind, with practical teaching on prayer, faith, healing, Spirit-
led living, and much more to help you live a victorious
Christian life!

For enrollment information and course listing call today!

1-888-28-FAITH Offer #604

(1-888-283-2484)